Remembered Re

Remembered Reading

Memory, Comics and Post-War Constructions of British Girlhood

To Derek
Thanks for the pointers!
All best
Mel.

Mel Gibson

LEUVEN UNIVERSITY PRESS

© 2015 by Leuven University Press / Presses Universitaires de Louvain / Universitaire Pers Leuven
Minderbroedersstraat 4, B-3000 Leuven (Belgium)

ISBN 978 94 6270 030 7
D/2015/1869/24
NUR: 617

Layout: Frederik Danko
Cover design: Johan Van Looveren
Cover illustration: detail from Corinne Pearlman, 'Girl Annuals', *The GirlFrenzy Millennial*,
Slab-o-Concrete Publications, 1998, p. 20.

Contents

Contents

Introduction

Comics aimed at British girls were a large and popular genre that appeared in the 1950s that largely died out in the 1990s. How these comics developed (and why the genre disappeared) are questions I address in this monograph. I'm also going to look at British women reader's memories of the texts they read, including titles beyond the genre of the girls' comic. I do this because, as a female comic reader and academic, I'm interested in the ways that, at various points in the history of the medium, discussion about comics and gender has tended to see the medium as very much about male readers and creators. Such debates have faded in relation to many genres, although not all, and the female creator and reader have become much more visible in recent years. However, this study looks at what was, until recently, a largely forgotten area of comics publishing in Britain and works with readers who had themselves often forgotten their commitment to the comic book.

Girls' comic culture encompassed over fifty titles within which a significant percentage of the material was in comic strip form. Thus, the sheer scale of British girls' comic culture represents an important history. In the heyday of *Jackie* (DC Thomson, 1964-1993) and *Bunty* (DC Thomson, 1958-2001), circulation was around one million and eight hundred thousand copies a week respectively (Ahmed, 1998, p.7) whilst each comic also had a second audience through swapping between girls and shared reading[1]. The existence of a large unrecorded circulation of titles is also acknowledged in some commentaries. George Pumphrey (1956), for instance, argues that each comic bought was read by up to eight readers other than the purchaser. Whilst this figure drops throughout the 1970s and 1980s it suggests that actual purchases were only the tip of an iceberg of comic reading.

The limited amount of writing on British girls' engagement with comics beyond those specifically aimed at them also intrigued me, given that reader surveys found that 30-60% of girls, depending on era and title, were regular readers of comics. The lack of focus on readers in general, has continued until fairly recently, although there have been attempts to encourage work on all audiences for comics. For instance, Robert G. Weiner and Mel Gibson's special edition on audiences and readership *Journal of Graphic Novels and Comics* (Volume 2, Issue 2, 2011) flagged up this potentially fruitful area and shared contemporary work.

The British girls' comic is a dead genre, although there have been various attempts to revive it, typically for the reprint market rather than in the creation of new work (for instance, there has been a long-running campaign to get the comic *Misty* (Fleetway, 1978-1980, back in print). There are now an increasing number of blogs and comic sharing sites focused on these titles, including *Girls Comics of Yesterday* (http://girlscomicsofyesterday.com/ accessed 3/7/14), *Comic Books +* (http://comicbookplus.com/?cid=2266 accessed 3/2/15) and Jenni Scott's *A Resource on Jinty: Artists, Writers, Stories* (http://jintycomic.wordpress.com/ accessed 3/7/14). Such blogs signal a welcome change from the sparse previous coverage. Until recently, it was very difficult to locate examples of these comics. The blogs mentioned above and others aim to offer complete stories online. These ongoing projects are a great boon to researchers. Finally, given that publication of these titles largely ceased in the 1980s and 1990s, the readers are now adults, their pleasure in comics and relationship with them generally only accessible through memory work.

Despite the potential limitations to research outlined above, such a major part of British girls' culture justifies study. Ignoring female readers of comics means that part of both popular and academic history is lost. In redressing this I aim to challenge definitions of female comic readers in the spirit of Rosi Braidotti's assessment of the function of feminist theory as a 'critique of existing definitions, [and] representations, as well as the elaboration of alternative theories about women' (1994, p.77).

I draw, in this monograph, on a number of disciplinary areas: primarily on comics' scholarship itself, but also on the fields of Children's Literature, Librarianship, Education and Media and Cultural Studies. I also draw upon my work with comics and gender beyond the academy. I have worked since 1993 as a consultant promoting the development of collections of graphic novels for both adult and child audiences, to libraries, schools and other organizations. This work started through my contribution of a chapter to a publication edited by Keith Barker (1993) about building collections of graphic novels in public libraries. This training work feeds into my research in that from the start I found that teachers and others typically saw comics as a solution to boys' reading difficulties, an assumption that has led in education to an increased focus on comics as a tool for literacy, but one which tends to dismiss comics as texts of wider merit.

The training work has also flagged up issues of status around the comic. If a medium is seen only as a solution to a problem, if not as problematic, then professionals' responses become important regarding readers' access. For example, Elaine Millard (1997) advocated the comic form as a way of drawing poorer readers into literacy (something which I have done too as a way of getting collections into libraries in the face of hostile fund holders. Once in place, collections become appreciated for their wide appeal and popularity instead). Until recently in education and librarianship the comic was primarily seen as problematic, but also as a useful tool. I still come across views today that see comics, graphic novels and manga in a negative light. For instance, I was recently told by some school pupils that they were not allowed to engage with manga in their art classes, as their teacher insisted manga was 'just doodling' (Interview 2/3/15). Thus, whilst this book is not about the historic low status of the medium, this status had a considerable impact upon the girls' comic. Consequently, I return to it in discussing British perceptions of the medium, especially in Chapter 3, which explains in some detail how the status of the comic both in and outside the academy developed.

British writing on comics, as we shall see, can be divided into three strands. The first, seeing comics as educational tool, is outlined above. The second is characterized by an interest or enthusiasm regarding the medium and the theoretical approaches that have been used to analyse it. A key example was written by Martin Barker (1989) entitled *Comics: Ideology, Power and the Critics*. Work from a number of disciplinary positions incorporating a positive view of comics increased during the 1990s, inspired, in part, by Barker's work.

In contrast, a much larger third body of work starts from the premise that comics are bad for readers, thus locating the research amongst that on 'media effects' and 'moral panics'. This research often, inaccurately but firmly, positions comics as only for children, as for instance in the work of Pumphrey (1964). Influenced by, rather than analysing the concerns expressed about the material, such studies see the comic negatively and readership is neglected except in relation to supporting notions of 'effects'. The crises within the industry stimulated by various groups' and individuals' fears that comics are harmful have been thoroughly documented. In the British context the most important account of the impact of these views is given in Barker's (1984) *A Haunt of Fears*.

In locating my research within audience or reader studies, it is worth noting that female comic readership is still under-researched internationally within any disciplinary field. Girl readers have been particularly neglected, something which has begun to change recently, with, for example, Casey Brienza's (2011) work on American girl readers and manga and Jacqueline Danziger-Russell's (2012) *Girls and Their Comics: Finding a Female Voice in Comic Book Narrative*, which also deals with the USA.

However, two areas of research regarding women and comics are more lively. There are increasing amounts of work on women as creators, for instance, with recent key examples being Trina Robbins (2013) *Pretty in Ink* and Hilary Chute (2010) *Graphic Women: Life Narrative and Contemporary Comics*. The other area in which there is more research activity is around images of women in the medium. Female characters do not, of course, necessarily imply sympathy for women, or the existence of female readers. For example, in the late twentieth century the representation of female characters in *Viz* (Dennis Publishing, 1979-date), such as 'The Fat Slags', was seen by some as insulting to women, as Roger Sabin (1996) recounts. This critical writing is often concerned with stereotyping and asserts that the medium is sexist and should be changed or banned. For instance, Sherrie Inness (1998) who explored changing representations of women in mass media, devoted a chapter to various comic book characters, but concluded that although gender stereotypes may have been reshaped, they are still affirmed by such fictions. However, even where negative views dominate, feminist thought does inform writing about the comic in a number of disciplines.

In addition, I draw on research from the discipline of Children's Literature. The study of children's books shares with the study of comics what Peter Hunt described as '[a tendency] to remain uncanonical and culturally marginalized' (1992, p.2). For Hunt children's literature is paradoxical: 'an amorphous, ambiguous creature; its relationship to its audience is difficult; its relationship to the rest of literature, problematic' (1992, p.1). Though not all comics are for children and not all children's literature is in comic book form, his comment also effectively describes the British girls' comic. Similarly, Jacqueline Rose (1992) describes the relationship between the child reader and adult producer of children's fiction as problematic and complex, an assertion which I shall show also applies when that fiction is in a comic book. Further, as the study of both comics and children's literature in Britain has largely originated in the subject area of Education, I consider the impact these origins have had on how comics have been researched and understood.

The problem with interdisciplinary research is, as Jackie Stacey observed, 'the breadth of academic debate which could be covered in order to put the reader 'in the picture'…an account of all [those] fields would constitute a book by itself' (1994, p.19). However, despite being problematic, taking an interdisciplinary approach is productive in allowing new aspects of the complex relationship between readers and texts to emerge. In writing this book, the nature of Barker's (1989) work proved influential. That he used multiple foci, looking, for instance, at class, historical specificity and production history, was also important. Following his example, I incorporate some initial analysis of production history in Chapter 2, whilst class and era (and therefore social change) are important factors with regard to reader accounts in Chapters 4 and 5. As will become clear in Chapter 3, academics and others have used many different tools to analyse girls' comics. As I also make clear, much of this analysis had an impact upon readers' understanding of comics, via the mediation of the form by various groups of adults, particularly teachers.

In the following example, where I look at a comic in various ways, I set up many of the concerns of the monograph and flag up some of the approaches that have been used in analysing girls' comics, establishing the context for much of what follows. I have purposely chosen a text that was important to me as a child, in order to offer a sense of what it meant to me at the time as a reader. The example is a four page story, 'Belle of the Ballet in Little Miss Nobody ', from the third *Girl* annual (Fig.1).

There are a number of ways of analysing 'Belle', for instance, putting the story into a personal context. Published by Hulton Press in 1954, the annual was kept at my grandmother's house, having originally been a gift to my mother. As a text shared with my mother, it stressed continuity in terms both of reading and as experience of girlhood (the comic strip was from the 1950s and I read it in the 1960s). It also reinforced my position as a female family member, linking me with previous generations of my family. This person-

Figure 1 George Beardmore and John Worsley, 'Belle of the Ballet in Little Miss Nobody', *Girl*, Hulton Press, No. 3.

al context suggests the way in which talking about memory involves talking about identity and text and their relationship (flagging up issues explored in Chapters 4 and 5). In addition, Belle, as the supportive and helpful mentor figure, offered me a possible role model (as an older sister trying to learn what one offered a younger sibling). Finally, the character Belle may have acted as an aspirational model of femininity. Her helpfulness and caring in the story, as well as her grace and femininity, is very much indicative of traditional female roles. The story reinforced my sense of self as female - even the title of the annual labelled me as such. Indeed, as is outlined in Chapter 5, the girls' comic has often been read by girls as directing them to behave in certain ways, both emotionally and physically.

One can also analyse the story in the light of Valerie Walkerdine's (1984), 'Some Day my Prince will Come'. Here Walkerdine sees comics as offering structuring fantasies that prepare girls for heterosexual romance, regulating and directing female subjectivity. Her approach is psychoanalytic, and centres on two points, the first that fantasies only work if they correspond to already existing needs and desires, and the second that the social cannot be separated from fantasy. The narrative could, then, be seen to offer fantasies of being the object of desire rather than desiring, of being admired, of being the ultimate in middle-class femininity in the mid-twentieth century in Britain: the ballerina.

In line with Walkerdine's assertion that the social cannot be separated from fantasy, my own feelings about school had clear links with the story, which related to Renee's desire to be part of a group (Renee is the 'Nobody' of the title, an outsider who watches Belle and her friends practice and copies them, despite her father's ignorance about, and disapproval of, ballet). Like so many children I fantasized about gaining the admiration of my peer group. However, whilst the story offers a satisfying fantasy, I found my actual peers and school confusing and alienating, something I never entirely overcame. This suggests that whilst the story may have spoken to my fantasies it also served to emphasize my feelings of isolation and so contributed in a small way to my increasing resistance to school and to traditional models of femininity.

Presenting Belle as admirable suggests a need to make femininity attractive to girls, perhaps implying, as Walkerdine states, that femininity is an area of struggle and that girls' 'adoption of femininity is at best shaky and partial' (1984, p.88). The story, after all, offers the potential of transformation for Renee (and the reader), into a 'somebody' (having been through a period of isolation and suffering) through a specifically female physical activity that trains one to be looked at, reinforcing the female as spectacle and as mutable within patriarchy. Renee might also be seen as passive, waiting to be saved, rather than acting for herself. Whilst I was attracted to the story, I was also ambivalent about it (as my childhood enthusiasm for reading superhero comics too might suggest) and finally rejected the model it offered. In reading both types of comic, I perhaps signalled my lack of comfort with the limitations I perceived regarding school and girlhood.

The story can be read as offering a second, rather different, aspirational model. Here, the 'special' group and community one is encouraged to aspire to is defined in class terms.

Ballet was an extremely popular physical activity for middle-class girls from the 1950s to the 1970s (when gymnastics began to challenge it in popularity), one that also had adult approval. Belle can therefore be situated historically and in a social context. The fact that Renee's father has never seen ballet signals that neither he nor his daughter belong to the middle-classes.

An aspiration to join the middle-classes is suggested by Renee's interest in ballet, this being, as it were, her first step. Her desire is signalled as 'natural' for a girl (suggested by her bare foot ballet practice) and her acceptance of Madame's authority spells out her suitability to join both groups. It could further be read as confirming to the middle-class reader the desirability of their class position (this was the primary intended audience for Girl) and as directing the working-class reader to aspire to that position. As such, it offers a narrative firmly focused within a specific social and historical context. In advocating conformity to middle-class norms Belle affirms the dominant ideology. Of course, there are many other ways of approaching this story. For instance, it could be seen as depicting an investigative heroine who identifies and solves a problem, something I pick up on in Chapter 2. Moving the action on rather than embodying passivity, Belle destabilizes the correlation of narrative as male and spectacle as female. Belle, in fact, not only moves on but initiates the action, both in finding out who the mystery girl is and in enabling her to learn to dance. Rather than simply embodying grace, her skills enable her to see Renee training, as depicted in a panel showing Belle on her points on a chair, which means she can see more of Renee.

Throughout the story the female characters' use of dance skills emphasizes their physical ability rather than helplessness. Given this, the absence of a demonstration by Belle of one key dance movement, the arabesque, is not surprising (although her performance of it is discussed). Whilst often seen as epitomizing ballet, the arabesque has other meanings, as E. Ann Kaplan (1983) notes. Kaplan (1983) argues that the arabesque

> ...represents the most perfect line that the female form can take, and yet it works only as long as the woman is "frozen," unable to move; she can only come down on one foot and is usually held in the position by her male partner' (p.157).

In the context of this 'Belle' story, which emphasizes dance as female agency, such meanings are counterproductive. To return to the notion of the active female character, throughout this story girls watch, investigate, imitate and take pleasure in the actions of other girls, an exchange of looks compounded by that of the female (real and implied) readers. The male ballet dancer, David, whilst also looking, is looked at by Renee, by Renee's father, and by Madame, offering the male as spectacle to the female viewer. Renee's father, the only character not specifically named, whilst holding the power to permit Renee to dance, is shown as finding that his initial assumptions, both about dance and those who perform it, are wrong. In entering the ballet school, a female dominated space (and in being guided by Belle and Madame) his permission and authority are both sought after and undermined. However, the story does offer a predominantly female spectacle as its climax, perhaps finally reinforcing his authority, as the final panel is depicted from his point of view as well as Madame's. Arguably, it is an adult point-of-view that is reinforced, making the child or young person the spectacle, rather than the female.

As in cinema, the comic offers a number of 'shots' from the point of view of the protagonists. The final two panels of the story, for instance, offer a shot/reverse shot positioning the viewer both as audience and as part of the spectacle. Looking at the two together, then, suggests a different interpretation from that given above. This suggests that another way of considering the comic is in terms of how the form works; how the reader reads. For instance, in this story the first and third pages end with a cliff-hanger panel, enticing the reader to turn the page. Whilst many aspects are similar to film, the comic offers still images that depict action and draw in the reader differently. As Scott McCloud argues, reader/text interaction in comics works primarily through the space between the panels, the gutter (1993, p.66-67). The gutter is part of the grammar of the comic, which McCloud feels allows readers 'to connect these moments and mentally construct a continuous, unified reality' (1993, p.67). In contrast to film, closure in comics, he suggests, 'is far from continuous and anything but involuntary' (McCloud, 1993, p.68). In effect, the reader performs an act of voluntary closure to make the comic format work, thus engaging them deeply with the text.

These analytical approaches interpenetrate, revealing potentially complex and contradictory meanings despite the seeming simplicity of the 'Belle' comic strip. I will build on the issues raised in this sample analysis, but my main concern is with female readers' responses to both comics for girls and those intended for other audiences. My research aims to recover some elements of girls' leisure and culture and open up a wider set of questions about reading, identity and British culture. The sets of texts and practices I discuss vary, as we shall see, according to the age and class of the reader, amongst other factors. In addition, I consider the figure of the girl as implied reader, as constructed within the text, and the responses of the historically positioned girls who read those texts and negotiated how far they would inhabit the identities that the comics offered.

I take also an historical perspective, complementing and extending explorations of girls' culture, such as those by McRobbie (1997), Pat Pinsent and Bridget Knight (1997), which tended to focus on contemporary audiences and texts. Since the 1990s, periodicals for the girl and female teenage reader have predominantly been versions of the women's magazine or focused on Disney princesses and other characters from television and film, with very few containing comic strips. In its historical approach, my research is related to the work of Penny Tinkler (1995, 2000) who drew attention to the role of the magazine for girls in the construction of the notion of girlhood and of girls as consumers in Britain during the period 1920-1958. What such research demonstrates is that girlhood has been, and remains, a slippery category: changing with each generation, girlhood is also interpreted differently within generations.

Chapter 1 sets out my approach to researching comics and girls, whilst Chapter 2 provides a brief history of the British girls' comic, outlining its chief characteristics. I also describe how the girls' comic correlates with constructions of girlhood, and why the girls' comic was seen as a marginal form. My intention is also to explore why the girls' comic disappeared. Chapter 3 explores the cultural mediation of these texts, which produced a climate of reading where comics were understood in certain ways (both academically and in educational practice). Such mediation has influenced both how later generations of academic writers discuss comics and how readers related to comics (as we shall see in Chapters 4 and 5). In this way, I aim to provide an historical and cultural context for the comic for girls and the relationship of girls with comics, showing how both may have been seen as problematic.

In the final chapters, I turn to readers' memories to help me to understand girls' relationships with comics. I firstly outline the pleasures British girls' comics offered the readers and make some assessment of the ways in which these comics fitted into their social experience; how they were implicated in issues of class, how they were consumed, what models they provided and why they became dislocated from girlhood. Moving on, in Chapter 5 I consider those readers who chose to read 'other' comic texts and how they positioned themselves in relation to readers of mainstream titles and sometimes as part of fandom, drawing on the work of Henry Jenkins (1992). The alternatives to which girls turned were usually British and American comics aimed at boys or at a mixed audience, although I also explore the limits of the term 'mixed audience' as accounting for comic reading patterns. My research indicates that some girl readers saw these other comics as offering different values and possibilities, suggesting a rather different picture of the girl reader from that offered in most accounts.

In writing about readers I chart something of the range of responses to comic book texts, revealing a complex set of relationships between readers and their texts. In discussing these issues I firmly locate the comic as one aspect of girl's culture during the 1950s and on and explore the relationship between identity and text. In conclusion, in exploring the status that these publications have held in Britain, my research opens up questions around what the comics offered to readers and how readers chose to use that material.

Inevitably, given my passion for the medium, my own memories of comics are incorporated and negotiated in this book. In a sense, this book is inspired by my own memories of reading American superhero comics and *Girl* (Hulton Press Ltd/Odhams Press Ltd/Longacre Press 1951-1964) at home. These comics, one genre predominantly targeting a male reader and the other targeting a female reader, seemed to contain conflicting messages about gendered behaviour and, indeed, these texts could have been seen as tools aimed to mould me into a 'proper' girl or boy.

In addition, my father triggered my interest in comics as an area for academic attention. I now recognize that in some ways I was 'taught' comics: my father would not simply share the story, but would talk about who the cover artist was, about an individual style and about who had written the text. His approach reflected his assumption that comics were worth serious consideration and criticism. This emphasis on the role and importance of the comic led to my fascination with this medium. My knowledge of my own reading patterns, within a genre seen as addressing a predominantly male audience, leads to my interest in the disjunction between the implied reader of the girls' comic and actual girls' reading practices.

I still read comics of all sorts for pleasure today, which, as someone in their fifties, means that I have only a comparatively small female peer group within my generation. That I am part of fandom makes me different from many of those involved in this research, as fandom offers a contrast to the experience of comics that most women interviewees had. Most had read comics only as children, or had, as parents, shared comics with their own children (some had additional experience of comics from a professional point of view, as teachers and librarians).

Titling this book *Remembered Reading* emphasizes that my concern is, above all, with readers' memories of comics. These memories dominate the final two chapters, allowing an exploration of discourses about the past. Lived experience is therefore a central element. My intention is not to present an alternative analysis of classic girls' comics but to explore in more depth the range of comics read by girls and the diversity of their reading practices. Both female readers and non-readers of comics from the early 1950s to the 1980s in Britain had an awareness of (or had read) a number of British and American comics aimed at both boys and girls. The readers' accounts included here are still more diverse in that they come from both those who enjoyed what comics offered to them as girls and those who rejected what was offered. Whilst the majority recalled that their reading had moved through *Bunty* to *Jackie* and thence to women's magazines, other readers resisted such a progression, or moved on to special interest magazines, predominantly about music. In both cases, from the 1950s to the 1980s the comic is revealed as an important factor in girls' lives. In acknowledging and working with their memories of a range of titles from *Commando* (DC Thomson, 1961-date) to superhero comics (as well as comics for girls) my research adds to the material contradicting the idea that comics can speak only to a male audience, addressing only their needs. I seek to disentangle the discrete area of the girls' comic (those texts with an implied female reader) from actual girls' reading (which was rather different).

Notes

1   When each comic first appears, I've added publisher and dates of publication, where known, in brackets after the title. The Comic Checklist at the end gathers this information together.

Chapter One

Picture This: Working with Readers, Comics and Memory

Researching British girls' comics and their readers offered some specific challenges, given that these were lost texts and usually neglected memories. I describe both the challenges and my approaches to them below. Further, I identify issues around working with girls' culture and with memory as well as outlining the arguments that have arisen within feminist research around memory, experience and the role of the researcher. Finally, I move on to flag up specific research that I looked to for inspiration in the task of integrating writing about texts and about readers.

On Analysing, or rather, on Finding, Comics

I had originally planned a much more text-orientated project about images of women, but the lack of access to British girls' comics meant that I needed to look for other ways to develop my work, including memory.

My first conclusions about girls' comics arose not from any textual analysis, but from the simple difficulty of finding any comics to analyse. Whilst I had access to the British Library and Newspaper Library holdings, there were no other archives containing girls' comics that I could work with. For example, key periodical publisher DC Thomson did not encourage visitors, although at the time of writing, in 2015, there are signs of a possible change in that policy. Getting access to comics was, therefore, a case of chance for me. Similarly, Barker recounts how, 'getting hold of them became an obsession all its own. I have spent a lot of money on buying rare copies…' (1989, p.vii). Here he is discussing a whole range of titles, of which girls' comics were only a part. In trying to find simply that material, my task proved difficult. I was initially reliant on oral sources, articles in fanzines and Denis Gifford's (1975, 1985, 1987) catalogues and encyclopaedias, rather than actual girls' comics, something that steered the research into considerations of memory.

> The lack of surviving girls' comics at that time was commented upon by Roger Sabin: It is a sad fact that titles for girls rarely feature in histories of modern comics: the 1990s collectors' market is essentially uninterested in them, and therefore they remain a forgotten story. (1996, p.81)

Even today and given the growth of on-line sales, there are comparatively few collectors of these comics. Those who do collect them, or original artwork for them, are aware, that, as Sabin asserted, innovations made in this area '...reshaped the medium forever' (1996, p.81). There is, by way of contrast, considerably more trade in comics that are primarily associated with boys. This is as true today as when my research began. It was confirmed in an interview very early on in my research with a second-hand book shop owner. Whilst part of a circulation, rather than a production, history, the information about the trade, unavailable had I focused solely on the texts, offers a number of insights about how British girls' comics were, and in many cases still are, perceived. Thus, rather than looking at texts in isolation, the comics became firmly located within an historic and cultural context, encompassing production, circulation and consumption.

The dealer, who handled a range of books and magazines, as well as British comics and annuals, regarded my interest in comics for girls as an exceptional occurrence[1]. As the interview developed, he outlined his image of collectors:

> Well, lads stay lads you know, and they get nostalgic. They've got more money now, see, so they start collecting the things that they either didn't have, or that their mothers threw away. Those that I see are looking for *The Beano* (DC Thomson, 1938-date), *The Dandy* (DC Thomson, 1937-2013), or *Eagle* (Hulton Press Ltd./ Odhams Press Ltd/Longacre Press, 1950-1969) depending on their age... mostly annuals. (Interview, 11/12/98)

He added that the demand was reflected in the prices, which at that time, in the case of annuals, ranged from £1- to £5- pounds for those aimed at girls, and from £5- to £50- pounds for those aimed at boys. The main factor in determining value was perceived to be a lack of interest from women in collecting these comics. A secondary one was that collecting, in general, was a habit established in childhood that was seen as acceptable if carried through to adulthood for boys, but often not so for girls. Male adult collecting was often spurred on, the interviewee suggested, by the fact that parents often threw out their child's comic collection when they felt their child had outgrown them. This, combined with poor paper quality and the fact that boys read comics 'to death', meant that existing copies had more rarity value. The assumption was that girls looked after their comics.

Yet, such an assumption seemed to be contradicted by the fact that I struggled to find any copies of girls' comics at all. The explanation given was that dealers would often find girls' comics or annuals in attics when house-clearing. The frequency of such finds further reduced their value. Several of the interviews for this project confirm that there are some sizeable collections in storage. Those that the dealers found were not 'live' collections, but forgotten troves. The perceived lack of demand, given the factors above, meant that the girls' comics were usually destroyed, as; '…there is no point in storing them' (Interview, 11/12/98). Annuals, the dealer suggested, might be kept for re-sale because of their comparatively robust construction.

The final argument offered by the dealer for the limited value of girls' comics provided another useful starting point for this monograph. It was that most of the annuals were presents from aunts rather than the choice of the female child and so were kept only because of familial feelings. Consequently, they were not important to the girls, not read, and so survived. The dealer argued that girls did not really like these comics, but did look after them and kept them for significant lengths of time, which rendered them valueless. Any that were found by dealers were destroyed, but this did not matter, for, as he saw it, women did not collect comics anyway. Keeping them signified duty, not pleasure, on the part of girls. Men, by contrast, were collectors, which, combined with their destruction of this material as children, forced prices up. Here destruction signified pleasure. Whilst the evidence from interviews contradicted some of what he said, this dealer's perspectives on comics reflected a market in which girls' titles had little value and their history and importance was neglected. Subsequent discussions with other dealers offered further confirmation that girls' comics were, in their eyes, the most ephemeral kind. On occasion, this worked to my advantage, as when one dealer gave me around two hundred comics free of charge saying that they would have been destroyed otherwise (and asked that I never tell anyone of his generosity)[2].

Eventually, between visits to the British Library collection and amassing a collection of my own, I moved on to looking at the texts themselves. By this point in the research, however, textual analysis had become less important. In mapping out the various different titles and forms of comics for girls, I read extensively, and selected the examples I finally used, predominantly from my own collection, with some confidence that they fairly represented the title discussed at a specific point in its development. I must add that most historical research about publishing for girls is blind to textual specificity. Yet whilst the magazine format for girls still thrives, the comic does not, suggesting to me the need to consider the comic separately and see how the two media interacted. As we shall see, the survival of the magazine and the disappearance of the weekly girls' comics can be seen as linked to the fact that some girls' titles were a hybrid form, incorporating elements from magazines as well as comic strips. In contrast, with very few exceptions, my sample reading of comics for boys and those aimed at a supposedly mixed audience revealed titles that typically consisted almost entirely of comic strips.

I looked at a range of titles to see what the balance was between elements in comic strip and magazine style content and then focused on the various categories that the content fell into. Whilst some titles were nearly all comic strip others included text-only stories, articles, adverts and other items. In many cases, a specific comic's content also changed over time. In effect, this gave a sense of the genre and confirmed that it was responsive, rather than an unchanging monolith. In addition, I aimed to identify the ways in which the age of the implied audience and their supposed class impacted upon a comic's contents. Aspects of production were, then, a factor in this analysis. The perception of the publishers as to target age and class, along with appropriate interests and behaviour proved to be a thread in many readers' accounts. Another important aspect of production was how the stories were depicted, given that the photo-story rather than the drawn cartoon largely dominated the later history of the girls' comic. The physical properties of these texts, such as whether the stories and other items were printed in colour or black and white, and even the type of paper, also became part of the analysis. In interviews, readers had described the importance of the paper on which a particular comic was printed. The stress laid on the way the paper felt, along with the size of publication (and whether it was tabloid or broad-sheet) indicated that comics were objects with a symbolic value that did not always relate to the actual content.

Next, in focusing more upon the content of the stories within the comics, I noted what type of story was offered by producers to a particular age group and class of reader, in what era. What was offered could be seen as a compromise by the producers, an attempt to attract readers but also make the comic acceptable to parents; thus the comics could be seen as representing, perhaps, an approved and 'appropriate' girlhood. That certain texts were seen as 'appropriate' by producers is to an extent speculative, but is supported by production information. Mapping the stories meant that I identified specific tales as located within particular genres, in addition to the overall comic itself belonging to the genre of the girls' comic. Shifts include the rise of horror stories in the 1970s and the slow disappearance of romance in titles for teenagers (as discussed by Barker (1989), as well as of the presence of the girls' school story, which consistently remained a generic marker of the girls' comic.

In analysing comics and girlhood I also draw on Penny Tinkler's (1995, 2000) exploration of the social construction of girlhood in periodicals for girls of the 1920s to the 1950s. In addressing an earlier era, Tinkler's work provides me with an historical springboard into understanding the ways in which the comic medium and models of girlhood have interacted. I explore the tensions and interaction between textual analysis and work with audiences. These approaches produce sets of results that productively fail to match.

However, in looking at academic writing about comics, I, in effect, treat this academic writing as a second group of texts that reveal a great deal about attitudes towards comics. These texts offer perspectives on the comic from various disciplines and eras. In addition, some disciplines, for instance the field of Education, have had a tremendous impact on the relationship the readers in my study had with their comics. In adding this layer to the research, I effectively end up with another very different story about comics. Production forms an additional story, albeit a somewhat tentative one given that I feel that much more work in this area is needed, something the *Comics Unmasked* British Library exhibition curated by Paul Gravett and John Harris Dunning (2014) and the accompanying catalogue, sought, in part, to address.

Media and Cultural Studies and Audience Research

Given my interest in audience, this project is located alongside a substantial body of research within British Media and Cultural Studies from the 1970s onwards. Audience research, even when that research questions the very existence of the audience, is a vital part of these disciplines. Such research is primarily ethnographic, drawing on the disciplines of sociology and anthropology, albeit in the context of studying one's own culture (and typically relying on interviews rather than participant observation). It differs from media industry research in that, as Shaun Moores suggests, it 'conceptualizes media audiencehood as lived experience' (1993, p.3). He adds, with regard to the media in general, that this 'ethnographic turn...[best] equips us to map out the media's varied uses and meanings for particular social subjects in particular cultural contexts' (Moores, 1993, p.1). It is this definition of, and approach to work with the audience that has been employed here as I chart the many uses and meanings that the comic had for British girls.

However, with regard to the British girls' comic, audiences first enter the Media and Cultural Studies research frame with McRobbie's 'Working class girls and the culture of femininity' (1978b) which contains a reference to *Jackie*. This comic is identified as being read in the classroom by girls as a way of resisting teachers and fostering their own friendships and solidarity. This reference was picked up on by Barker (1989), who saw it as flagging up the need for audience research, both historical and current, in relation to comics. In addition, Elizabeth Frazer's (1989) article, also mentioned by Barker (1989), on *Jackie* confirmed the potential of work with audience.

I am involved here with issues of pleasure and of media use in the context of the home and school. I am also engaged with the differences between the implied and real reader, and so with, as Ien Ang (1991) states the incisive distinction between "audience' as discursive construct and the social world of actual audiences' (p.13). Thus, I look at how producers envisaged the readers, the audience for the girls' comic, and at academic and educational work that predominantly addresses notions of the girl 'audience'. The final chapters, 4 & 5, engage with actual audiences, actual readers, and I also map some of the meaning 'clusters' around these texts and audiences.

Audience, Class and Girls' Culture

To return to McRobbie's observation about girls reading Jackie, she had addressed current working-class girl readers of the girls' comic in the 1970s. McRobbie's work impacted on this monograph in two key ways. Firstly, she flagged up as important the ways that comics involve the reader in acts and contexts of consumption specific to the medium. Secondly, that this was a specifically working-class readership alerted me to the ways that comics may be considered 'classed' (both through subject matter and medium).

How the comic may have connoted class is a theme running throughout this monograph. In particular, readers' understanding of taste and class in relation to girls' comics is discussed. In part this engages with the work of Pierre Bourdieu. In considering notions of respectability and taste, I return to Bourdieu's (1986) argument:

Taste classifies and it classifies the classifier. Social subjects, classified by their classifications, distinguish themselves by the distinctions they make between the beautiful and the ugly, the distinguished and the vulgar, in which their position in the objective classifications is expressed or betrayed. (p.6)

However, it is Beverley Skeggs' (1997) feminist reassessment of Bourdieu that has had the most impact on this research. This is primarily because of the lack of focus on gender in *Distinction*, but also because, as Skeggs (1997) describes, '[it] does ultimately code behaviour in a cold and mechanical classificatory manner which does not bring out the pleasures and pain associated with gender, class and sexuality' (p.10). In using, but also moving away from Bourdieu, Skeggs focuses upon the impact of the correlation of femininity, respectability and middle-class-ness upon the group of women in her study and their sense of gendered and classed identity, as I attempt to do here.

In looking at British girls and their comics, I draw attention to the tendency to neglect girls' culture. One can compare, for instance, the media coverage of the girls' comic *Bunty*'s 40th anniversary in 1998 with a film that appeared in the same year. *Velvet Goldmine* (Haynes, 1998) reworked glam rock, nostalgically revisiting the 1970s. Media coverage made much of the nostalgia that both film and comic inspired, but the coverage for both also shared a discomfort with girls' involvement in popular culture, albeit expressed in different ways.

The film and the coverage of it privileged male nostalgia. For example, one article, more about the involvement of writer Peter York (1998) with glam than about the film, spoke of two distinct aesthetics, the first 'consumed as kultur' (represented by Roxy Music and Bowie). The second, in contrast, was given the credit for marking 'the point at which pop became fun again' (represented by Slade, Sweet and Gary Glitter) and described as particularly for girls (York, 1998, p.4). In effect, the former version of glam as popular culture was to be taken seriously (and coded as male). The latter version of glam, seen as focused exclusively on the pop charts, was to be largely dismissed (and seen as female, reiterating the notion that girls are not involved with subversive subcultures). Beyond gender, this could be seen as a binary opposition which constructs a monolithic mainstream seen as of little value.

The coverage of *Bunty* suggested that, as it was representative of girls' culture, it belonged to a different sphere from 'proper' popular culture. This was partly articulated through the (relative) lack of attention given to the *Bunty* anniversary in comparison to the coverage of *Velvet Goldmine*. Where it did exist, coverage was enthusiastic, although it also tended to gently mock the comic. The stories were depicted as exclusively set in a privileged and isolated world of girls' boarding schools (although *Bunty* features other types of stories, as we shall see). The sole exception to this mild mockery was an edition of *On These Days* (BBC Radio Four, 17/1/98), but it seemed to imply that all girls had embraced *Bunty*, recasting girlhood as monolithic and allowing minimal space for divergent or critical voices. The coverage illustrates how girls' relationship with popular culture is typically rewritten, excluding them from certain areas and containing them within others. In effect, girls' culture is simultaneously criticized for 'not going far enough' and encouraged not to go too far.

In the coverage of *Bunty*, femininity, consumption and passivity were interwoven: a model explored and critiqued by a range of writers including Janice Winship (1987) and McRobbie (1978a, 1978b, 1981, 1984, 1991, 2008). The coverage of *Velvet Goldmine*, in rewriting popular culture as wholly masculine where it is seen as 'valuable', is also mildly reminiscent of the slant taken by work on subcultures in the 1970s at the Centre for Contemporary Cultural Studies in Birmingham. The relationship between subcultures, masculinity and academic writing was explored by McRobbie and Jenny Garber (in Hall, 1976) who questioned the general absence of girls in accounts of subcultures in their essay in the collection *Resistance Through Rituals*. They critiqued the other contributions in terms of gender. For instance, they enquired of Paul Willis' research about bikers:

> Is this simply a typically dismissive treatment of girls reflecting the natural rapport between a masculine researcher and his male respondents? Or is it that the researcher who is, after all, studying the motor-bike boys, finds it difficult not to take the boys' attitudes to and evaluation of the girls, seriously? (in Hall, 1976, p.210)

In answering these questions, McRobbie concluded that female participation in subcultures was downplayed in male academic writing. Girls' culture (specifically that of the teenybopper in the 1970s) was largely dismissed as passive consumption of feminized mainstream popular culture. In contrast, male dominance of subcultures was portrayed as threatening to the mainstream, in an attractive way, and as 'oppositional and creative' (in Hall, 1976, p.220), a distinction offering a gendered reading of audience engagement with popular media. The focus on the masculine could be seen, as suggested by Hall and others, as emerging from an interest in notions of working-class resistance and so part of their Marxist approach to the study of subcultures.

Sarah Thornton (1995) later argued regarding dance cultures that much academic writing about subcultures tends to construct binary oppositions 'ultimately depicting 'mainstream' youth culture as an outpost of 'mass' or 'dominant' culture' (p.145). Thornton (1995) argues,

> When investigating social structures, it is impossible to avoid entanglement in a web of ideologies and value judgments. Nevertheless, it is important to maintain analytical distinctions between: empirical social groups, representations of these people and estimations of their cultural worth' (p.145).

As a younger reader I dismissed comics for girls as less significant, showing my own entanglement with value judgments and ideology as a child reader. Further, Thornton speaks of Hebdige (1979) as constructing a mainstream whose role is to be shocked. She states that this 'hardly does justice to the bulk of young people who are left out of the picture' (p.146). I try to follow her lead in this monograph by attempting to counter a dualistic paradigm regarding comics.

In the case of the comic for girls, these binary characterizations of male and female popular culture are examples of what Jean Grimshaw (1986) described as the '"official' (and often male) definition of [women's and girls'] identity' (p75). In the girls' comics industry what Grimshaw describes can also be seen in the relationship between producer and reader, where editors (often, but not always, male) made decisions about what girls want to read, typically with minimal audience research. However, at times they did support the development and growth of girls' culture. For example, McRobbie's conclusions focused on the idea that the neglect of girls' culture was due in part to its very difference, but also that the importance of comics and magazines in this culture cannot be overestimated. McRobbie (1976) noted:

> The important question may not be the absence or presence of girls in male subcultures, but the complementary ways in which young girls interact among themselves and with each other to form a distinctive culture of their own, one which is recognized by and catered to in the girls' weekly comics and magazine (in Hall, 1976, p.219).

The ways in which girls organize their cultural life, both as part of subcultures and in general are articulated in terms of a separate sphere:

> It might be suggested that girls' culture... operated within the vicinity of the home, or the friends' home. There was room for a great deal of the new teenage consumer culture within the confines of the girls' bedrooms (in Hall, 1976, p.214).

This separate girl reality may itself be deceptive, McRobbie suggested, in assuming a single type of girlhood isolated from participation in subcultures. The idea that bedroom culture is specifically female and monolithic has been critiqued further in more recent research by Sarah Baker (2004) and Sian Lincoln (2012) who show that boys and young men also make use of this physical space (as well as virtual space). The ideas of play around texts and group reading practices, which I flag up in Chapter 4 regarding historical practice and bedroom culture, continue.

However, McRobbie did suggest that subcultural theory was limited in relation to teenage girls in that they 'play little, if any, role in shaping their own pop culture and their choice in consumption is materially extremely narrow' (McRobbie, 1991, p.86). McRobbie argued that the texts do not allow much room for play, but can still be used 'as a means of signalling their [the girls'] boredom and disaffection, in the school, for example' (1991, p.83). This last assertion provided a hint as to what I might discover in working with the women who had once made up the audience for the girls' comic.

Working with Readers

McRobbie's observations offered other food for thought. In focusing on child readers in the 1970s, McRobbie was looking at current audiences for girls' comics. Yet, given the collapse of the girls' comic, I could not map current reader communities in relation to those texts. Nor could I directly immerse myself in the culture of the readers, as is often the case in ethnographic accounts of groups of media fans. In addition, there are few historical accounts of readers between the early 1950s and early 1980s that offer a perspective on how girls felt about comics aimed specifically at them. The earlier accounts that do exist are themselves filtered through the perspectives of the librarians and teachers who wrote them.

Given the factors outlined above, I instead explored girls' varied uses and meanings for comics through readers' comic reading autobiographies, through their memories. The initial circumstance of having no access to texts led, then, to a focus on lived experience and memory. In practical terms, this meant that the research was largely based on interviews and written pieces received from women about reading comics.

Although McRobbie and Barker offered the primary theoretical stimulus for this research, the shift from texts to readers was compounded by my work in libraries, schools and other organizations across Britain. The aspect of my training work that feeds into this monograph is about developing the participants' understanding of the pleasures of reading comics and graphic novels. I asked participants to consider those comics that they had read as children (as most had read no comics since). Given that the majority of participants at training events were female, the resulting discussions about childhood reading often focused on girls' comics.

The responses from participants followed an unexpected, but consistent, pattern. After much laughter, participants started to talk about specific titles or characters and what comics had meant to them as girls. Such discussion included issues around the culture of a given period or generation, in that both content and use varied across time. I encountered a range of responses to, and interpretations of, what the texts were thought to offer, echoing Umberto Eco's notion of 'variability of interpretation' (1986, p.141) dependent on the context of reception. It was clear, for instance, how aware readers of girls' comics were of issues such as class. Comics and stories were seen as connoting or promoting class interests (again something that could shift over generations). One of the most exciting discussion of comics and class I participated in culminated in an impromptu debate about the merits of specific titles between a panel member and parts of an audience of two hundred and fifty, in a concrete example of what Annette Kuhn describes as the 'collective nature of the activity of remembering' (1995, p.5). Such discussions indicated both that these publications had been an important part of childhood reading, and that few had spoken about that reading since childhood.

In effect, not having copies of the comics, I used their names, particularly that of *Bunty*, to identify readers and so locate possible participants in this research. The gatekeepers who enabled me to contact readers were the organizations (e.g. councils or charities) employing me to run a course or event, which distributed publicity across their own networks. Coined by Kurt Lewin (1943), the term 'gatekeepers' refers to those who must approve of a proposed change before it can be successfully implemented (Lewin started from domestic settings, but here I flag the concept up with regard to institutional ones). My courses and events were often seen as helping to implement an approved change in relation to policies regarding reading or changing collections, or changing attitudes amongst participants. The size and function of the organization determined access to potential participants in my research. The targeting of courses and promotional events meant that some were open to all, often as part of literature or media festivals. Promotional events drew those interested in comics from a specific geographical area, both men and women. Other events aimed to attract a specific group, for instance librarians working with books for adults. Course and event costs were also a factor in defining potential participants, although most were offered free to participants.

These training courses and promotional events offered me access to large groups of women, both readers and non-readers of girls' comics. The subsequent interviews, letters and e-mails involved women from across Britain, aged from around nineteen to beyond retirement, who were from a range of backgrounds. In relation to their childhood reading, what participants had in common was a largely shared culture of British girlhood, whether wholly or partially accepted or rejected. The interviews and other accounts served to emphasize how important these periodicals had been for those who read them (and those who rejected them) as well as suggesting that several constructions of girlhood (in terms of class and era), partly generated by these publications, had existed.

The geographical spread amongst those taking part was matched by an educational spread from minimal qualifications through to higher degrees, including participants who had gone through private, secondary modern, grammar and comprehensive schools. Most of these readers felt that they had begun life as working class girls, but also that education had moved, or was moving them, into the middle classes. For the most part, participants in training courses were now working in schools, colleges or libraries of one form or another at a number of levels and with different roles. Some also worked for arts or charitable organizations, and others worked at home either as freelance workers or in caring for their children. I attempt, in later chapters to show the shifting, slippery sense of girlhood and self that emerged in the accounts.

As I outline above, the readers involved were primarily contacted through my freelance work with comics, a process that took place over a number of years. Participants generally wanted a degree of anonymity and so the names given above and in the following chapters are pseudonyms. Of the fifty-six readers who offered accounts, twenty-eight became involved as a result of attending sessions I ran at public events and training days in a range of settings. A further seven were contacted through events I attended. An additional fourteen contacts became involved through an article by Pat Hagan called 'What happened to the comic heroines?' that appeared in the Newcastle Upon Tyne (UK) based paper *The Journal* (15/2/1999, p.42-43). The same article, predominantly an interview with me about both my research, also inspired an editorial by Rosie Waller in the same edition of *The Journal* offering a personal account of reading. Finally, seven contacts came forward in response to a comment I made about my research, which simply outlined what I was doing, in discussion groups that I had been a member of for several years. In addition, several women involved in the creation of comics came forward, offering accounts of their involvement with the medium.

Generally, in interview my role was simply encouraging readers to speak, to construct a comic reading self. There were occasions, however, where I was positioned by those interviewed in the role of 'expert', and questioned about comics, something evident from the sample of longer interview material used at the start of Chapter 5. Discussions about reading comics sometimes evoked memories in participants that were intense and revealing. The way that reminiscences of reading comics evoke uncomfortable, rather than nostalgic, affective memories about identity and childhood, is a theme I return to. In other cases, readers felt they had opened themselves up to possible recriminations from colleagues in 'rubbishing' comics that they felt were important to those colleagues. Concerns about offending other girl readers, especially for those who had chosen to read what were seen as boys' comics, also emerged as an issue within the readers' accounts of childhood reading.

Besides the individual interviews there were also two group interviews. These interviews offered the opportunity to focus on group norms. What emerged in both cases was an agreed collective perception of certain kind of comics and what being a reader of such comics entailed. In the first group, the focus was on superhero and non-mainstream comics (from the point-of-view of fans and new readers in the area) and the second was concerned specifically with girls' comics. In both, the emphasis was less on the readers' personal history with a set of texts, although some material of that nature did appear, but instead on issues around the comics. For instance, in the former group, discussion touched on what response being an adult reading a comic in public generated. In the latter, there was discussion about peer pressure in relation to reading and about contemporary girls' magazine publishing in comparison to comics. There was also some exploration of what comics the group had in common, something typical of individual interviews as well.

Whilst interviews were dominant, the accounts also include e-mail correspondence and letters. Clearly, sending letters and e-mails enabled those readers to have a tighter control over what they wished to say. In addition, the letters in particular allowed readers to offer a monologue rather than participate in a dialogue. Yet many asked questions or made comments that invited responses from me. Equally, the speed at which most were composed, being sent on the date (or within several days), of the article being published, and their often conversational tone, suggests a less thought-out and more intuitive response than I had anticipated.

I have used autobiographical information from other sources alongside those personal interviews and written accounts I have gathered. The press and radio coverage celebrating *Bunty*'s 40th year provided some material, especially the radio show *On These Days*, (BBC Radio 4 17/1/98) which also featured interviews with readers. I have also drawn upon three published personal accounts of comic reading; from Corinne Pearlman and Jenni Scott in the *GirlFrenzy Millennial* (1998) and Ju Gosling's e-book, *Virtual Worlds of Girls* (1998). I have, in addition, drawn on Liz Heron's (1985) collection of personal histories from the 1950s. Finally, the analysis has been informed by accounts of children's comic reading that involved interviewing children. A brief summary of key points can be found in Appendix 1. Whilst always filtered through the adult experts' perceptions of the comic (which characterized comics as a cause for concern), in reporting readers' comments these accounts do offer some insight into the child reader of the past.

Working with Readers and Memory

Research involving memory (both the writer's and those of interviewees) occurs in a number of fields. Such work has often been feminist, as for example, Stacey's (1994) account, Sheila Rowbotham's (1973) juxtaposition of official and personal accounts of feminism, the use of the personal by Walkerdine (1997), and Kuhn (1995). Memory and the role of the researcher are discussed and theorized in these accounts in a number of ways. For my research, the most inspirational model is Kuhn's description of memory as:

> driven by two sets of concerns. The first has to do with the ways memory shapes the stories we tell, in the present, about the past-especially stories about our own lives. The second has to do with what it is that makes us remember: the prompts, the pretexts of memory; the reminders of the past that remain in the present. (1995, p.3)

Kuhn sees memory work as archaeology or 'police work', looking for hints and clues, making deductions (1995, p.4). In following this model I have found patterns in the interviews that could be seen as suggesting either a rewriting of personal history that was similar for each participant or a history which represents a series of common sets of girlhood experience, or both.

My research shares with the works above a pre-occupation with the status and use of experience within the academy. Kuhn, for instance, in her exploration of her own childhood memories, asserts that avoiding memory and experience means omitting important aspects of cultural research: 'experience is undeniably a key category of everyday knowledge, structuring people's lives in important ways' (1995, p.28). She goes on to ask:

> Can the idea of experience not be taken on board -if with a degree of caution- by cultural theory, rather than being simply evaded or worse, consigned to the domain of sentimentality and nostalgia?' (Kuhn, 1995, p.28).

Kuhn's reference to nostalgia emphasizes how vital it is to remain aware that individuals rewrite their history over time and that research needs to recognize the partial nature of any conclusions drawn. Her question also asserts the importance of work on experience while articulating the concerns that the use of experience in research evokes. The use of experience in analysis needs to be thought of as complex. As Elspeth Probyn (1994) argued, experience is always incorporated within theorizing as the researcher's 'enunciative position', whether admitted, explicit, or not. To Probyn, the researcher is always speaking from somewhere, a somewhere that leaves a trace in everything they do.

In explicitly using both my memories and those of others, I cross boundaries between public and private. These boundaries may be seen in various ways. Stacey (1994), for instance, describes how 'public' discourses have shaped how specific eras are seen, creating popular versions that interact with 'private' narratives. In dealing with material that has often been pushed to the edge of academic interest in the past, those working with memory (much like those working with comics) are on the boundaries of a number of worlds, interpreting from one to another. Work with memory creates tensions between listening to people's words (and their own interpretive frameworks) and the need for a theoretical framework through which to read them.

The selection and construction of memory and of identity is a central issue here. As Hall asserts, identities are not stable: 'Identity is formed at the unstable point where the 'unspeakable' stories of subjectivity meet the narratives of history, of a culture' (1987, p.44). Clearly what we read, along with many other aspects of childhood, influences who we become as adults. We write and re-write our autobiographies as we remember, going through a continual process of selection and construction. Chris Jenks flags up this issue, in discussing childhood and sociology: 'When we talk of the child we are also talking about recollections of time past, images of current forms of relationship and aspirations towards future states of affairs' (Jenks, 1996, p.11). The relationship between history and memory is a complex one. For instance, commenting on the connection between history and memory, Walter Benjamin wrote that: 'To articulate the past historically does not mean to recognise it 'the way it really was' (Ranke). It means to seize hold of a memory as it flashes up at a moment of danger'. (1970, p.257)

In discussing childhood, then, one explores moments that are fraught with danger, touching on the creation of one's sense of self. Readers' stories were centred more often on their relationship to these texts than on actual content. This also spilt into discussion of other aspects of the texts, in line with Henri Bergson's (2004) arguments that memory can be re-ignited through the senses and I return to this concept in Chapter 4 in relation to the materiality of the comic.

Comic reading, interviews revealed, was not an isolated activity, but overflowed into other activities and relationships. As Jenkins suggests, regarding memory and Batman, '[r]emembering Batman evoked images of a personal past and also of the intertextual network of 1960s popular culture' (1992, p.35). Even though there were obviously differences of period, class and geography, the interviews incorporated both wider memories triggered by these texts and memories of the texts themselves. Readers might identify themselves as having been *Jackie* girls, or as having gone through a *Bunty* phase, connecting a range of activities and attitudes to the name. As Kuhn states, 'an image, images, or memories are at the heart of a radiating web of associations, reflections and interpretations' (1995, p.4). Although her own work starts with photographs, she considers a number of possible triggers, including film. Her discussion of the film *Mandy* (Ealing, Norman, 1952) indicates how texts less intimate than the family photograph may also have important roles in memory work, particularly in how 'we use films and other images and representations to make our selves' (Kuhn, 1995, p.39). The texts then act as a trigger for all sorts of buried memories and their associations went far beyond individuals. In effect, comics are tied to the construction of identity. More specifically, I see comics in the light of Spence and Holland's (1990) definition of the family photograph where they acknowledge that they:

> are objects which take their place amongst the other objects which are part of our personal and collective past, part of the detailed and concrete existence with which we gain some control over our surroundings and negotiate with the particularity of our circumstances. (p.10)

Seen in this way, objects can illuminate both personal histories and a sense of the changes that generations of readers saw during the period of the emergence of the comic strip story and its subsequent rise and decline. Spence and Holland (1990) see this interrelationship of texts, history and memory as:

> blurring the boundaries between personal reminiscence, cultural comment and social history, paying attention to the overlap between history and fantasy, using popular entertainment, reading official histories between the lines and against the grain... (p.9)

Here blurring boundaries is seen as a way of creating histories that act as a counterpoint and a challenge to the official histories of an era, something I emulate in this monograph by offering a readers' history of the comic.

In conclusion, I have charted here how I approached research around comics and readers. I suggest that the nature of the diverse 'private' reading practices associated with the comic book form often serves as a contrast to what textual analysis of the 'public' text reveals. This is not to deny the value of either, but to see both the experience of reading and textual analysis as acts of interpretation. In addressing readers' memories I agree with Tinkler's (1995) comment that '[o]ral history would seem to offer one of the most fruitful sources of the study of magazine readership' (p.59). Despite the problematic nature of research on memory, the contradictions, mismatches and overlaps between readers' accounts, production history, academic accounts and textual analysis proved productive.

Notes

1   I do not discuss the sale of original artwork in this book, a rather different market, but simply the comics themselves.
2   Many of these comics are now part of the 'Femorabilia' collection of twentieth century periodicals for girls and women held by Liverpool John Moores University, UK.

Chapter Two

The Rise and Fall of the British Girls' Comic: The Comic and Post-war Constructions of Girlhood

McRobbie said that comics, along with women's magazines 'define and shape the woman's world, spanning every stage from early childhood to old age' (1991, p.83). The comic strip format in periodicals for girls began in the 1950s and steeply declined during the 1980s, eventually ending at the turn of the new century. However, the history of publishing for girls stretches from the nineteenth century to the present. This chapter outlines how the comic fits into the wider history of publishing for girls, looking at titles from *School Friend* (Amalgamated Press, hereafter AP, 1950-1965) to *Oh Boy* (IPC Magazines Limited, hereafter IPC, 1976-1985). The chapter also looks at the age range, from *Twinkle* (DC Thomson, 1968-1999) aimed at under-fives to *Jackie* for the teen. I do not consider the range of texts actually read by girls in this chapter, but only those titles published specifically for them.

Most British girls' comics were weekly publications containing a number of stories that continued in serial form over a number of weeks, along with shorter strips. Some were accompanied by a pocket-sized version containing a complete single story, of which there typically one issue a month. All had accompanying hard- back Christmas annuals or 'gift books'. It is important to note that writers and artists did not automatically have their names on their work for UK comics. Consequently, in interviews readers tended to refer to titles and characters, not creators. Finally, I will address the way that notions of girlhood, age and class expressed in periodicals for girls before the 1950s are inherited and modified by comics after that date, outlining the structures within and against which readers consumed or rejected the girls' comic and the models of girlhood it offered.

Despite shifts across time and specific inflections in texts depending on the age and class of the reader, there is nonetheless a degree of consistency in what is seen as appropriately 'girlish' throughout publishing for girls, confirming Tinkler's (1995) argument that girlhood is, 'a cultural construct, one which embodies the cross cutting of gender by age' (p.183). Simply the title of *Princess* (Fleetway Publications/IPC hereafter Fleetway, 1960-1967) has connotations of traditional femininity, evoking paternal comments about daughters being 'little princesses' that are partially supported within the text. As Tinkler (1995) suggests:

> Constructions of 'modern' girlhood in the period 1920-1950 were...characterized by continuity with pre-established, 'old-fashioned' conceptions of girlhood which were the product of past attempts to culturally manage gender and social change and negotiate the interests of capital and patriarchy. (p.187)

I would argue that titles such as *Princess* offer some continuity, as well as breaks, from the attitudes, ideologies and subject matter found in the earlier publications for girls that Tinkler analyses.

From their origins in the nineteenth century to the present day, publications for girls offer a perspective on how girlhood was seen by adults and children, a sighting of how it was defined in a particular era. It would also seem that publications for girls offer a perspective on how producers felt girlhood should develop. The producers of these publications are, as Tinkler suggests, implicated 'in the construction of the 'girl'' (in Andrews & Talbot, 2000, p.99). For the most part, the publications present adult, and especially the editors', perceptions of what is appropriate to girlhood in terms of both entertainment and education. However, this does not mean that the titles were ideological monoliths, rather that they offered tensions, contradictions, complexity and change around girlhood.

Context: Periodical Publishers and Girlhood as a Cultural Construct

The emergence of girlhood as a cultural construct has economic as well as ideological determinants. According to Tinkler periodical publishers, '[were] amongst the first to recognize the commercial possibilities of 'girls' as distinct from 'children' or 'women'' (in Andrews and Talbot, 2000, p.98). Today children are often seen as constructed as consumers, often accompanied by an assertion that this is a contemporary phenomenon, but similar processes are evident with regard to girls throughout the twentieth century. Tinkler, for example, argues that girls were encouraged by the periodicals published from the 1920s to the 1950s to inhabit an identity distinct from that of the child or the woman, an identity in which consumption played an integral part. Thus, concerns about how to both mould and appeal to girls are central to publishing for girls from the beginning of its consistent publishing, making the girls' comic a tool in the management of change around gender.

Where comics differ from the girls' magazines of earlier eras is primarily in the way that perceptions of the medium in general are at odds with the ideological work of the earlier magazines. The comic as a medium in Britain has often been defined as addressing a male audience, and as having a negative effect upon boys' behaviour. This has changed in recent years, and has always varied according to genre, but remains a trope.

There is a tension, then, when the comic is combined with girlhood. Perceptions of the comic as a 'bad influence' may mean that even the idea of comics for girls can undermine or destabilize notions of femininity. In effect, given the way that the overall medium became seen by the 1980s as male-orientated, the existence of the girls' comic could almost be seen as a contradiction in terms. Conversely, the absorption of the girls' comic back into a magazine format to some extent represents a solution to that tension.

Adults were not reacting simply to the social conditions of girlhood in relation to publications for girls. Adult concerns about girlhood, and what is appropriate to it, are revealed within these texts, often through the way that the periodical for girls constructs subjectivities for the readers. The texts address an implied rather than actual reader, offering teenagers, for instance, images of heterosexual romance, in an assumption that such romance is of primary importance. It may not be important to the real reader, but the model of teenage girlhood in the 1950s located it as a central concern, leading to a flurry of romance titles such as *Roxy* (AP/Fleetway, 1958-1963). What the comics, and other periodicals, offer the readers of any given title and era is an image of girlhood, complete with a range of behaviours, attitudes and activities determined by the adult producers and policed by interested adults such as parents and teachers. What readers made of these titles is something that shall be explored in later chapters, but it is important to note that comics reveal values and assumptions around models of girlhood.

The models of girlhood offered to girls by comics and their sister texts may tell us more about adult concerns around the female child than about girls themselves. Tensions with regard to these publications tend to occur when adult commentators see the publishers as including content they identify as stepping beyond the bounds of 'appropriate' or 'respectable' behaviour and attitudes in girls. This also suggests that perceptions about girlhood, responses to the comic and attitudes to class might be linked. This adult clash of interests omits another interested group, girls themselves. These texts must also, obviously, engage the reader (or they are unlikely to be profitable for the publisher). Publishers had to represent the interests of readers, alongside those of the company and adult stakeholders, mediate the interests of children and adults and gain consent from all groups, to succeed. Thus, despite having titles like *Princess* (with their overtones of traditional femininity) publishers offered, for instance, adventure stories like 'Robbie of Red

Hall' in *Girl*, which featured images of physically active girls investigating mysteries, to attract readers. The juggling of interests is evident within the texts. Whilst dealing with girlhood, publishers also dealt with girls.

Publications for girls may have served other functions, primarily in the recuperation of the reputation of the comic. In the 1940s and onwards, there were various national campaigns by teachers, parents and others attempting to ban or modify comics. The campaigns triggered the creation of new kinds of comics and a movement into new markets, including that for girls. From the publishers' point of view, comics for girls were unlikely to shock or anger commentators, although this subsequently proved inaccurate. The assumption suggests a construction of the girl as decorous. Arguably then, the girl's comic was partly intended to act as good publicity for the comic in general, in addition reinforcing the 'niceness' of British material in comparison to American comics. From the start, the industry, and commentators upon it seem to have simultaneously associated female audiences with worthless material and seen them as potentially improving the reputation of comics (as well as a source of profit).

Comic publishing for girls responds to, and partially initiates, a number of gradual transformations in the readership and the social definition of girlhood. Such transformations were due to, amongst other things, changes in education and the growth of consumer culture. The comic both benefits from and stimulates an expanding working-class readership, the emergence of the teenager and shifting attitudes towards youth throughout the twentieth century. I would argue that the comic for girls, like the story paper before it and the magazine after it, is a sensitive medium. It reflects significant variations over time in the activities and upper age limit that define girlhood revealing its fluid and shifting nature.

The *Girl's Own Paper* Before the Comic: Nineteenth and Early Twentieth Century Periodicals for Girls

Fluidity around definitions of girlhood is evident in the periodicals of the nineteenth century from which British girls' comics developed, such as the evangelistic and self- consciously wholesome *Girl's Own Paper* (Religious Tract Society, 1880-1956). Mary Cadogan's (1999) research on publishing for girls and her work with Patricia Craig (1986) argues that the *Girl's Own Paper*, in the late nineteenth century, depicts the concerns of the adult and child as identical. The implied reader is an avid consumer of school stories and biographies of the great and of items on housekeeping and fashion.

Cadogan's analysis of early editions is largely confirmed by Tinkler's comments. However, Tinkler offers an analysis of adverts as well as stories and articles in later editions, extending Cadogan's work. For example, Tinkler notes that adverts for further education appear in the *Girl's Own Paper* in the 1940s (in Andrews & Talbot, 2000, p.103).

These and other advertisements reinforce the importance of certain concerns to readers and suggest how both advertisers and producers see them. By the 1920s, Tinkler (in Andrews & Talbot, 2000) argues that there is clear evidence of a notion of the 'girl', a definition increasingly focused on the unmarried female under twenty. She also shows that this notion incorporates both the working woman and the young child, in that the periodicals in general came to be divided into those aimed at schoolgirls (10/11-15 years old) and the 'working' or 'modern' girl (15-20 years old).

An indication of how conceptions of girlhood can shift and change is apparent from the way in which the *Girl's Own Paper* reverted to a model including both schoolgirl stories and material about home and family in the mid-1940s after a period of dividing content by assumed age of reader. This suggests that shifts in how girlhood and womanhood were perceived were unstable and fluid. As Cadogan (1986) explains:

> [From] 1931 to 1945 ...someone at the Religious Tract Society had the sense to make the distinction by bringing out two separate journals: their *Woman's Magazine* then catered for adult readers whose main interests were considered to be home, family and fashion; and the "G.O.P", at a time when schoolgirl fiction was in its heyday, for ashort time lived up to its name. (p.73)

As outlined by Cadogan, the girls' magazine shifts constantly between elements that she identifies as regressive, or conservative, with regard to women and girls, and those she sees as progressive, encouraging female education, independence and activity.

As age became a factor in niche marketing of publications, so did class. Publishers, rather than target the 'mistress and servant' with the same magazine, developed separate titles. For instance, the *Girl's Own Paper* came to be predominantly concerned with the middle-classes, although earlier it had, as Cadogan states 'addressed itself to both mistresses and servants' (1986, p.74). The various changes indicate some of the ways in which girlhood developed, or was assumed to be developing, within the middle class in the late nineteenth century and the first half of the twentieth century. Tinkler (in Andrews & Talbot, 2000, p.100) shows these same developments in the pre-1950 schoolgirl papers, showing how they divide into two types, one for the elementary schoolgirl and another for the secondary; the former contained mostly fiction set in schools, and was principally aimed at working-class readers. In addition, working girl papers before 1945, according to Tinkler, can be divided into three types. One was aimed at 'business girls' (seen by producers as working and lower-middle-class), whilst 'millgirl papers' (whose themes of struggling girls were to re-emerge in comics of the 1950s) were wholly aimed at working-class readers. Such magazines were largely aimed at girls in their late teens and early twenties and influenced both the romance and story comics of the 1960s. The 'millgirl papers' included AP titles *Girls' Friend* (1899-1931), *Girls' Reader* (1908-1915) and

Girls' Home (1910-1915). Many of these were AP publications intended as entertainment, unlike the *Girl's Own Paper*, which saw itself as educational. The final category consisted of 'monthly' titles aimed at upper-working-class and middle-class readers.

Tinkler argues that self-discovery and consumerism become linked in all of these publications. It is also clear that a predominantly middle-class model of girlhood emerges during the 1920s and 1930s which is offered, with slight variations, to all. Cadogan (1986) describes the stories as containing, 'endlessly successful school themes, 'tales of bygone days', ghost stories, mystery and detection, exploits of gypsies in disguise, poor little rich girls and rich little poor girls' (p.233). The school stories must have functioned as fantasies for the majority of readers given that they featured all-girl private schools, which, given the widening readership for these publications (in text and comic forms) would have been outside readers' direct experiences of education. School and supernatural stories continued into the 1930s, remaining staples into the comic strip period. However, they were increasingly located in publications aimed specifically at younger age groups, whilst those aimed at older readers emphasized their futures as wives and mothers. Non-fiction articles were an important element of story papers and this mixed model of stories and non-fiction is common throughout the history of girls' publications. So, for instance, in the earlier periodicals, pets and fashionable activities for girls, such as the Guide Movement, were included. This tendency to offer middle-class models is continued in the comics of the 1950s, even in the titles that explicitly target working-class girls such as *Bunty*.

However, a textual emphasis on upper and middle-class values does not mean that those classes formed the actual audience for these periodicals. One of the few surveys made of girl readers was by A. J. Jenkinson (1940). It involved 1,330 girls aged between 12 and 16, going to two types of school. One set attended state run fee paying schools. These were mostly attended by middle class children. In contrast, senior schools, similarly state run but free of charge were attended mainly by working class pupils. Jenkinson concluded that the story papers were more popular with the working class girls, and they read more as they aged. In contrast, the middle class girls tended to stop reading them as they grew older.

In the story papers and the comics that followed, the editorial teams were confident that they knew what girls wanted (Tinkler, 1995, p.70). Whilst they may have been right in terms of subject matter, the social values and judgments of the staff about girls and girlhood tended to conservatism. Girls in the period from the 1920s to the 1950s were, Tinkler (1995) argues, 'described as natural servicers of others... 'adolescent' behaviour was regarded as abnormal in girls' (p.72). This construction of girlhood creates a tension with regard to the content of comics as they develop.

Girl and Others: The Start of the Girl's Comic

The girls' comic itself appears in the 1950s as part of an expansion of publishing that followed the post-war relaxation of paper rationing regulations. The Amalgamated Press had cut its activities across the board during the 1940s due to paper rationing and the loss of paper stocks during bombing, leaving *Girls' Crystal* (1935-1963) as their sole periodical for girls. A significant number of periodicals (including *Girls' Crystal* from number 909 in 1953 (Gifford, 1975, p.70)) adopted a comic strip format, typically printed on poor quality paper that absorbed any coloured ink.

The shift to comic strip format was often a slow conversion rather than a single wholesale re-vamping. For instance, *School Friend*, defunct as a story paper, was reinvented as a comic but still contained a number of prose stories and items (Gifford, 1975, p.141). Though these periodicals incorporated comic strip materials they nonetheless retained elements of the old model in the new format. For example, 'The Silent Three', which ran in *School Friend* from 1950-1963, featured boarding school girls who solved mysteries (Fig.2). Innovation was also present, in that stories featured the new state grammar schools, family life stories and contemporary pastimes such as ballet and ice-skating. Such shifts in stories and interests, some superficial, but some, particularly those reflecting changes in education, actually fundamental, also represented the further growth of the middle-classes and the dominance of middle-class models within girlhood.

The new publications proved very popular, with *School Friend*, for instance, achieving a circulation of around one million in the early 1950s (Tinkler, 1995, p.60). However, in the development of titles aimed at the girl audience, it is *Girl* rather than *School Friend* that is typically seen by comic historians as a watershed. This was partly because *Girl* was printed on glossy, high quality paper in four-colour rotogravure and was rather more expensive than the competition. This may have accounted for the smaller circulation, which, as mentioned by Gravett (2006, p.133) stood at 650,000 per week in 1952. Sister comic to the *Eagle*, *Girl* was followed by two more 'companion papers', as they were known, *Robin*, aimed at the youngest readers, was launched in 1953 and lasted until 1969 and *Swift* for a slightly older age, was launched in 1954, lasting until 1961. It is clear from the fact that the other titles are bird's names that *Girl* was, in a sense, 'othered' in that both comic and girl were seen as different from the child and boy.

Girl has also been seen as a watershed because the editor, Marcus Morris, was a clergyman. Consequently, Hulton publications had a high moral tone and therefore more likelihood of parental approval. The tone of these publications was also, in part, a response to other British comic publishing, especially the slapstick and anarchy of *The Dandy* and *The Beano*. The initial intention of *Girl*'s producers was to develop adventure themes whilst creating a middle-class comic inculcating sound Christian values, as with *Eagle* for boys. *Girl* also attempted to offer girls a wide range of models of girl and womanhood, as was

Figure 2 Horace Boyten and Evelyn Flinders, 'The Silent Three and the Kidnapped Dog', *School Friend*, Fleetway, 1958.

clear from the cover story of the first edition in 1951, 'Kitty Hawke and her All-Girl Crew' about women pilots. Unfortunately, the protagonists did not appeal to as wide an audience as 'Dan Dare' in *Eagle* and such stories were replaced within two years by schoolgirl investigator stories like 'Wendy and Jinx' (Fig.3). The change was motivated by the findings of a reader survey and dropping sales, after which Morris concluded that adventure stories did not translate directly from boys to girls' comics. In their biography of Marcus Morris, his daughters Sally Morris and Jan Hallwood (1998) report that Morris said of these changes that

> [w]e had received reports that quite a number of girls were reading *Eagle* and drew the wrong conclusion; we had made *Girl* too masculine. We therefore made it more romantic in its approach, more feminine. (p.164)

The change of style meant that female protagonists were given personal reasons to act, unlike male protagonists in the *Eagle* who would be depicted as responding to more abstract motivations, like national pride, for instance.

Eagle also contains a model, or models, of boyhood (which, like girlhood, is likely to shift and change during the life of the periodical). However, to summarize, adventure stories were dominant and often included authority figures such as policemen. Investigators in the stories of *Eagle* were typically adult males, whilst those in *Girl* were schoolgirls, or at the start of their working life. *Eagle* also contained news and sport sections, rather than simply stories about sport (sport featured much less in *Girl* than in *Eagle*). News was much less significant in *Girl*. Further, *Eagle* included educational cutaway diagrams of sophisticated machinery, something entirely missing from *Girl*, reflecting an assumption that girls would have no interest in technology or engineering. Religious stories were also included, in line with Morris's views, but those in *Eagle* were dominated by male characters and *Girl* female. Consequently one can see that the *Eagle* positioned a boy/young man as sporting, engaged with the wider world and involved in gender appropriate activities and interests.

Girl's gender appropriate activities and interests did include the world of work, offering aspirational narratives. It focused on professions for girls quite extensively, including what might be seen as glamourous ones. To illustrate this, I selected, after some sample reading, Vol. 8, No. 28, Aug. 1959, as a typical edition. It begins with the ongoing cover story, 'Susan of St. Bride's' about a nurse (Fig.4). 'Angela, Air Hostess' is another ongoing story that focuses on career, introducing the working life of the central character. These stories also focused on training the characters undergo. A working life for women is proposed as 'natural' in this title, if the career is 'appropriate'.

Alongside these career-focused characters are stories of private, all-girl schools inherited from the story papers. In this particular edition of *Girl*, there are two examples of

Figure 3 Stephen James and Peter Kay, 'Wendy and Jinx in The Girl from Norway', *Girl*, Hulton Press, Vol. 8, No. 28, p. 6.

this type, 'Wendy and Jinx' (see Fig.3) and 'Lettice Leaf', the former mystery, the latter, shorter strip, comedy, from which it is clear that the model of girlhood offered by the story magazines remained dominant. Girlhood and genre could be seen as intertwined in these periodicals. However, although producers were generally conservative, in the case of *Girl*, the readers rather than the publishers (as the changes brought in after the reader survey of the early 1950s suggest), conformed to the dominant ideology with regard to girlhood, rejecting alternatives. The readers' choices suggest a form of self-policing, as if they had accepted that their roles as 'proper' girls, even in imagination, limited what they could engage with.

The emergence of ballet as a theme reflected fashion and also reinforced the centrality of school stories in offering images of schools devoted to dance. In the sample 1959 edition, the school stories are accompanied by ballet school story 'Belle of the Ballet' (see Fig.1). The importance of ballet was further reinforced by *Girl*'s Ballet Scholarship Scheme which was linked to the Girl Adventurers' Club. The scheme began in 1955 in association with the Royal Academy of Dancing and Sadler's Wells School. By 1957, 150 scholars got tuition from the RAD and two were full time at Sadler's Wells (Morris & Hallwood, 1998, p.166). Other features are a text story 'Kit Hunter-Young Horsewoman' and a photo-story about sailing. There is also an advert for a Hulton Press Limited sponsored the Junior Inter-County Team Show Jumping Championship for both boys and girls. Other activities which were shared across boys and girls included an art competition. It had, however, started in *Girl* and then been extended to include boys. Both fictional and true-life stories are thus concerned with physical activity. Riding and ballet themes emphasize middle-class pastimes and activities.

Both sport and dance were seen as acceptable activities, as the above suggests, although it had not been long since ballet had been seen as a problematic profession. Sport had also been an issue for some commentators with regard to earlier publications for girls. For example, Cadogan (1999) identifies *Girl's Realm* (Hutchinson/Bousefield/Cassell, 1898-1915) as having a progressive approach as it featured gymnastics in 1899. However, Cadogan (1986) adds that this 'prompted frequent articles in the national press suggesting that sport was damaging to girls (and particularly to their capacity for producing babies)' (p.78). In this case, the girl's role as future mother was physically at stake. This means that *Girl* indicates how what is appropriate activity for girls has changed over time.

Whilst the comic strip was adapted to suit a female audience other aspects of *Girl* were derived directly from the women's magazine. *Girl* introduced the first fashion page in a comic in 1958, and pin-ups in the form of the 'Girl Picture Gallery' in the mid-1950s (the first was Tommy Steele, regarded by some as Britain's first teen idol and rock and roll star. Other pin-ups included Harry Belafonte the American singer, songwriter, actor, and social activist and members of the royal family). However, there were limits to this type of engagement with popular culture, as Morris preferred that celebrities profiled should

Figure 4 Ruth Adam, Ray Bailey and Philip Townsend, 'Susan of St. Bride's in The Foundling', *Girl*, Hulton Press, Vol. 8, No. 28, p. 1.

be British, or have links with Britain via what was called, at the time, the British Commonwealth. In the 1959 edition that I sampled, the focus is on Christmas, with features on the pantomime season and circuses, as well as the official Readers' Carol Services. *Girl* also developed a problem page, harking back to nineteenth century periodicals. 'What's Your Worry?' began in response to unsolicited letters received from readers (Morris & Hallwood, 1998, p.168).

The mixed format model came to be predominantly associated with British girls' comics, despite titles like *Eagle* and *Look & Learn* (IPC Magazines Ltd /Fleetway Publications 1962-1982) also employing it. A mixed format meant that *Girl* and some later titles contained text stories, puzzles, non-fiction strips, biographies and handicrafts as well as comic strip stories. The 1959 edition includes a number of non-fiction picture and comic strips including a biography of 'Marie Curie', 'Real Life Mysteries' on 'The Mystrey of Eilean Mor, and cookery instruction. In an earlier edition, Vol. 8, No. 18, 2 May 1959, one of the strips is an adaptation of 'Vanity Fair'. Bible based strips were also common. This range of stories and activities suggests that *Girl* was intended to be 'improving' for the reader. Adverts also addressed a range of ages and concerns. In this edition, they included coats for school, shoes, camera film, toys and sweets and a geometry set. The editors clearly had school holidays and the start of term in mind.

Nonetheless, whilst much of *Girl* seems to contain a cosy middle-class-ness and focussed on what were considered appropriate activities, certain elements suggest a much less comfortable notion of girlhood. The letters page, for instance, often addressed dramatically different issues from the rest of the comic. The existence of the letters page reveals a tension at the heart of *Girl* and a fracturing of the ideal girlhoods put forward elsewhere in the text. Letters received by *Girl* in the 1950s, for example, featured cases of sexual abuse and requests for information about sex and childbirth as well as fashion and beauty (Morris, 1998, p.169). The editors attempted to offer answers, even if it had to be under a general comment anonymising the correspondent. Those dealing with the letters were well aware of the differences between the idealized girlhood of the comic and the actual lives of the letter writers.

Roxy, Romance and Teenagers: Developing Comics for Young Adults

Publications for girls continued coming out in comic format in the late 1950s, but the market altered with the further growth of the notion of the teenager. The 'teenager' is also a changing construction, which, like the 'girl', as Tinkler (1995, 2000) notes, varies in age across and within generations. This is illustrated by Mark Abrams' (1959) research on consumption and the young in which he defined the teenager as an unmarried 15-24 year old (current British perceptions of the teenager usually suggest someone from 12-19 years of age). However, in common with current assumptions about the teenager, Abrams saw them as closely linked with consumerism. Cadogan also identifies this link, seeing teenagers, like the comics of the 1950s, as wholly commercialized (1986, p.329). The connection with consumerism is apparent in the way that titles aimed at readers at the older end of the scale of teenager, such as *Roxy* and *Valentine* (AP, 1957-1974) frequently based romantic stories on popular songs and featured music stars (in Andrews & Talbot, 2000, p.106). This contrasts with titles for younger readers, which appeared comparatively untouched by popular and consumer culture. *Bunty*, for instance, contained few adverts until it was revamped.

The emphasis on romance in teenage comics suggests that producers and audiences saw both the experience of romance and the consumption of it as part of what it meant to be a teenager. In Britain, the romance comics of the late 1950s included *Marilyn* (AP, 1955- 1965), *Romeo* (DC Thomson, 1957-1974) and *Valentine*. These titles were based on ones that publishers developed in response to the popularity of imported and reprinted American romance comics in the late 1940s (but they also inherited romance narratives from the British story papers of the pre-war era). *Marilyn* et al were innovative in many ways, from actually using a girl's name as the title and the advertising (for clothes and jewellery rather than toys) through to their links with popular culture, such as the weekly pop broadcast, '*Hullo, Marilyn!*' on Radio Luxembourg.

The comics came both to reflect and confirm the notion that the late teenage years were a transitional period in which romance was central. Although adults and what we would now see as the older teenager were both audiences for the romance comics from the start, younger teenagers (the audience for *Jackie*) were *not* part of the target audience. However, as the Royal Commission on the Press reported, '*Mirabelle* (C. Arthur Pearson/ IPC, 1956-1977) was originally intended as a 'romance comic' for girls of 18 and upward, but its publishers later were surprised to discover that it was most popular with 13-16 year olds' (1977, p.11).

The realization in the late 1950s and in the early 1960s that there was a younger audience for romance comics produced a shift in perceptions of these texts. What was offered by publishers to a late teenage and adult audience in the late 1950s and in the early 1960s became, stripped of the context of an older readership, perceived as a moral problem. Despite the fact that these romance comics were comparatively bland texts, typically putting forward unquestioning images of conformity to a heterosexual norm, their accessibility to younger readers meant they could be seen by adults as encouraging girls to 'experiment' with romance (and, implicitly, sex) at a younger age than was deemed appropriate. Given that the readership was under eighteen, romance comics came to be seen as potentially able to influence or manipulate 'vulnerable' readers, revealing a 'blank slate' model of the girl.

The Royal Commission on the Press suggests that the success of the romance with a much younger group was accidental. The publication of *Jackie* is, I would argue, both an acceptance of this finding by the industry and an attempt to exploit it. *Jackie* (1964-1993) differed from the romance publications before it in being aimed squarely at younger teenagers. With an eye on parental concerns about *Jackie*'s younger audience, publishers DC Thomson reinforced their strong moral line on marriage and 'true love' that had appeared in publications for older readers.

However, this did not prevent *Jackie* from being seen as problematic reading by adults. *Jackie* became a marker of a transition from child to teenager to adult, although what type of material is 'proper' for a specific group varies across class and period. There were debates amongst adults over what material was suitable for readers of specific ages (as there still is regarding magazines, manga and other media). The balancing act undertaken by publishers, especially editors, in mediating between the readers and adult interest groups slips, as I have indicated, when other adults see the producers as failing to act in loco parentis (for instance when the content of comics is seen by parents as encouraging an engagement with sexuality).

The same issue emerges with regard to magazines of the late twentieth century aimed at young women. Pinsent and Knight (1997) show that problem pages of titles such as *Mizz* (IPC, 1985-date) were attacked by parents and media commentators for being more explicit than *Jackie* and other titles starting before 1980. This shows a shift regarding views of what is appropriate for girls given that *Jackie* had been considered controversial. Other magazines were also censured, notably *More* (Emap, 1988-2013), primarily because of its feature 'Position of the Fortnight', which illustrated how to achieve various ambitious sexual feats.

Notions of what was appropriate for girls meant that some publishers refused to respond to how girls' lives changed, preferring to offer a model of middle-class propriety. An extreme response to the changing concerns of young women, particularly around sexual activity was that of *Jackie*. The publishers, according to Sabin (1996) stated that they ended the title in 1993 rather than update their approach (p.84).

Whilst *Jackie* grew from the romance comics it also differed from them. The romance comics were, above all, comics, despite their inclusion of elements from the women's magazines. The first edition of *Roxy* (March 15, 1958), for example, had only three and a half pages of non-comic strip material out of twenty-eight pages (Fig.5). These were devoted to a horoscope, 'Alma Cogan's Glamour School' (beauty tips) and interviews and competitions related to pop music (choosing a 'Top Ten' of Tommy Steele's songs could win someone a record player). Stories are mostly three to four page romances, although there is one serial called 'The Passionate Prince' (which revisits 'The Sheik' with a 1950s makeover). Of the shorter stories, Tommy Steele supposedly narrates the first. Popular music also appears elsewhere in the comic, in the form of adverts for the *Roxy* show on Radio Luxembourg and for a Six-Five Special songbook that was to be part of the next edition.

In contrast, *Jackie*, as the forerunner of *Mizz* and the other teen magazines of the 1980s and 1990s, applied the format of the woman's magazine to material for younger

Figure 5 Anon., 'Tommy's Lucky Little Guitar', *Roxy*, Amalgamated Press, No. 1, 15 March 1958, pp. 1-4.

people. *Jackie* was made within the women's magazine department, rather than the one responsible for children's comics. Those working on *Jackie* were mostly young and female and allowed some degree of freedom in choosing stars to interview and other aspects of the title. In that sense, they had a good idea of what might appeal to readers. Along with *Diana* (DC Thomson, 1963-1976), which was aimed at a younger audience than *Jackie*, it was DC Thomson's first venture into the full colour gravure printed market. *Jackie* served to increase the potential audience for women's magazines, showing readers as young as twelve in what to expect from them. Despite being published by the same firms, comics and magazines were, in effect, competing over a female audience. The success of the magazine becomes apparent in the mid-1960s when the romance comic began to fail for both the older teen and adult audience. The magazine became the primary mode of address to women in their twenties and over, and slowly came to dominate the market for younger readers. Cynthia L. White (1970) in her account of women's magazines in the 1960s, reported that:

While the story monthlies have generally been putting on circulation, the 'romance comics', the staple fare of the secondary modern school-girl in the fifties have lost popularity. Since 1958 *Boyfriend* (City, 1959-1967), *Marilyn*, *Marty* (C. Arthur Pearson, 1960-1963) and *Roxy* have all folded, although *Mirabelle* is managing to hold its own, and *Jackie*, a more recent entrant put out by DC Thomson is doing well. (p.177)

The romance titles that continued into the 1970s, such as *Romeo* and *Valentine*, increasingly adopted a magazine layout (Gifford, 1975, p.139).

After the introduction of *Jackie*, the magazine format increasingly dominated the teenage and adult markets. The anonymous author of *Mum's Own Annual* (Fleetway, 1993), a celebration of comics for girls, characterizes magazines as forcing girls to grow up and accuses magazines of being streetwise and disrespectful, so creating a nostalgic model of the comic which was also 'safe' from an adult point-of-view, which was not necessarily the case when one looks at the content of the comics. Aspiring to womanhood could be seen as reading texts similar to those women read, which suggests one reason why magazines rather than comics became part of the construction of girlhood. Comic strip materials, having been part of publishing for women, were pushed down the age range, replaced by a mixed and then wholly magazine format. The use of the comic strip in publishing for girls comes, during the late 1950s and 1960s to indicate a definition of the teenager differentiated from adulthood. Comic strips subsequently become an indicator of girlhood, differentiating the girl, through use of a specific format, from teenagers and women.

The inclusion of magazine elements in *Girl* became something of a Trojan horse in later titles. *Jackie*'s popularity, with a circulation of one million per issue by 1973 (Winship, 1987, p.166) hastened the shift to the magazine format. *Jackie* has been described both as a comic (Sabin, 1996) and as a magazine (Alderson, 1968 and Winship, 1987). Just as *Woman* (IPC, 1937-date) had included teen pages (Andrews & Talbot, 2000, p.101), *Jackie* blurred the boundaries between comic and magazine, as well as between child and adult female reader. Whilst McRobbie insisted that *Jackie* 'expresses the natural features of adolescence' (1991, p.83) the format, I would suggest, increasingly offers a model of continuity between the teenage girl and adult woman as the comic strip elements disappear, as Barker (1989) indicates.

Bunty and *Princess*: New Comics for Younger Girls

Teenage and romance titles were not the only publications launched in the late 1950s and early 1960s. In response to a drop in sales of comics across the board, there was a burst of publishing aimed at pre-teens. These changes in publishing for younger readers were initiated by DC Thomson. After their initial success with *Bunty*, the first in the field, DC Thomson launched *Judy* in 1960. Competitor Fleetway responded with *Princess* for pre-teens and younger teenagers, and then *June* in March 1961. In turn, DC Thomson's *Diana* (1963) followed. *Diana*, in particular, showcased as broad a range of stories as possible, adding elements of science fantasy and horror. Again, this suggests more diversity in what were perceived as the interests of girlhood by publishers than some critics have suggested. *Mandy* completed the DC Thomson range of titles targeting 8-12 year olds in January 1967.

For DC Thomson, launching *Bunty* was a new initiative. Ron Smith, an illustrator for the comic, described their lack of experience of publishing for girls:

> The problem was that no-one at Thomson's amongst the journalists, writers and illustrators had produced a girls' comic. This was, for them, the first, so the managing editor obviously had to scout around the various papers within the company and pull out illustrators from *Wizard* (DC Thomson, 1922-1978) [and others]... someone who was probably adaptable, and would draw girls. (*On These Days*, BBC Radio 4, 17/1/98)

Despite the previous history of publishing for girls, none of the staff had worked on such a periodical. In addition, the use of the phrase 'would draw girls' suggests that many of the staff were unenthusiastic about the prospect of working on a girls' comic.

In drawing staff from the part of the company that produced comics, DC Thomson's periodicals for younger girls were very much separate from *Jackie*, produced by the woman's magazine department. Initially the story comic was almost entirely separate from the magazine format papers and contained minimal amounts of non-comic items. Even non-fiction tended to be in strip format as in the case of writer Benita Brown's 'Winning Ways' series, a five-frame sports strip (Interview, 9/8/99). In a typical edition of *Bunty*, Number 832, Dec 22, 1973, which I selected from sample readings only four of the thirty-two pages do not contain comic strip. The first is the title page featuring the 'Bunty' picture story, where there are captions, but no speech balloons. Of the others, one is the 'Cosy Corner' which features letters on a range of topics from readers; another advertises the *Bunty Annual*, *Bunty Picture Story for Girls*, *Bunty* subscriptions and a game, while the last has a cut-out doll.

Bunty was aimed at a younger age group than comics like *Roxy*. Before the arrival of *Jackie* in the 1960s and the decline of the romance comic for older readers, readers would graduate from one to the other familiar with the format, if not content, in that *Bunty* reflects the interests and concerns that producers saw as belonging to younger girlhood. However, as the model of magazine (incorporating a comparatively small amount of comic strip) associated with *Jackie* overtook *Roxy* to become the norm in teenage reading in the late 1960s, the high percentage of comic strip content in *Bunty* and other titles became associated with a progressively younger audience. The comic medium, in not continuing through to periodicals for adults was reinforced as an indicator of childhood.

Bunty changed girls' comics considerably. DC Thomson aimed to publish comics that would particularly appeal to working-class readers, consequently creating new markets by further differentiating the audience. However, whilst the introduction of *Bunty* in the late 1950s might seem without precedent in terms of narratives, it could be seen as referring back to the tradition of the millgirl paper which typically featured stories about put upon Cinderella figures, although those characters typically worked in laundries or shops. They also incorporated romantic tales for older readers, telling stories 'from the viewpoint of the skivvies, shop-girls and factory hands' (Cadogan, 1986, p.127). Comics such as *Bunty* incorporated similar motifs, although without the romance and so owed some of their approach to papers aimed at older readers who had also been defined as girls, again showing shifts in girlhood and publishing for girls over time and in relation to age.

There was also (*Princess* being a notable exception) a great deal of continuity between comics like *Bunty* and *Judy* (DC Thomson, 1960-1991) and the narrative themes of the story papers of the 1930s, such as *Girls' Crystal*. In particular, there was a continued focus on the figure of the schoolgirl, most notably through 'The Four Marys' in *Bunty*. Such stories, part of both middle and working-class girls' papers, can also be firmly linked to changes in education during the twentieth century. *Bunty* and others reworked the schoolgirl stories in response to a changing experience of school in the 1950s, by, for instance, making one 'Mary' a working-class scholarship (non-fee paying) pupil. *Bunty* also had an increased focus on state schools and home life as well as private and boarding schools. Even *Princess* adopted some of the narratives DC Thomson initiated, as in the case of the series 'The Happy Days' which focused on family life.

Where *Bunty* differed from earlier publications especially those aimed predominantly at middle-class readers was that many of the school stories focused on the problems of being a working-class outsider. The stories tended to be concerned with the struggle of such outsiders to deal with the snobbery of, and bullying by, both staff and pupils in private schools. This theme continued into the 1970s with examples such as 'Outcast of the Pony School' in *Bunty* 832, Dec 22 1973, where Laurel Clark wins a free place at a boarding school that specializes in riding and is bullied because of her status. In this, as in similar stories, there is a form of 'justice' in that the bully is finally exposed and fails to defeat the heroine. This theme of the outsider and the bully is rather double-edged, making the reader aware of the possibility of private education, whilst presenting it as potentially nightmarish. These particular stories often potentially undermine the aspirational intentions of the publications through their dark view of the world (increasingly the case in the 1970s), and extensive use of the victim heroine. In addition, as Cadogan (1986) suggests; 'It is possible that many working-class girls did not think of themselves as 'council-school' pupils until the authors of popular fiction hammered home the difference between their environment and that of more wealthy families' (p.251).

Like school stories, ballet stories were incorporated in *Bunty* and similar titles, adapted from the middle-class papers like *Girl*, as well as from the earlier story papers. Again, the heroines were often disadvantaged. In the story 'Moira Kent', which ran in *Bunty* from

1958-1964, the focus is on an orphan's desire to become a ballerina despite overwhelming obstacles. In describing how he learnt to draw stories for girls, Ron Smith focused in interview upon his experience of creating 'Moira Kent'. He was sent to a ballet school to do some life drawing and said,

> It was a little hazardous really... I had to sit on the floor with a sketchpad and when these buxom Scottish ladies appeared I had no idea of the noise that would then be created with them bouncing up and down. I'd be leaving the floor by an inch or two every time they hit the deck, so it was really not working terribly well. I went out to a Menzies bookshop and I bought a book, an introduction to ballet, swotted it up, looked at the diagrams and really started from there. (*On These Days*, Radio 4, 17/1/98)

What this anecdote illustrates is that the image of graceful girlhood in these comics is truly a fiction several times removed from reality. The images construct a myth of girlhood that has little relationship to actual girls. This story also shows Smith's understanding of the process of creating a myth of girlhood.

Another common theme was the Cinderella figure, extended well beyond its use in the millgirl papers. Cinderella in these girls' comics was often trapped, misunderstood or exploited, a victim of female bullies, gossips, wicked stepmothers and aunts. There were also evil uncles, employers and trainers, although they tended to feature less. Thus, the comics of the late 1950s and early 1960s expanded upon the older titles in that, as Sabin (1996) describes, '[they] hit upon an entirely new formula, typically involving a child alone in the world, away from fondly remembered parents, trying earnestly to do the right thing' (p.82). Such formulae were usually combined with moral intent and became, with various twists, a dominant mode of storytelling in titles aimed at the pre-teen reader. These narratives also suggest tensions regarding notions of girlhood.

Fleetway's *Princess* for pre-teens and younger teenagers was a rather different type of periodical to *Bunty* and *Judy* in that it was a deliberate attempt to court what was perceived as *Girl*'s middle-class market. In terms of subject matter, *Princess* was also both similar to and different from comics like *Bunty*. Inevitably, it too focused on ballet, but not typically through stories. Instead, the sample edition of *Princess* (from July 9, 1966) contains photographs of productions and performers. It also incorporated a wide range of other non-fiction text and photograph based items rather than stories. Thus, the dominance of non-fiction here could be seen as carrying class connotations. Like *Girl*, *Princess* laid emphasis on factual items, whilst *Bunty* was more focused on fiction. The former publications target a middle-class audience, the latter working-class. The sample July 9, 1966 edition begins for instance, with a feature on keeping a camel as a pet. Other items include an article on giving horse riding lessons, a 'pop pictures' page featuring Cilla Black, The Seekers and Herman's Hermits, a nature column on lapwings, knitting patterns, a pet feature on the Bedlington Terrier and the Princess Club page. In addition to being focused on non-fiction the majority of features do not engage with popular culture (although they do so much more than DC Thomson publications) but are about what might be considered 'improving' activities, such as pet care and crafts. Again, overall there is a range of activity depicted that goes beyond models of passive femininity.

The final section of *Princess* is devoted to 'My Magazine', a six-page supplement consisting of contributions from readers, something rare on this scale. Here the subjects are wide in scope, including items on dolphins, going on a school coach trip to Italy, stories written by readers, poems, art and photographs, some of which are accompanied by the editor's comments. There is also a question page predominantly focused on factual and homework queries (rather than advice about private life). As with *Girl*, many of the items are clearly linked to middle-class models of feminine interests, with ponies, ballet and pets at the forefront, although I feel it was meant for a slightly younger age range, as the focus on pets rather than beauty might suggest. The readership was also envisaged as having access to cameras, or the funds to buy them, as the adverts and reader-generated photo-items suggest. This participation in creating the periodical is distinctive. Whilst most titles encouraged girls to write in, few went as far as *Princess*.

In the main body of the magazine, there are also four serial text stories, one about knights, one about an American pioneer family, and two about family life. Another serial, more heavily illustrated than the others although not a comic strip, has a science fiction theme and there is a short fantasy story about a wizard. In comparison to titles like *Bunty* there are few comic strip based pages, totalling eight out of thirty two in this particular edition. Most are one page long, with only 'The Happy Days', written by Jenny Butterworth, being longer. Of these strips, several are humour based, including 'Lettice Leaf' (the only school story) which had first appeared in *Girl*. There are also three mystery stories, one featuring an actress under threat from a sinister director 'On Stage', one about a nurse who uncovers a case of blackmail 'Beth Lawson - Nurse of the Outback', and one about a swimming teacher involved in solving a murder 'Alona – The Wild One'. Careers, mystery and girls as investigators dominate over school stories, suggesting a deliberate attempt to move away from that genre's dominance whilst maintaining links with the *Girl* approach. In addition, there is an adventure story called 'Mary Jo' about two girls involved in a plane crash in the jungle making their way back to 'civilization'.

Even the cover offered a dramatic contrast in that it had a full-page image, not a comic strip, making it look even more like a woman's magazine. The edition I selected shows a girl reading a collection of Sue Day stories from the series 'The Happy Days'. It also mimicked the format of women's magazines by using full colour on glossy paper for at least some of the contents. *Bunty*, in contrast, was cheaply produced on newsprint rather than the higher quality paper. Another statement of the publisher's intent was that the annual was instead called a 'Gift Book', a term associated with middle-class women's publications.

Thus, format is clearly marked by the producers as being related to class. *Princess*'s magazine format signalled who the intended audience was and offered a model of middle- class girlhood consistent with that of *Girl* (the introduction of the family life story being the key exception). In contrast, the comic was deemed more appropriate in addressing a working-class audience. The comic format came to connote, I would argue (to producers, parents and readers) working-class-ness and childhood. *Princess* was clearly intended as a challenge to comics like *Bunty*, particularly through being marketed as more sophisticated. *Princess* suggested that even at a point where girls' comics were the more dominant of the two forms it was the magazine that would become central to girls' culture.

Changing Markets: *Tammy* and the New Wave of Comics

The drop in sales of all types of comics in the late 1960s meant that there was a search for new formulae for both teenagers and younger readers. As we have seen, the romance and teen comics were ailing. Consequently, many comics were reworked into magazines in an attempt to mimic *Jackie*'s success. The magazines also cashed in on the emerging 'teenybopper' market created by the growth of music acts like The Osmonds and the Bay City Rollers. This process of cashing in on pop music was started by IPC, who launched a pop-oriented magazine, *Pink*, in 1973, which did contain comic strips, although the bulk of it was concerned with fashion, advice, pop stars, horoscopes and short stories.

Comics lost out since the marketing of music acts through television and other coverage was, effectively, an advertisement for the magazines as well as the magazines being adverts for the acts. The only exception to this failure to capitalize on other products' marketing was the practice of basing comics on popular television programmes from the mid-1960s on. Thus, there were comics like *Lady Penelope* (City Magazines Ltd, 1966-1969), which in addition to the titular character being from *Thunderbirds*, a British science-fiction television series featuring marionettes, also featured strips on The Monkees (the American pop band) and *Bewitched*, an American TV situation comedy fantasy (Gifford, 1975, p.95). Other comics included strips based on television, but were less dominated by them. *June*, for instance, ran a story in 1966 called 'The Growing up of Emma Peel' (based on the character from *The Avengers*, a British action television series). The new magazines and music publications of the 1970s and 1980s were very profitable in comparison to the comics, but often had even shorter lives. Some readers reported graduating, not onto women's magazines, but into music publications associated with a range of musical genres rather than focussing on what they saw as mainstream pop. Comics were not generally part of the synergy around other forms of popular culture and so became lower profile, increasingly detached from the more consumerist model of girlhood offered in magazines. This detachment is ironic given the earlier titles' involvement in establishing models of girlhood built around consumerism.

Only *Twinkle*, a 'nursery' comic for very young readers, was to expand the girls' market significantly. Other attempts included, for example, *Tina* (Fleetway, 1967), which was launched with the intention of trying to capture an international audience. The aim was to create stories that could be easily translated and from which British bias could be removed. In accordance with that aim, stories featured, 'Jane Bond', 'Moira, Slave Girl of Rome' and 'Westward the Wagons' which featured a cowgirl heroine called 'Glory Gold.' It was a success in Holland where it was the first of its kind, but failed in Britain and was merged with *Princess*. IPC tried again with a more traditional title in 1969, *Sally*, but this did not last long before succumbing to the same fate. Change was needed if girls' comics were to continue, and in interview with Barker, Pat Mills identified the comic *Tammy* (Fleetway, 1971-1984) as 'the beginning of what could be called the 'new wave' comics' (Barker, 1989, p.17).

The 'new wave' could be characterized as more responsive to readers than previous comics.

The girls involved in the market research for *Tammy* (aged 8 to 13 years old) generally confirmed the editors' assumptions about preferred content, but the readers' enjoyment of stories that made them cry came as a surprise (Anon, 1993, p.13). Consequently, *Tammy* and *Jinty* (Fleetway, 1974-1981) differ from titles of the 1960s in their heavy emphasis on suffering central characters, although both comics (and particularly *Jinty*), had humorous stories as well. Suffering central characters added realism and many stories showed girls learning through difficulty. In *Tammy* 15 Jan 1983, for instance, the first story, 'Romy's Return', focuses on two friends, one of whom, Linda, is dominated by the other, Romy. After Romy leaves, Linda starts to stretch her wings and discovers that she likes being in charge. When Romy is transferred back to her original school, the two girls, far from being friends, end up competing. The theme of the story that follows is the emotional turmoil that this competition engenders. However, this is not about suffering leading to passivity, but about both girls' attempts to actively establish themselves as individuals. *Jinty* contains similar narratives. For instance, in 'The Slave of Form 3B', (12 June 1976) the central character is a girl hypnotized into putting herself, and others, in danger, something from which the bully who has hypnotized her gains much amusement. Whilst these stories are from very different genres, they share a similar focus on the emotional turmoil of the heroine. There were also new twists on the sports story. 'Bella at the Bar' (Fleetway, 1974-1984), for instance, featured a working-class orphan gymnast whose guardians attempt to persuade her to become a criminal. The story (far from being miserable) is about the wit and resilience of the central character[1].

The impact of *Tammy* encouraged DC Thomson to produce harsher stories, so whilst 'The Four Marys' continued to appear in *Bunty*, this new kind of story became dominant. Brown states that many of the stories had this tendency to cruelty. However, rather than always criticizing this tendency, sometimes she and other writers wanted to push it further to get rid of constraints upon their creativity within some texts.

There was one I was talked into doing called 'Blind Bettina'. She was an orphaned pop-singer whose only friend was her guide dog and her cruel aunt and uncle were her theatrical agents. Well, I got sick of the dog because if you were writing a script you always had to make provision for [it]…Well, this little girl's life was supposed to be miserable, so I thought, right, I'll make you really miserable and at the end of one episode I drowned the dog. And my editors said 'you'll have the little girls weeping into their pillows'. [I asked them] Isn't that what you wanted?' She argued that she would have to re-write the episode, but the editor instead gave her the opening caption of her next episode 'Brave Laddie swam across the loch to the other side'. (Interview, 9/8/99).

Where some stories feature supportive siblings, others feature a girl alone and isolated. 'Hateful Heather', written by Brown, ran for fourteen issues in *Mandy*. In this story, the heroine looked after aged grandparents in real life but was also an actress playing a 'bitch' in a glamorous soap-opera. The story played on the idea that the public would choose to believe she was like the character she played and treat her accordingly (one part of this story appears in the 23 June 1984 edition). In the 22 Dec 1973 edition of *Bunty* there are a number of similar stories, including 'Wildcat of the Court', in which a Princess's snobbish cousins hate her and 'Outcast of the Pony School' about bullying. Even the humorous stories tend to feature isolated girls: 'Powder Potts', for example, is about a girl working in a store who finds it is under threat of closure. She saves everyone's jobs, but because she is seen as 'dizzy' no one thinks she has had anything to do with it. In effect, the common element in many of these stories was a lone, misunderstood girl, a secret heroine, who puts things right in one way or another, whether it was an injustice at school, home or elsewhere. Again, the emphasis is on activity, not passivity. Indeed, 'Powder Potts' shows an understanding of how stereotypes of femininity may misrepresent individuals.

Interestingly, the *Mum's Own Annual* account of girls' comics denies the existence of humour of any kind in comics for girls. The author argues that humour is inherently insulting to the reader and so will be unattractive to girls (Anon, 1993, p.40-41 & 48). This assertion makes clear the author's assumptions (as a representative of the publisher IPC) about gender. Despite being one of the few supposedly nostalgic popular books about girls' comics, I have long suspected that the author is mocking the readers of the book through the tone of voice they adopt, which is that of a fussy, prissy and rather snobbish older woman. It may be an adopted persona that is a pastiche of an actual reader, rather than the actual writer's views[2]. Nonetheless, the reader is depicted as having 'feminine' qualities, which seemingly do not include humour or laughter.

There were other kinds of narratives in the comic book of the early 1970s, most notably fantasies and stories with historical settings. These narratives shared the harder edge of the new school stories. The majority of fantasy stories in the pre-1970s titles featured a magical helper, invisible friend, or a heroine transported to another world. This continued into the 1970s, but with a rather different feel. For example, Brown's first story for

DC Thomson in *Mandy* in 1972 featured a magical helper, but was actually about the need to solve family, personal and emotional problems. Brown described 'Cathy's Friend from Yesterday' as,

> all about a little girl who was playing in the park, who went through a gate that was hardly ever used and found herself solving family problems. Actually, her own family problems, 'cos the little girl she met with was her grandmother' (Interview, 9/8/99).

Brown also mentioned other examples, including an invisible friend story that appeared in *Jinty* about a ghost skater coaching a girl from an underprivileged background, again an orphan living with a wicked aunt and uncle (neatly combining the fantasy and cruelty that became more common in the late 1970s).

Despite changes in narrative, the girls' comic continued to decline in the mid-1970s, something noted by commentators outside the industry. In 1970 White had attributed the rapid turnover of titles to the 'transitory nature of current crazes' (1970, p.177). Here the end of the girl's comic was seen as symptomatic of a youth culture different from the experience of earlier generations. White characterizes this difference as based around the swift transition from one consumer-based trend to the next (linked with the rise of the 'teenybopper'). The collapse of the genre was also sometimes attributed to more literal changes in the readership. The Royal Commission on the Press (1977) claimed that:

> Largely due to a fall in the age of puberty, older teenagers were now enjoying periodicals once considered suitable only for their mothers and grandmothers, whilst younger girls had graduated from comics featuring 'Bunty of the Vth form' to the strip-weeklies and their sagas of love in the typing pool. (1977, p.11)

Further, the Royal Commission on the Press linked the decline of the girls' comic to publishing practices. Their report suggested that '[i]t is possible that publishers' own expectations, and the approaches built upon them, have become self-fulfilling prophecies' (1977, p.39). The tendency to combine titles when one dropped below the break-even point rather than drop it was seen as evidence of a lack of commitment. This could be seen as a circulation-boosting exercise, but The Royal Commission argued that, 'The prevailing policy has been to 'launch and merge' with the result that titles in this group have mostly appeared and died within a single decade or less' (1977, p.39).

This approach was commonly combined with the repetition of stories, a feature of comics since the 1950s. The recycling of stories usually took place on a seven-year turnaround (although it could be as low as four years). This seven-year period was envisaged as the length of time that it would take a reader to get into and grow out of a title. Such repetition could be either of a story as it originally appeared, or of a story which was re-written, sometimes with only minor adjustments for the new era, or of a translation into photo-story format. Whilst readers would not necessarily realize that stories were repeated, they described some as 'old-fashioned' in their interviews. These production approaches could be seen as creating the preconditions for the failure of these titles.

Endgame: Photo-stories and Horror

During the late 1970s, attempts to make the girls' comic relevant coincided with the emergence of adult feminist-inflected work on comics. In these adult comics, the intent was to create alternative texts, as for example, was the case in the creation of *Heroine* (1978), a feminist and punk informed one-off from the Birmingham Arts Lab edited by Suzy Varty. Much of this work emerged from the underground but was also a response to its perceived sexism. Underground and American superhero comics, rather than British mainstream or girls' comics were generally the stimulus of such work. In contrast, the work of young feminists incorporated responses to the British girls' comics (alongside magazines) and shared their mixed format. Both feminism and punk influenced *Shocking Pink*, for instance, published in the 1980s by a collective of young women. It was based on *Jackie* and teen magazines which it pastiched mercilessly. One can, for instance, compare their treatment of the nurse narrative, which is full of aggression, lack of deference, political overtones, and has an anti-romantic theme, with the very traditional 'Susan of St. Bride's', which is romantic, deferential and features the nurse as selfless 'angel' (Fig.6). However, they saw *Bunty* and similar titles as potentially positive, albeit in a slightly tongue-in-cheek way, particularly in seeing the all-girl worlds of the school stories as promoting lesbianism.

There were various attempts in the late 1970s to reverse the decline of the girls' comic for a teenage audience. One problem was that romance *in* the comic, like romance comics, had failed to hold an audience, as noted by McRobbie (1991, p.136). Attempts were also made to stop the erosion of the market for the story comic for younger readers. Changes included the use of photo-stories and modifications in the content of the drawn stories. Whilst the former, given the photographic medium, added a social-realist edge, the latter drew on horror and melodrama. Even darker themes of loss and difficulty emerged in comics at both IPC and DC Thomson in the late 1970s while standards like the ballet story largely disappeared. The intensification of the theme of cruelty continued throughout the 1980s, for instance in the popular 'Nothing Ever Goes Right', (*Judy*, DC Thomson, 1981) discussed by Barker (1989, p. 234-8). Here the heroine ends up buried anonymously in an unmarked grave.

The supernatural had an increasing importance in girls' comics of the late 1970s, again in attempts to refresh the genre. *Spellbound* (DC Thomson, 1976-1977) was an ex-

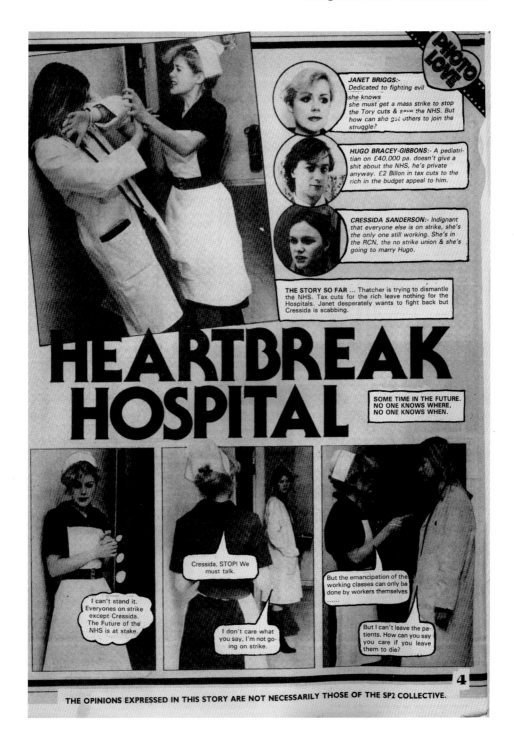

Figure 6 Shocking Pink Collective, 'Heartbreak Hospital', *Shocking Pink*, SP2 Collective, pp. 4-5.

periment, the first British horror title since the 1950s. These horror stories tended to be self-contained short stories narrated by a linking host character. One example given by Brown, who also wrote some of the 'Man in Black' stories, was a 'Damien Dark' story (the character featured in the comic *Spellbound*, but also appeared in *Judy*) about a girl stealing a paperweight that she ends the story trapped inside (Interview, 9/8/99). Fleetway took up the idea, launching their horror title, *Misty* (Fleetway, 1978-1980). Both *Spellbound* and *Misty* were rather short-lived, but indicative of what was to be a major type of publishing for girls in other formats. However, other kinds of periodicals continued to grow in popularity. Comics, in contrast, offered narrative in a format increasingly seen as only for boys (confirmed by the fact that narrative for girls became located in prose novels) and so were increasingly dislocated from models of girlhood across class during the 1980s.

Despite offering powerful narratives, the overwhelming shift to magazines continued as the 1980s progressed. The teen papers adopted and further adapted *Jackie*'s magazine format. In contrast to the minimal market research done for comics, titles like *Mizz* were reportedly researched very thoroughly, a process that included input from readers (McRobbie, 1991, p.136). McRobbie commented that publishers claimed to have moved beyond treating teenage and younger readers 'with amusement if not downright ridicule' (1991, p.136). This implies that the comic for girls was patronizing (although, as I've suggested, that was not always the case). An emphasis on magazine and feature, rather than comic format and story, then filtered down into pre- teen comics as well. Although elements of the comics were recycled in magazine and book format, it was clear that the comic no longer defined and shaped female lives. IPC followed up *Pink* with titles like *Mates* (1975-1981) and *Oh Boy*. DC Thomson eventually followed with *Blue Jeans* (1977-1991) and *Patches* (1979-1989). One attempt at a new comic was more of a return to earlier titles in IPC's re-launch of *Girl* (along with *Eagle*).

Factors around production may also have had an impact on the girls' comic in the 1980s in the shape of staff concerns about employment. As Sabin (1996) argues, the British boys' comics (rather than girls' comics) could lead to the possibility of other, more lucrative work. It was generally felt that the British firms were not good employers and that American firms offered slightly better pay and conditions. By the 1980s these same firms recognized the talent of those working on *2000AD* (IPC/Fleetway/Egmont Fleetway/Rebellion, 1977 to date) for instance, and actively recruited British creators (Atkinson, 1997, p.6). British comics for girls had few equivalents in the USA so these titles would not be a place that head-hunters would automatically consider looking in the search for new talent. That artists worked on both boys' and girls' comics, but that only the former would be a truly effective forum to showcase one's talents for potential new employers, meant that girls' comics were, in career terms, redundant.

The decline of the 1980s was compounded by one particular change, ironically intended to breathe new life into the genre but which instead hastened conversion to the magazine. Photo-stories were initiated by IPC in *Oh Boy*, aimed at 14-15 year-olds and *My Guy* (IPC, 1978-1994), for 16-17 year-olds. The success of these titles forced DC Thomson to go over to photo-stories during the 1980s. Benita Brown worked on these in *Blue Jeans*, *Dreamer* (IPC, 1981-1982) and others, initially as a writer, and later with her partner, as a photographer, which meant finding models. Brown said that, in a reversal of the drawn strips, the boys tended to be more idealized figures, but not the girls. They also had to be inventive, for instance using three different shirts in a strip to show the passage of time. Eventually, one of their stories was used as an example to newer photographers. She later stopped writing for photo-strips as she felt that the format meant that stories were less exciting and more conservative than the drawn strips had been. Sometimes creators were offered older stories and asked to update them by changing them into photo-stories, another form of the recycling of pre-existing material.

These comments from a creator are very much in line with critical commentary on the photo-strips. McRobbie (1991) reports an interview with an Assistant Editor at *Jackie* in the late 1980s, which characterized them as problematic 'With the advent of the photo-story we found that the scope became much more limited... It all became much more realistic, like the problem page set to pictures' (p.146). According to McRobbie (1991) photo-strips represented a move towards both a degree of social realism (seen as potentially positive) and increased conformity, restricting the heroines' activities in girls' comics during the 1980s (p.135-188). I would contend, however, that 'Heartbreak Hospital' in *Shocking Pink* (1987) suggests that the technique had largely unexplored possibilities (See Fig.6). McRobbie also argues that photographs signal class, in ways that the drawn stories had not. She argues that class is shown predominantly through the absence of middle class interests like tennis and ballet and the inclusion of television viewing, the youth club and the disco, reflecting more accurately how working-class young people lived.

McRobbie argues that the documentary nature of the photograph ruled out the fantasy elements that drawing had allowed and had a wooden-ness that contributed, finally, to the phasing out of comic strips of any sort. She identifies this as part of a 'generic crisis' of romance in which readers rejected stereotypical romantic behaviour and the stories that contained it. I would add that the wooden quality of the photo-stories and the changing relationship between girls and comic strip materials are as much about the failure of the form as a rejection of romance. In essence, this was a crisis of format (not content) in relation to gender, which reveals itself first in the teen magazines and is then replicated in the titles for younger readers. The titles for younger readers, after all, had no focus on romance, and yet the strips undergo similar shifts.

Ironically, while the girls' comic finally faded out and magazines became dominant there were some attempts to develop an adult female audience for comics. As part of the growth of comics for adults, female creators, audience and characters became, if not in vogue, then certainly a discussion point. Some characters emerged at this time that continue to be known and influential with a female (as well as male) audience, notably 'Tank Girl' in *Deadline* (Deadline Publications Ltd, 1988-1995), 'Halo Jones' in *2000AD* and 'Eve' in *Crisis* (Fleetway, 1988-1991). There was also a rise in female readership. *Deadline*, for instance, had a 25% female readership in 1989 (Sabin, 1993, p.233) which Sabin also argues was due to the input of female creators, particularly Julie Hollings, Carol Swain and Rachael Ball. There were also more women taking an active part in fandom. Whilst adult sales to both men and women increased, little thought seems to have been given by publishers to where the new female readers of the future would come from (given the increasing lack of familiarity girls had with the medium) and so the girls' comic market finally collapsed.

In institutional terms this may also be partly explained by the breakup of IPC, following Robert Maxwell's death, and its subsequent purchase by the continental publishing corporation Gutenberghus, whose interest was in developing special interest magazines. This institutional change, damaging in the context of boys' reading of comics was fatal to that of girls. DC Thomson rethought its publishing for girls and was left, alongside *Twinkle*, with a trio of graduated titles, *Bunty*, *Judy* and *Mandy*. These were aimed at slightly different age groupings. They continued to be printed on cheap paper: whilst the narratives had changed, the appearance had not. By the late 1990s, the disappearance of *Mandy* and *Judy* (which finally appeared as a glossy combined comic *M & J* from 1991- 1997) left *Twinkle* (which itself ended in 1999) and *Bunty* as the last British-originated strip-based publications for girls. *Bunty* had 'gone glossy' in 1989, although it kept its familiar mix of stories. It finally stopped publication in 2001.

Meanwhile, women were once more working predominantly in 'alternative' publishing. Women artists in the late 1990s were typically based in the independent sector. Fiona Rattray suggested that this was because women entering the big companies tended to contribute to the success of other (male) creators, in roles as colourists or letterers rather than being centre-stage (Rattray, 2000, p.21). Whilst arguing that increasing numbers of women entered the profession in the 1980s and 1990s, Sabin confirms that their roles tended to be, '[As] inkers or colourists, or sometimes even as editors' (Sabin, 1993, p.222). As with the feminist publishing of the 1970s, titles of the 1990s like *Women out of Line* (Knockabout, 1997), *The GirlFrenzy Millennial* (Slab-o-Concrete, 1998) and *Unskinny* (Quartet, 1997), the latter by Lucy Sweet and based largely on *Jackie*, are mostly aimed at adult women. What these titles show is reactions to the comics the creators had read as children, reworking and radicalizing some of the content. This shows a recognition of the potential of the original comics. These changes in the market were accompanied by the rise of the pre-teen magazine, a further trickling down of the woman's magazine model.

Periodicals for Girls After the Comic

Lifestyle magazines dominated the periodicals market for girls in the 1990s and on, before the growth of manga publishing in English drew a new audience to the comic medium (albeit in book rather than periodical form). A trawl made in early 2001 revealed few titles incorporating any comic strips at all. The shift in the nature of publishing for girls was confirmed by a report from the mid-1990s by the Children's Literature Research Centre, Roehampton Institute (1996), *Young People's reading at the end of the century*. At Key Stage One (4-7 years) children's favourites were *The Beano* and *The Dandy*, *Sonic the Comic* (Fleetway Editions/Egmont Magazines, 1993- 2002), *Barbie* and *Tots TV* (Redan Co, 1996- end date unknown). Of these, only the latter two had a large female readership. Few comics appealed to both boys and girls in the seven to twelve years old bracket. *Sonic the Comic* had been successful although the majority of readers are boys: the readership ranges from four to sixteen years. By Key Stage Four (14-16 years), whilst half of the boys read comics, less than 20% of the girls did so. Instead of comics, the vast majority of the girls read magazines. The survey indicated that from Key Stage Two (7-11 years) onwards *Big* (EMAP Metro, 1990- end date unknown), *Shout* (DC Thomson, 1997-date) and *Fast Forward* (BBC Magazines, 1989-1995) were girls' favourite titles. In addition, *Smash Hits* (EMAP, 1978- 2006), *Just 17* (EMAP, 1983-2004) and *Horse and Pony* (Redan Co/EMAP Active, 1995-2010) had a large following. By Key Stage Four *Just 17*, *Big*, *Mizz* (IPC Magazines, 1985-date), *Sugar* (Attic Futura/HFUK/NatMags/Hearst, 1994-date), and *Smash Hits* dominated. These latter titles appear in many sources, including Whelehan's (2000) account of feminism and popular culture in which they are seen as preparation for women's magazines and their focus on lifestyle, body and partners (2000, p.53).

Whilst it is clear that the increasing dominance of the magazine format resulted in the disappearance of the girls' comic other factors also played a part, for instance, as *Tots TV* and *Sonic the Comic* suggest, there was a rise in magazines that were spin-offs from other media or licensed characters. Further, male audiences had become seen as the 'appropriate' ones for comics as a medium. The recognition that the female audience was disappearing, (a situation that some publishers had helped create in developing the teen magazines that came to be in competition with the comics that they also published) came to confirm, for producers, the need to develop other products for girls. This decision, in turn, further exacerbated the erosion of the female market for comics. That the comic, whilst it continues to represent girlhood to adult women readers in a nostalgic sense, became detached from models of girlhood in Britain can be ascribed to the gender associations of the comic format, but also to other aspects of production. Thus, working conditions, international interest in British comic creators, 'teenybopper' culture, the transfer to magazines for girls inaugurated by *Jackie* and perceptions of the comic as addressing a male audience combined to undermine the girls' comic and the idea that it represented or was attached to notions of girlhood. The completion of the long slow shift over several generations of readers to a woman's magazine format from the comic strip shows how completely the magazine format came to be associated with both women and girls (even given the arrival of men's magazines). This both implies a potentially shorter childhood and returns us to the early periodicals and their inclusion of material seen as suitable for 'girls' of all ages.

Notes

1   I wrote a short piece on this strip for Paul Gravett's (2011) *1001 Comics You Must Read Before You Die*.

2   Apologies to the writer if this is not the case.

Chapter Three
Mediating the Text: Academics, Teachers, Librarians and Others

In Britain, the way that both adults and children understand the comic has been, in part, shaped and guided (sometimes indirectly, sometimes with rather more immediacy) by teachers, academics, librarians and a range of other commentators since comics first emerged. In particular, perspectives on mass media and education, as described by F.R. Leavis and others in the 1930s and onwards, created a climate of reading where perceptions of comics were mediated in certain ways. These perspectives influenced both childhood reading and adult practice, as commentators' perceptions of the medium filtered through to parents and teachers. It also influenced the subsequent practice of child readers who, as adults, mediated understandings of the comic for following generations (particularly in the case of those readers who became teachers). In effect, readers were poachers and gamekeepers, both approving and disapproving of comics, a point to which I later return.

Inevitably, such mediations of the comic as text also had an impact upon future generations of academics. As I chart here, the legacy of how the comic has been understood in education is visible in writing on comics in a range of disciplines in Britain, shaping how comics have been discussed. This chapter attempts to outline the context within which readers' understandings of the comic partly developed, as various writers' work made an impression upon librarianship, education and the academy. As such it offers a counterpoint to the previous chapter on the history of the girls' comic and leads into the readers' accounts of comics.

Comics and Criticism: Mass culture, media effects and moral panic

Much of the scholarship about the medium in Britain identifies the comic as problematic mass culture. Throughout the twentieth century, British commentary on the comic has been dominated by the discourses of 'media effects' and 'moral panic' seen against a background of debates over high versus 'low' or popular culture. Yet, as Barker and Julian Petley state (1997), terms like 'media effects' and 'moral panics' can be seen as contentious. For example, even the way that regular comic readers learn the rules of the genre can be seen to undermine a notion of 'media effects'. As Barker and Petley (1997) argue,

> [i]f media materials obey certain rules then it makes no sense at all to detach little bits from the programme and count them to see what 'effect' they might have, because their meaning and possible effects are not detachable from the rule-governed form in which they occur... And if audiences have to learn those rules, have to be able to make sense of the media they encounter, then the more they have learnt the rules, the less likely they are to be 'vulnerable' to those media. (p.9)

I explore here how 'moral panics' and 'media effects', as part of a 'common sense' conception of how media work, have had an impact upon how comics have been received and understood. Although work revealing a shift in attitudes towards the comic can be found in a number of academic disciplines, generally beginning in the late 1980s, it is the earlier critical work that has dominated discourses. It is to this latter writing that I now turn, both outlining what has existed and looking at how it may have influenced children's and adults' understanding of comics.

In a British context, a number of traditions have had an impact upon much of the work on comics, especially within the education sector and so, in turn, upon attitudes to the comic in Britain. Debates in America and Britain around popular culture, whether located in traditions of 'culture and civilization', the Frankfurt School or mass culture criticism have (mostly indirectly) resulted in the form being dismissed. With regard to the official discourse about comics, some accounts have had a high profile with the wider public and a negative impact on attitudes. To many the comic has been something someone else reads, usually those less well off, less educated and of lesser status than themselves. Further, as the format that is used for such publications is the 'other' of the text-based book, so the readership of such texts is depicted as the 'other' (in terms of class, age, or gender) to those who lodge complaints about the form.

The worries expressed in writing by educators and academics about young people's reading have a history which includes the 'penny dreadful' which was felt to encourage immorality amongst the young in the 1880s. The 'solutions' proposed by reformers to the problem of the 'penny dreadful', partly involved developing gendered magazines like the *Girl's Own Paper*.

In fact, the comic was also born partially from concerns about the supposed effects of the 'penny dreadful'. From the start, then, comics were bound up with notions of what was acceptable and respectable entertainment for the young or for the working-classes, notions based on middle-class judgment and informed by the need for social control. This indicates what Nyberg (1998) suggests, which is that '...the debate over comic books fits into a broad pattern of efforts to control children's culture' (p. viii).

Comics first came in for criticism in Britain in the 1890s, initially along class lines. *Ally Sloper's Half Holiday* (WJ Sinkins/The Sloperies, 1884-1914), usually seen as the first British comic, was very popular, and offered its adult audience a working-class anti-hero. Capitalization on the success of this paper by a variety of publishers, particularly Alfred Harmsworth's Amalgamated Press, meant that there was an explosion in the number of comics produced. Harmsworth ran an anti-'penny dreadfuls' campaign and intended his comics, including *Comic Cuts* (1890-1953) to be an alternative. As a result of the increased quantity of comics they swiftly became seen as problematic. It was argued that they were a threat to the literacy of the working classes, as Sabin (1996) explains, both because they were picture-based and because the type was too small to read where it did exist (p. 19). In their turn comics became the dangerous new mass medium of their day, liable to have an effect upon the young or working-class reader. A number of recommendations were made to control their further development. These included increasing the number of 'improving' texts, and producing comics for children rather than adults.

Concerns about literacy, morality, class and comics continued to be the keynotes in later debate, emerging with most vehemence in the 1950s, predominantly amongst librarians and teachers. These debates were a pivotal influence on how comics were seen. Many story papers were translated into comic format during that decade and the fears that existed with regard to British titles were further intensified due to the arrival of American comics. However, whereas America saw the comic publishers as the problem, the British identified the problem as American comics (and the values they were thought to represent), seeing them as particularly gauche, crass and commercial. In reality, the large scale of the campaign belied the fact that the case in Britain was against a small trickle of imported material, initially available via US troops stationed in Britain, rather than a flood. Anti-American sentiment, mass media criticism and fears of cultural imperialism were combined, again setting comics at one extreme of a high versus 'low', or popular culture, paradigm.

British concerns about comics in the 1950s originated with the Communist Party which felt such comics were insidious propaganda attracting children to capitalism, but the campaign later involved the teaching unions and the Comics Campaign Council[1]. The teaching unions shifted the campaign onto a moral position and, ironically, used the blueprint of the American campaign against comics, whilst also expressing anti-American sentiment. The similarity of left and right positions in seeing popular culture as problematic (although for very different reasons) meant that the British campaign begun by the left could end as a right-wing one. One result was that in Britain, the *Children and Young Persons (Harmful Publications) Act 1955* made publication or distribution of the wide category 'horror comics' (a shift from the term 'American-style') illegal.

The assumption that the comic is a potentially dangerous medium was central to the writings of Pumphrey (1954, 1955 and 1964), a member of the Comics Campaign Council and can also be seen in P.M. Pickard's appraisal of British comics (Comics Campaign Council, 1955). The latter expressed concern about levels of violence and racism, in, for instance, *Eagle*. The campaign was felt by participants to be even-handed in not wholly banning comics but engaging with and judging individual texts (Pickard, 1955, p.3). This 'even-handedness', however, started from a viewpoint held by the clergy, teachers, academics, and librarians of the council that comics were a cause of social problems. For example, Pumphrey saw himself as attempting to minimize the damage caused by children reading comics by advocating censorship. He identified comics in general as worthless and indecent literature, arguing that there were two kinds of comics 'harmful and harmless' (in Barker 1984, p.81), adding that the best they could do was no harm to the child. As Barker (1984) notes, from the campaigners' points of view '[it] was not simply that horror comics were around, but that better things -more suitably written but making concessions to their intended readership- were not' (p.54). Similarly, Pickard (1955) concluded that at best British comics were 'average' (p.12) in respect of the writing and artwork that they contained. However, in looking at British comics, I must comment that the range of art and narrative is broad and often of very high quality. I would suggest that commentators chose to report negatively, usually without offering examples, to strengthen their case.

Pumphrey set the tone for much of the British post-war educational analysis of comics. It was both Leavisite in tone, and an interpretation of Fredric Wertham's perceptions of the relationship between juvenile delinquency and comics. Wertham's work, particularly *The Seduction of the Innocent* (1954), had a profound influence upon British attitudes to the comic. As Nyberg writes of the American experience: 'The major factor in the success of the campaign against comics was the linkage of comic book reading to juvenile delinquency, a problem representing the ultimate loss of social control over children' (1998, p. ix). However, Nyberg sees Wertham's work as attempting to offer an alternative approach to the question of 'media effects' through a multidisciplinary study of mass media (Nyberg, 1998, p. x). Wertham did produce an ideological analysis of comics, which Nyberg (1998) describes as 'relatively unsophisticated... [but, considered as a predecessor] ...not out of place in the company of media scholarship today' (p. 95). Nyberg also suggests that in his use of the interview Wertham might be considered one of the first scholars to engage with audience analysis. Similarly, Pumphrey and Pickard (1955) in a British context saw interviews as a useful tool in gaining an understanding about 'what children of different ages regard as interesting, amusing, funny', because 'it may well be that the infiltration of violence...is not in accordance with their wishes' (p.19).

Thus, the critical approach to comics in Britain amongst teachers, librarians and others is explicitly linked, via Wertham, to academic accounts of media. However, both the Frankfurt School and Wertham could be generally categorized as offering, albeit from a left perspective, a Leavisite discourse of 'us and them'. In the final account, Wertham, whilst using tools that are recognizably part of a left commentary on media, did have a specific agenda. As Nyberg (1998) puts it, '[Wertham] de-emphasized the intellectual roots of his argument in order to ally himself with the conservative groups who seemed most willing to take action against comic books' (p. 97). Although he did show that readers were not simply passive consumers, he also asserted that comics *did* have a direct influence on readers. Hence, British educational responses to comics, which were often influenced by Wertham, can be framed within both the 'culture and civilization' *and* the Frankfurt School traditions.

Wertham's work consistently associated violent or criminal behaviour with comic content, whether read by children or adults, male or female readers. In general, Wertham emphasized male reading of comics, because the juvenile delinquent was generally characterized as male and the comic book was seen as a predominantly male preserve, yet many of the comics coming in for the harshest criticism were those attracting a female audience. Wertham saw female violence in the comics as especially shocking. He feared that these examples would encourage female readers to be more violent themselves, positioning the comic as an instruction manual for crime with regard to women (another 'blank slate' model). In particular, adult orientated comics from American publisher EC were condemned for tales of vengeance where domineering husbands were killed by their wives. In material produced for a readership of both men and women, such stories were seen as an incitement for other wives to follow suit.

In terms of images of women and the female audience, the assertion that reading comics of any kind will lead to criminality is common throughout Wertham's writing. The female reader is depicted as more likely to turn the reading experience into criminal activity, suggesting a greater degree of susceptibility to the 'messages' of the texts. In general, as Nyberg reports, women were '...objects to be abused or to be used as decoys in crime settings. Women who did not fall into the role of victim were generally cast as villains, often with masculine or witchlike powers' (1998, p.95). The male reader, it was suggested, would have no respect for women, and the female reader, it was implied, might end up like the '...seventeen-year-old girl [who] earned $1000 per week through the sale of narcotics' (Wertham, 1955, p.26). Romance comics were also unhealthy in Wertham's analysis. In this instance, the harm to the female reader was in the portrayal of women as victims, humiliated in love. Wertham reports that a 12-year-old, addicted to love comics, ended up stealing money from a lodger (1955, p.41). He attributed this to images of girls as thieves, and to associated images of criminal male partners in love comics. Thus the male readers of the crime and superhero comic, and the female readers of the romance, would come to see the female as either evil or weak; and in either case not in her 'proper' role as homemaker, wife and mother.

Alongside horror comics, Wertham included what would now be considered superhero comics, which were classified as crime because the superheroes combated it. Further, he was insistent that '[s]pecific comics had specific dangers: superhero comics were essentially fascist …often with homo-erotic undercurrents' (in Sabin, 1993, p.158). A notion of 'effects' upon the reader was central here. For instance, the girl may desire to be like 'Wonder Woman', which is seen as problematic. Wertham (1955) said:

> [Wonder Woman] is always a horror type. She is physically very powerful, tortures men, has her own female following, is the cruel, "phallic" woman. While she is a frightening figure for boys, she is an undesirable ideal for girls, being the exact opposite of what girls are supposed to want to be. (p.35)

Wertham (1955) later characterizes this comic as '[a] crime comic which we have found to be one of the most harmful' (p.64), a judgment related to his concerns about appropriate behaviour for girls. He argued that '[i]f it were possible to translate a cardboard figure like 'Wonder Woman' into life, every normal-minded young man would know there is something wrong with her' (p.235). Thus, he places himself and the 'normal-minded' young man as the right-minded citizen against the deviant female, including those females in the audience who might admire Wonder Woman.

The policing of girls' reading generally took place at a local level, within the family and school, rather than achieving national significance (unlike that of male readers). Sabin (1996) suggests that the way in which titles were scrutinized until the end of the 1960s was as a result of a 'heightened sense of protectiveness about female children' (p.90). The fear that girls will grow up 'too soon' as a result of their contact with 'unsuitable' texts has remained a common argument in relation to periodicals for girls. The fear of the effect that comic reading might have upon girls was often combined by adult commentators with nostalgia for what they saw as a disappearing model of girlhood, that of their own childhood. In such an argument, the actualities of girls' lives and reading practices become overlaid with an assumption that there was once a golden time when girls read 'appropriately'. As my previous analysis shows, there have consistently been tensions around models of girlhood and narratives offered in these texts. However, nostalgic accounts suggest previous titles were 'respectable', a quality identified by Skeggs (1997) as 'one of the most ubiquitous signifiers of class' (p.1). In relation to adult fears, the 'girl' is not an individual, but a symbol of vulnerability, in need of adult protection from wider social change. In addition, the concept of the 'girl' carries connotations of middle-class respectability, also seen by commentators as under threat from comic reading. Girlhood and girls exist in tension in such a climate, with the former under threat from the latter. That is, girlhood is (potentially) undermined by girls' actual choices. From this perspective, control over reading becomes part of protecting children from themselves. That fears about girls' reading are a consistent feature in adult accounts of that reading indicates the work involved for adults in maintaining girlhood as a structure. This notion of the dangers of comics, a key way in which these texts were mediated, is also reflected in the way that some readers saw them as a vehicle for rebellion.

'Appropriate' and 'respectable' reading for girls was a central part of Pumphrey's (1964) survey. Pumphrey utterly dismissed American titles and expressed concerns about subject matter, literacy, and the vulnerable reader with regard to British ones. His stated aim was to refocus British children on periodicals whose 'producers are not satisfied with mere entertainment' (1964, p.35). In terms of gender, Pumphrey rated as highly 'appropriate' reading those girls' comics containing '[u]seful information and occupation' (1964, p.39). These include cookery, home decoration, and a crossword in *Diana*, dress patterns in *Girl*, hints on deportment in *School Friend* and the rather vague 'things to make' (Pumphrey, 1964, p.39) in *Princess*. However, Pumphrey's most positive comment is 'traditional' (1964, p.39), suggesting both the conservative nature of his analysis and his focus on specifically British culture. The periodicals aimed at teenage girls get consistently lower marks than those aimed at younger readers, except for *Honey* (Fleetway/IPC, 1960-1986), which also apparently contained useful information. Pumphrey clearly sees some British girls' comics as potentially a tool for guiding the girl into what he considers appropriate behaviour. Pumphrey identified the two models of girlhood as on offer in girls' comics, of which he saw the homemaker as more 'appropriate', rejecting what he saw as consumerist teenage girlhood. This, just like Wertham's assertion that comics will lead girls into criminality, is based on a 'blank slate' model of the girl.

Both of the models mentioned by Pumphrey (domestic and consumer based) became targets for criticism in educational analysis and elsewhere in the late 1960s. The deceptively titled *Magazines Teenagers Read* (Alderson, 1968), for instance, is an analysis of reading matter for teenage girls, combining a textual analysis of selected issues of *Trend* (City Magazines Ltd, dates unknown), *Jackie* and *Valentine* with some interview material. It is regularly cited in accounts of *Jackie*, such as, for instance, McRobbie's (1991). Written from an educational point of view, Connie Alderson (1968) sees what is described as the 'pop scene' along with the teenage and woman's magazines as a pernicious influence upon girls in terms of both literacy and achievement, insisting that, 'The harm from this type of literature is the persistent encouragement to 'dream' rather than to 'do' and participate' (p.109). Alderson's approach consists of an uneasy alliance between feminist-inflected thinking about political action, conservative educational rhetoric and Leavisite commentary. Her analysis ignores the fact that many of the narratives were about activity, through working lives in titles for older readers, or 'righting wrongs' in titles for younger ones.

The impact of Leavisism upon Alderson, writing in the 1960s, but also upon the educational curriculum in English in general, from the 1930s and onward, was immense. Leavisism proposed direct intervention in schools to develop students' critical skills in ways that would ensure that they resisted mass culture. This intervention took the form of a campaigning educational politics represented in a range of texts including *Culture and Environment* (1933) written by Leavis with Denys Thompson, and Thompson's journal for English teachers, *The Use of English* which further developed the connections between Leavisism and schooling. Leavisism was a considerable influence upon the educational curriculum in English and in turn on pupils, for a number of reasons, particularly through the way that practical applications in the form of exercises for students were offered in the texts. In addition, the image of English as a bastion against the 'barbarism' of mass media, and the seductive notion of the role of the teacher as cultural missionary and as part of a cultural elite must also have played a part. The negative and moralistic attitude to media Leavisism encouraged is still visible today (often revealing itself in concerns about 'media effects'), but it also paved the way for teachers more sympathetic to popular texts in creating a space for popular culture to be studied.

Seeing the titles from a Leavisite point of view as addictive, escapist and limiting is only part of the story, however. In concluding, Alderson refers to what she considers to be the greatest problem facing young people. This is not the periodicals, but the education system, which she sees as failing to help the development of critical skills, again bringing her in line with Leavis. Her analysis refers specifically to girls attending secondary modern schools, and argues, in effect, that Leavis' (1933) proposal to 'introduce into schools a training in resistance [to mass culture]' (p.188) should be revisited in relation to these schools. As Alderson (1968) stated

> We shall continue to have two nations as far as enjoyment of what is valuable and lasting in the arts is concerned as long as we have a system of education where children are segregated at 11 and the majority become young workers at 15. A developing taste for what is good in a child of 16 can be reinforced, but where no initial flowering is possible there can be no strengthening and the child is most vulnerable to the pressures of all that is bad in mass media (p.112).

Thus, comics and magazines are implicated in the underachievement of girls within a school system in need of reform. The inheritance of Leavis can be seen in the way that pupils, in a range of schools over a long period, were told of the horrors of mass culture. The cultural climate with regard to comics, as mediated through education, might be seen as one in which comics are (officially, at least) seen as dangerous (or addictive) rubbish.

The focus in Alderson's work on vulnerable female readers is inflected through class, identifying the young working-class as particularly under the influence of their reading material. Such concerns can again be traced back to commentators on the readers of the 'penny dreadfuls' of the nineteenth century. Readers were felt to be at risk in ways specific to their gender. As Edward Salmon (1888) wrote of girls in *Juvenile Literature As It Is*:

> the injury is more insidious and subtle. It is almost exclusively domestic. We do not often see an account of a girl committing any serious fault through her reading. But let us go into the houses of the poor, and try to discover what is the effect on

the maiden mind of the trash the maiden buys. If we were to trace the matter to its source, we should probably find that the higher-flown conceits and pretensions of the young girls of the period, their dislike of manual work and love of freedom, spring largely from notions imbibed in the course of a perusal of their penny fictions. (in Barker, 1989, p.101)

Salmon couches fears for the female reader in domestic terms, but also suggests that reading 'trash' might encourage ideas about 'freedom'. Wider literacy skills were seen as opening up dangers that young working-class women might not 'know their place'. Thus, concerns about girls' reading go back to the nineteenth century, although with a very different slant from that found in commentary about *Jackie*. Whether leading girls astray, radicalizing them, or encouraging their passivity and attachment to traditional femininity, the very range of concerns about periodicals for girls creates a much more complex image of both girlhood and the publications over time than many critics suggest.

The Impact of Feminism

Librarians, like teachers, were represented on the Comics Campaign Council, and were also involved in analysing material, predominantly with the aim of informing parents and fellow professionals. Librarianship, as well as education, may direct the reader towards more 'suitable' texts, again mediating the form on behalf of young readers. Hence, although the publication by the London Borough of Camden Libraries and Arts' (1988) *Survey of comics & magazines for young people* reveals concerns that are very different from those of Pumphrey, Whitehead et al and Alderson, they have much in common with them in terms of both tone and approach.

In the 1970s Whitehead et al (1977) turned 'with relief' (p.265) to *Bunty* after *The Beano*, arguing that it contained more words, better grammar and sections in prose as well as offering 'appropriate' activities for girls. Whitehead et al (1977) in the most significant survey of children's reading of the 1970s, argued that in comics, pictures force words out, and surmised that if comics were not available reading would improve (p.256, 270). Strangely, given this assertion, they also concluded that heavy periodical reading goes hand in hand with heavy book reading but did not see that as worth commenting on further (p.274).

In the later Camden report the 'problem' of comics (at least from the point-of-view of the report's authors) is that they are racist (an issue Pickard had raised) and sexist, as well as poorly written. British debates about the comic in the 1970s and 1980s, then, also emerged from both right and left politically and theoretically. As Barker notes, by the late 1980s it was a common assumption that 'magazines like *Jackie*, but perhaps that one especially, have done long term damage to girls' psyches' (1989, p. 134). He identifies this generalization, as one which, combined with concerns about the comic as a form, had a significant impact upon how these texts were received.

Feminism had a major impact on debates about comics incorporating any representations of girls and women through identifying comics as generally sexist. Sabin (1993) indicates how various types of comic were criticized,

> ...from a feminist perspective. The early comics in the genre ...were attacked for being unnecessarily twee and reinforcing notions of girls as inferior to boys; the romance comics for promoting the message that a woman's purpose was to make herself attractive in order to find a mate; the American female- superhero comics for merely being imitators of the male variety and so on. (p.224)

Concerns about sexism were also to found in writing about children's books, including Rosemary Stones' (1983) *Pour out the cocoa, Janet*. In relation to the girls' comic, both sets of critical writing are relevant.

Stereotyping was a particularly important issue in critiques of children's books and comics. Rosemary Auchmuty's (1992) discussion of the school story flags up the approach to this issue. Auchmuty stated that,

> In the educational sphere feminists launched an attack on 'sex-role stereotyping' in the classroom and children's reading material, considered to be damaging to both sexes, in the hope and expectation that the removal of sexist imagery and its replacement by sexually interchangeable role models would create a climate of true educational opportunity. (1992, p.18)

Further, the victim heroine was seen as a particularly damaging stereotype. For example, Cadogan described comics as undermining the girl reader by encouraging her to embrace victimhood rather than feminism. She saw this trend as starting in the late 1950s. Calling the texts worthless, she was particularly angered by lurid death scenes. In particular she criticized one story, 'No Time For Pat', a story from *Jinty* in the mid-1970s. Cadogan (1986) described it as 'one of the most tasteless serials of all' in which 'a girl is told that she has six months to live and decides to devote them to looking after a crippled child at a nearby orphanage' (p.330). Her conclusion, like Wertham's, was that the medium was irredeemable.

Creators, however, argued that their intention was often directly feminist. Brown, for instance, insisted that the intention was to create characters with problems, but ones who could also solve them. She points out that, '[They might be a] victim hero, but little wets would not have got anywhere in the girls' comic, you couldn't be a little whingy wet. You might be a victim, but by God you were going to put that right!' (Interview, 9/8/99). From her point-of-view many of the heroines were valid feminist role models for girls in encouraging self-reliance. Further, that girls were often apart from their parents, had to make decisions and be independent was a model of girlhood Brown saw as positive.

Concerns about stereotyping were also central to the Camden Libraries report. Here the comic for children was seen as full of negative stereotypes. Girls' comics in particular were criticized with only *Shocking Pink* (Shocking Pink Collective, 1982, 1987), being seen as having any merit. However, Myra Macdonald (1995) suggests that this type of stereotyping analysis could be criticised, for, '[a]t its crudest... [it] even disregards how the stereotype is integrated within the text and is blinkered to the possibility that the same stereotype can be presented within the narrative context...as either victim or as the protagonist' (p.14).

Walkerdine (1990) identifies two other problems with such an approach. On the one hand, it '...assumes a passive learner...who will change as a result of receiving the correct information about how things really are' (p.89). On the other, such thinking assumes that when the girl has 'the veil of distortion lifted from her eyes, she too will want to engage in those activities from which she has been precluded by virtue of her gender' (Walkerdine, 1990, p.89). The critical writing from education and librarianship had what was in the best interests of the child at heart, however, it also assumes a 'blank slate' model and does not engage with actual children in terms of their interests.

Much of the writing about sexism in the 1970s and 1980s simply demanded the removal of materials perceived as sexist and their replacement with more positive texts. Simultaneously, however, the appearance of less traditionally feminine (and possibly feminist) heroines *also* drew criticism, making comics a suspect medium in relation to the depiction of women from both feminist and anti-feminist perspectives. For instance, the *Mum's Own Annual* (1993) account of *Tina* is very critical of the active heroines in this title, including 'Glory Gold', describing them as macho, inappropriate role models, and above all, unfeminine. In addition, the author asserts that an active heroine is simply a man in disguise. Discussion of super-heroines in American comics similarly led to assessments of characters such as 'Ms Marvel', as male, or simply mimicking male characters, for instance, in Richard Reynolds' writing (1992, p.80). Such comments, of course, relate to an underlying set of assumptions about what is female, respectable and feminine. For a comic with central female characters, these perspectives could be seen as leading to a dead-end in that the 'properly feminine' seemingly do not have adventures.

The idea of tension between girlhood and adventure had resulted in a number of strategies being used by publishers from the 1950s onwards. One was to have the character associated with a 'properly feminine' activity, such as ballet, which (despite being very physical) acted as a guarantor of femininity no matter what else that ballerina might do. Another strategy was that in a story with a female lead, motivation should be personal. As Marcus Morris reported in relation to *Girl*, 'The adventure and the danger can be there but the reason for it must be the search for a long-lost uncle or father' (Morris & Hallwood, 1998, p.164). However, by the time of the writing outlined above, such strategies were also under criticism.

With the emergence of second wave feminism, the comic also became a suspect medium because of the male domination of the profession. It is argued that women were discouraged from entering the profession at college and were instead redirected into children's books, fashion or fine art (Lanyi, 1979, p.740). Sabin (1993) suggests a slightly different model, arguing that 'it seems that the comics industry was seen as such a 'closed shop' that women wishing to become involved in this kind of work tended instead to drift into book illustration (especially children's book illustration)' (p.288). I would add, anecdotally, that those studying illustration at university or polytechnic in Britain, whether male or female, were very rarely encouraged to work on comics, such was the perception of the medium, well into the 1990s.

Comics were also seen as sexist with regard to views of the reader. If one assumes a wholly male group of editors, artists and writers making decisions, as reflected in the stories, about what would be suitable entertainment for girls it could be seen as inherently sexist. In addition, there actually were some unpleasant examples of poking fun at the readers through the narratives, and a knowing quality in some that seemed to be at the expense of the reader. That editors felt they could take decisions about narratives without recourse to market research with girls, suggests confidence in commercial decisions, buoyed, in the 1950s and 1960s, by high circulation figures. These figures may have fuelled an attitude that these comics only required limited input from female creators or readers. When the sales of girls' comic declined, conversely, this could be seen confirming that comics were only a male interest.

These assumptions have led to a suggestion that there were no female writers, artists or editors involved in the creation of these comics (or that they were conservative and compliant if they did exist). It also suggests that male artists and writers were hostile towards girls' comics. However, whilst the dominance of male artists and editors means that comics will reflect their perceptions of the readers and the material, as Macdonald (1995) suggests, '[t]he relation between the gender of the producer and gender representations is a complex one' (p.4). In addition, Sabin (1996) said that whilst there were few women artists or editors in mainstream comics before the 1990s they did exist.

Further, as the production history of the girls' comic is slowly becoming better known, more women writers and artists are talking about their experiences (such as Benita Brown, interviewed for this monograph) undermining the image of the profession as consisting solely of male creators and female consumer/victims. Brown saw her writing as informed by *School Friend* and *Girl's Crystal*, which she had read as a girl. Like many of the other creators, she inherited an understanding of girls' comics from previous versions she had read, or worked on, and consciously operated within that tradition and often moved beyond its limitations.

Finally, a number of men involved with girls' comics as creators, readers, or editors, including Alan Grant, Pat Mills and Neil Gaiman have spoken about various aspects of comics for girls and women. Gaiman has spoken about the high quality of the stories in comics for girls, Grant on working on romance comics and Mills on the significance of the girls' comic in changing approaches in UK comic publishing. Paul Gravett has also held events where women creators and editors are celebrated, for example the 'Draw Misty for Me' event held as part of the Comica Festival in August 2014 which was intended to showcase the work of artist Shirley Bellwood.

The lack of focus on the female creator is partly because, on many comics, artists, editors and writers were unnamed. This was compounded by the fact that many of the writers for DC Thomson, for instance, worked from home. Individual creators were not necessarily aware of who else worked for the firm or whether they were male or female, although Brown said that during her period of writing the majority of writers that she found out about, in both IPC and DC Thomson, were women (Interview, 9/8/99).

Mills, however, in an article by John Freeman (no date given) argued that there might be another reason for a lack of female writers in the field, arguing that women

> wanted to be working on trendy, glossy pop magazines as a stepping stone to older magazines like *19* and *Honey*. So they stressed the feature content of publications like *Pink* and paid little attention to the comic side, which they saw as a necessary evil, rather than a vital selling aspect of the publication.

This moves away from notions of female exclusion onto notions of comics not being useful enough to engage with, or as Mills (no date given) put it 'that's also why male writers worked on girls strip stories – because many female writers found them uncool. Pure snobbery!' As argued above, however, there were more women writers and artists than has often been seen to be the case.

Another aspect that made it less clear who worked on what, was that authorship was often shared and writers could end up working on other peoples' ideas (and their own may well have gone on to someone else). If we consider these factors, it is clear that the male domination of the profession was interpreted as sexist in a rather too simplistic way within feminist critiques of comics. The anonymity of writers and artists in many British comics, then, hides a more nuanced story about comic production and gender.

Perspectives on the Comic in Education and Librarianship since the 1990s

Publications produced about comics for librarians and teachers since the 1990s generally show a less judgmental approach than the writing of the 1970s and 1980s. Millard (1997), for instance, whilst she says she sees comic reading as a stage before 'proper' (i.e. text-only) reading, distances herself from previous perspectives. She criticizes Whitehead et al for describing comics as 'a time-consuming drug' (Whitehead et al, 1977, p.255). That Millard both flags up this report and takes a step away from it suggests a climate of reading that is changing, but where comics may still seen as problematic.

Further, work like that of Morag Styles and Victor Watson (1996), also aimed at teachers, asserted that '[many] teachers are aware that the comic is one of the best and most motivating genres for teaching reading' (p.179). At the same time, they acknowledged that these same teachers '[are also aware that] this is too unsettling for those with fixed views of what children should read and how they should learn to do it' (Styles and Watson, 1996, p.179). What these comments suggest is a profession divided between those who see the use of comics as entirely unacceptable and those who see them as a useful teaching aid, or simply as highly motivational reading for pleasure. Contemporary educational and library interest in comics, is, in part, linked to fears about the internet and mobile technologies undermining literacy and not by any understanding or enthusiasm for the medium in its own right. In addition, worries about boys' perceived weaknesses in reading mean that comics have been seen as a way of drawing them back into an engagement with printed texts.

Manga has been seen as similarly problematic, with initial media coverage in the 1990s offering 'moral panic' headlines about content. In dealing with periodicals rather than book formats, manga and graphic novels aimed at girls are beyond the scope of this book. However, the success of shojo manga (titles for girls) from 2000 and on has had an impact upon how both manga and graphic novels are seen in schools, and, indeed, has resulted in an increase in the number of British female creators.

In summing up the tropes that appear throughout educational and librarianship accounts of comics, emphasizing their currency and use in 'common sense' understandings of the comic, comments made at training days I have run with librarians and teachers provide an illustration of negative views and, more importantly, reflect the impact that the educational discourse about comics had upon professionals. Whilst many are prepared reflect on their views of the medium, and others are enthusiasts, others again hold to a cultural stereotype of the comic as a dangerous, or at the very least suspect, medium. In this we see the inheritance of the ways in which comics were mediated to the child reader in current professional lives. For some, as in Jenkins' (1992) research on 'Batman', their own memories of comics did not just involve pleasure, but, 'evoked a more reactionary response – an attempt to police contemporary children's culture and to regulate popular pleasures' (p.35), tying in with those sentiments expressed by the Comics Campaign Council. These stereotypical understandings of the comic, reflecting official discourse about the comic, were held simultaneously, by some, with pleasurable personal memories. Thus, readers were both policing and policed with regard to the medium. In effect, the regulation of the child, the worker and the female form a part of the history of the comic, even when those policing current readers have themselves been the policed readers of previous generations.

Concerns about comics expressed by female teachers and librarians at training days have been wide-ranging. For example, some participants argued that they could not justify buying comics because there were so few words in them. Others refused to buy them on the basis that reading comics was not 'real' reading. In offering images rather than solely text some argued that comics would ruin the imagination of young people or make readers 'lazy' because there were pictures to support the words. The view that comics weaken readers was a contradictory position given that professionals' interest in the comic book is commonly about its potential role in encouraging the less able reader. There were also worries that this was an addictive form of reading, which would mean that readers never progressed to 'proper' books. For some, the problem was not their own perspectives, which they characterized as sympathetic, but those of head teachers and governors. How to justify buying in such material even if it did serve to encourage reading was a significant worry. Thus, the divide between high versus 'low' or popular culture remained firmly in place.

The final area of concern centred on the content of comics. It was assumed that violence and the objectification of women was common to all comics. Statements were made about how weaker young male readers might be influenced in their behaviour by such material. This kind of concern is described by Barker & Petley (1997) when they ask in their critique of notions of media effects with regard to film:

> Upon whom are the media supposed to have their 'effects'? Not the 'educated' and 'cultured' middle classes, who either don't watch such rubbish, or else are fully able to deal with it if they do so. No, those who are most 'affected' are the young, and especially the working class young. Here 'effects' theory meets up with what Pearson (1983) has called 'the history of respectable fears' and Cohen (1972) 'folk devils'. (1997, p.5)

There was a clear fear that whilst people like the audience, that is middle-class and largely graduate, were immune to the effects of comics, the young, uneducated and working-class pupil would be vulnerable.

To conclude, there are changes in relation to education and libraries in relation to how practitioners feel about comics, although a discourse of media effects still exists. There are now a number of initiatives which work directly with young people and comics in educational settings, including the Excelsior Award (http://www.excelsioraward. co.uk/ accessed 4/3/2015), which encourages comic reading in schools. This, in itself, reflects a major change from previous attitudes. In addition, it should be noted that lack of approval amongst authority figures can serve to make the comic more attractive to young readers. This in turn may lead, as Styles and Watson suggest, to a cycle being established, in that '...the fact that children take such pleasure from these texts is enough to convince some commentators that they must be harmful' (1996, p.179).

Media Studies, Cultural Studies and Other Disciplines

The perspectives outlined above appear in some academic writing beyond the areas of Librarianship and Education. Whilst this writing may not have the same impact upon child readers as that of those involved with teaching and librarianship, academic accounts do reflect the mediating context for comics (as well as forming part of a new mediating context for future readers). Academics, like the readers I interviewed, are part of the cultural climate around comics. Writing about the comic in Britain has emerged from a range of disciplines including Media and Cultural Studies, as well as Sociology, Art History, Psychology, Literature, the study of various languages, and Children's Literature, where there is a growing interest in periodical publishing for children. That research appears in a number of locations is unsurprising given the ambiguous position of the comic in relation to the academy, itself a product of perceptions of the comic over many generations. Each discipline also usually reveals a shift from hostility to an interest, sometimes grudging, in what the comic is, how it works and whom it attracts. Again, such shifts must be seen against both a paradigm of 'high' versus 'low' or popular culture and changes within the academy in the understanding of mass media texts. Later debates are, then, indicative of a change in the cultural climate, a loosening of views around comics.

Children's Literature

Whilst all of the disciplines above reflect changes in how the comic has been mediated for its readers, some are more closely related than others to the educational accounts mentioned earlier. In the case of Children's Literature, for instance, teachers are one of the discipline's primary audiences. A typical example is the survey by the Children's Literature Research Centre, Roehampton Institute, whose survey and report on young people's reading at the end of the century (1996), mentioned earlier, is part of the educational tradition of Whitehead et al (1977), and that which Pumphrey establishes by asking children what they read. Where the Roehampton account differs is in the lack of emphasis on what adults might want to children to read. Instead, the focus is much more upon what children say they read and what pleasures they feel reading offers them. This research indicates a shift to a more child-centred approach in terms of how the comic has been viewed, both in relation to the children who took part in the survey and to the adult audience for the report.

Similarly, a shift is clear in the way that some research focuses on the feelings that publications for children may inspire in adults, attempting to analyse mediating contexts. For instance, Pinsent and Knight (1997) study, rather than participate in, the moral panic that emerged around girls' magazines in the 1980s and 1990s. Pinsent and Knight (1997) described a situation in which,

Many mothers of adolescent girls have perused with surprise and some disquiet the magazines read by their teenage daughters. *Just Seventeen* (EMAP Elan, 1983-2004) and *Mizz* seem to be very different from the magazines these mothers may have read when they were young themselves, such as *Jackie*...The romantic stories, usually told in comic strip format, seem to have been replaced by explicit material about sex...Are these magazines destroying our daughters' innocence, and encouraging them to form sexual relationships before they are ready for them? (p.6)

The writers assume nostalgia on the part of parents for texts like *Jackie*, which, as I suggested in the previous chapter, were seen as equally problematic in their time. Their focus on the magazine and girls is very much in line with the work of McRobbie (1991, 1997) in that they all start from the position that such texts are seen as a problem, although they differ in their use of the texts and in their conclusions. McRobbie (1997) uses these texts as a way of interrogating feminism and looking at generational change. In contrast, Pinsent & Knight do not address feminism as an issue, instead concluding that there is no real cause for anxiety on the part of parents and teachers in titles read by eleven to sixteen year olds. They add that these titles represent a shift in defining what girlhood is and what the concerns of girlhood are.

A similarly close relationship with educational writing on the comic is apparent in histories of books and magazines for children. The comic is peripheral here partly because of the period typically covered by writers in this field. Tinkler's (1995, 2000) accounts of girls' reading, for instance, stop at 1958, coinciding with the period when girls' comics increased significantly in number, and Kristen Drottner's (1988) study of English children and their magazines ends in 1945. Similarly, Pinsent and Knight, mentioned above, focus on periodicals produced only after the death of the girls' comic. Whilst this may be coincidental, for some writers the comic is clearly an issue. In her writing on the girls' magazine, Cadogan draws attention to the forerunners of the girls' comics, but rarely discusses comics themselves. *You're a brick Angela!* (1986) locates the comic strip material firmly in the tradition of the girls' story 1839 to 1985, but dismisses such material in comparison to longer text based fiction and to the story papers from which comics evolved. Cadogan turns in relief to novels for girls stating that, '[i]t is fortunate that the decline of the girls' papers has occurred at a time when they are most dispensable; it has been paralleled by an unprecedented diversification in 'reputable' children's books' (1986, p.332). The deterioration, as she sees it, is exemplified by a '[d]readful *School Friend* picture strip serial, 'Anita-Beloved Princess' (1956), in which all the worst aspects of the decade were aired: princess worship, vapid romanticism, a teenage dreamworld more gaudy than glossy' (Cadogan, 1986, p.329). Cadogan combines nostalgia for a lost world with distaste at more recent publications. In effect, her overall argument is that the comics emerging between the mid-1950s and the 1980s are not worth bothering with.

My own work on comics acts as a counterpoint to Cadogan's views about the worthlessness of the medium and is represented in publications forming part of the discipline of Children's Literature in Britain. It has focused on gender, childhood and comics (Gibson, 2013, 2008b), but also on picturebooks, graphic novels and comics (Gibson, 2010). Few others work in this area and the comic for girls still tends to be neglected.

As with Education and Librarianship, then, research in this area covers a spectrum ranging from strongly anti-comic through to seeing them as part of childhood. In addition, much of the work looks at comics in historical context, interweaving them with constructions of girlhood, boyhood and childhood.

History and Comics

It is useful to contrast the above studies with those done in Britain as part of a history of comics. Histories of comics, in both academic and popular arenas, have often responded to the perceived low status of the form by asserting its importance, rejecting (and often referring to) other, more negative, assessments of the medium.

Comparing and contrasting these two areas of research, however, it appears that the girls' comic has often fallen between two stools. Whilst histories of reading for girls in Britain tend to omit the comic book form, possibly influenced by a mediating context in which comics have been seen as a male interest, or as 'bad' mass culture, histories of comics tend to make limited analysis of material for girls. I feel this may be because, within British comics, girls' titles have been seen as a genre of their own.

There are exceptions to this rule. For instance, Denis Gifford produced a number of histories of British comics including work on titles for girls. Gifford's catalogues of comics (1975, 1985 and 1987) also incorporate girls' comics and stories. In addition, a number of writers flag up, or offer chapters on, titles for girls. These include Roger Sabin (1996), who devotes a chapter to comics for girls. Further, Paul Gravett's (2006) and (2011) publications include material on girls' comics, as do James Chapman (2011) and Graham Kibble-White (2005).

In addition, my own work offers a range of material on the subject of childhood, especially girlhood, and comics (Gibson, 2007, 2008a, 2008b, 2009, 2010a, 2010b, 2011, 2013). Much of it develops themes identified in this book. There is, however, no British equivalent of the body of work created by Trina Robbins in charting both images of women in comics and women as creating comics (1985, 1992, 1996, 1999, 2009, 2013).

Media and Cultural Studies

Within Cultural Studies, comics are mentioned in Richard Hoggart's (1957) *The Uses of Literacy* and Raymond Williams' (1961) *The Long Revolution*, which form part of the foundations of the discipline of Cultural Studies. They both challenge and share some the assumptions of Leavis. Consequently, these texts have been described as being of the 'break', as well as 'left-Leavisism' (Arnold, 1960, p.6). Critical approaches to mass media have been profoundly influential on the commentary of teachers and librarians on comics and, therefore, in turn, on child readers. Here the impact is similarly direct, this time in forming and compounding discourses about comics within the academy.

Williams (1961), only refers to comics once, but it is indicative of the writer's perspective in that comics appear as part of a discussion of 'bad art'. Williams argues that neither jazz nor football should be categorized as bad. Evidently, comics remain a step too far, as he then goes on to ask,

> Can we also agree, though, that the horror film, the rape-novel, the Sunday strip-paper and the latest Tin-Pan drool are not exactly in the same world, and that the nice magazine romance, the manly adventure story (straight to the point of the jaw) and the pretty, clever television advertisement are not in it either? (Williams, 1961, p.336)

Hoggart (1957) mentions two types of periodical aimed at children in the main body of his study. One is the story paper, which he seems to see as unproblematic, 'He is, say, a boy of eleven going to the paper-shop for his Saturday magazine, for the *Wizard* (DC Thomson, 1922-1978) or the *Hotspur* (DC Thomson 1933-1981)' (Hoggart, 1957, p.64). Here he refers to the text-only versions of those periodicals, the story papers, before they incorporated comic strip material. When children's periodicals are mentioned, the audience is identified as male. The nostalgia about a lost world evident from Hoggart's remark about the story papers can be contrasted with his omission of titles such as *The Beano* and *The Dandy*. Given that *The Uses of Literacy* celebrates the 1930s as a having a rich, less commercial culture and the 1950s as substituting for that culture shiny and insubstantial candy-floss, that both comics began in the 1930s and were highly popular serves to undermine the image of the era he depicts, given his view of comic strips. They are only mentioned in the notes where Hoggart acknowledges that they sell around one and a quarter million copies each per week (Hoggart, 1957, p.355). His relegation of those titles to footnotes arouses suspicions about his view of the medium in general, which associates the comic with fragmentation, passive consumption and an overwhelmingly American commercialism, all of which serve to undermine British working-class culture and particularly that of the young male. Nor is there any mention of the girls' comics.

Hoggart's perspective on comics is confirmed by the only mention of comics in the main text. Of the spread of the comic strip in newspapers and periodicals, Hoggart states that,

> The 'strips' spread like a rash, from the bottom corner of the back page through all the inner pages, take over a page of their own, and still crop up here and there elsewhere. There has to be some verbal guidance to the action, but descriptive com-

ment is kept to a minimum: the aim is to ensure that all necessary background information is contained in the dialogue which bubbles out of the characters' mouths. (1957, p.201)

The evocative use of language, drawing an analogy between comics and disease, gives a clear indication of how Hoggart sees them. The image of popular fiction as infectious disease is used to conjure up a melodramatic sense of horror and disgust. This language of disease and addiction is mirrored in criticism aimed at earlier texts. James Greenwood (1869), a crusader against the 'penny dreadfuls', asked in *The Seven Curses of London* 'Which of us can say that his children are safe from the contamination?' (p.97). He also added,

Granted, my dear sir, that your young Jack, or my twelve year old Robert, have minds too pure either to seek or to crave after literature of the sort in question, but not infrequently it is found without seeking. It is a contagious disease, just as cholera and typhus and the plague are contagious, and, as everybody is aware, it needs not personal contact with a body stricken to convey either of these frightful maladies to the hale and hearty. A tainted scrap of rag has been known to spread plague and death through an entire village, just as a stray leaf of Panther Bill or Tyburn Tree may sow the seeds of immorality amongst as many boys as a town may produce. (p.100)

Hoggart (1957), having described comic strips as disease, then goes on to expand on what he feels is the lowest form that such strips may take, the American comic:

At the lowest level all this is illustrated in the sales here of the American or American-type serial-books of comics, where for page after page big-thighed and big-bosomed girls from Mars step out of their space- machines, and gangsters' molls scream away in high powered sedans. Anyone who sees something of Servicemen's reading, of the popularity of American and English comics (with the cruder English boys' comics serving their turn where the supply of hotter material runs out), knows something of all this. The process continues, for a substantial number of adolescents especially; a passive visual taking-on of bad mass-art geared to a very low mental age. (p.201)

Hoggart's observations on comics, made in a book published at the time of the work of the Comics Campaign Council, act as a reminder of the debates around the comic to the readers of the book, reflecting, in part, a fear of American cultural imperialism.

Hoggart's comment above also reveals his perspective on gender and comics. The 'problem' of the American comic is identified with what are seen as aberrant females.

These active aliens and criminals are the opposite of the mothers Hoggart describes elsewhere. The shapeliness, activity and sexuality of the fictional women of comics can be contrasted with his images of mothers, defined by their children and their shapelessness of form. Instead of adventure, as he describes it, they have, 'a hard life, in which it is assumed that the mother will be 'at it' from getting up to going to bed' (Hoggart, 1957, p.42). It is the mother that Hoggart approves of, despite (or rather because of) the hardship she endures. In linking the comic, deviant female sexuality and America, Hoggart suggests the seductive 'otherness' of these comics, equating them, it seems, with both the 'easy life' and venereal disease, seeing them in a similar light in respect of the effects on the readers. Hoggart clearly sees the comic as addressing only one audience, vulnerable young men whom comics lead astray, in terms of literacy, morality and national identity, an understanding of the comic very much in line with the views expressed by Wertham, Pumphrey and others.

It might seem unlikely that such a climate with regard to comics would prove productive. However, as with those of Leavis, Hoggart's comments allowed a space for work on comics to develop within Media and Cultural Studies. Like histories of the comic, later studies analysed perspectives on comics. Such work includes Barker's on the British Horror Comics Campaign (1984) and his *Comics: Ideology, Power and the Critics* (1989). In addition, by the late 1970s, feminism mediated some academics' and female readers' understanding of comics (along with having an impact on accounts by teachers and librarians). Consequently, some of the Media and Cultural Studies work (as well as some of the readers interviewed for this monograph) evinces similar views to librarians' accounts in being concerned with sexist images.

Media and Cultural Studies research on Girls' Comics

Comics for girls and girls as readers of comics feature in Media and Cultural Studies research, as well as histories of comics and children's literature. It is in these areas that Sabin's (1996) hope that girls' comics and girl readers in Britain 'should not remain a forgotten story' (p.81) is answered. Barker, McRobbie and Walkerdine's accounts are key contributions. The other writing that exists usually owes a debt to these writers, including this monograph. All three have made important studies of the role that comics play in girls' culture. Their debates are very different to those discussed in education and librarianship, in largely moving away from notions of high versus 'low' or popular culture (or worth). Instead, these accounts offer alternative approaches that are potentially liberating with regard to researchers as well as readers.

Barker and Walkerdine both engaged with comics for younger readers in this academic space, such as *Bunty*. There are few other studies of comics for younger girls, with an exception being the brief article 'Jinty come back!' by Jenni Scott in the *GirlFrenzy Mil-*

lennial (1998), which begins with the writer's memories of the title, but swiftly moves into textual analysis. With regard to *Bunty*, Walkerdine (1990) argues that the comics act as an 'ideological preparation for adolescent sexuality' (p.87), analysing the fantasies embodied in these texts using a psychoanalytic approach. She refers to the role of comics *Bunty* and *Tracy* (DC Thomson, 1979-1985) in preparing the girl for the model of heterosexuality offered by publications like *Jackie*. Walkerdine (1997) later revealed that her fascination with these comics was that she could not see them in the same way that most feminist thinking of the time did. She (1997) argued that she wanted to challenge the assumptions that such comics were 'the worst, most offensive and stereotyped literature around' (p.46).

According to Walkerdine (1990), all of these periodicals are part of a system of implicit guidance '...as to how young girls may prepare themselves to be good enough to 'win' the glittering prizes: the man, the home, the adventure, and so forth' (p.90). Like other fairy tales, they present happy endings such as finding a new family. Controlling girls' comics is part of an effort not only to control the female child (in the sense of a 'natural' child that resists control) but also to produce girlhood in specific ways, regulating female subjectivity. Walkerdine sees the narratives in the comics as classic fairy tales that produce the heroine and the implied reader as suffering, often orphaned, victims. In this she continues to see the comic as problematic. As I suggest in the introduction in relation to 'Belle of the Ballet', such stories offer what Walkerdine (1990) described as 'structuring fantasies' which produce a sense of self. The stories in comics are powerful, she argues, because they play out the audience's inner tensions, offering oedipal resolution (p.90). The implied reader of *Bunty* and *Tracy* was not passive, then, but engaged in emotional struggle and reorganization, developing selflessness and helpfulness to achieve passivity within patriarchy. Walkerdine (1990) argued that 'anger signifies as wholly negative...nor is rebellion ever sanctioned' (p.96). The stories locate bad desires and anger as outside the girl and activity is equated with selfishness. Only passivity is related to rescue, goodness and eventual success. The conflicts and miseries then lead the reader, within a few years, to the solution of romance offered by *Jackie*.

Walkerdine returned to *Bunty* in the 1990s in what was in part a response to Barker's (1989) analysis of her theoretical approach and analysis. This is only one element of his research, which looks at a wide range of comic genres and tests out and critiques a number of methodological and ideological approaches. Barker argued that a more historically specific understanding of the girls' comics Walkerdine identified was needed and that reading across a larger number of titles might reveal a different set of conclusions. In addition, in contrast to Walkerdine's assertions about the selflessness of the heroines, Barker maintained that the happy endings in the two sample comics were usually accidental. The end of those stories, according to Barker, is not arrived at through the action, or rather, inaction, of the heroine, but through a 'deus ex machina'. A variation is that the outsider may enhance the heroine's understanding of what is going on, enabling her to solve the problem herself. Thus Barker (1989) concluded, 'In as much as there may be ideology in these stories...it is in the stressing of self knowledge' (p.231). The emphasis one may argue, then, is on knowledge on the part of characters and readers, not desire or emotional re-organisation.

Walkerdine (1997), in her response, argued that Barker was 'pointing to something important, but also conveniently ignoring the place of femininity and of the place of the psychological in girls' struggles' (p.49). She felt he depicted the working-class girl as put upon victim and argued that this denied women's class mobility and ambitions. In effect, Walkerdine argues that saying these are accidental endings creates powerlessness, yet arguing that the ending creates passivity does not seem to engage with class mobility or ambition, unless it is wholly focused on marrying someone of a higher class than oneself. Walkerdine (1997) also felt that 'comics for Barker are examples of grim realism, whereas I read them as anti-realist texts' (p.50) and developed a thesis about how what might act as empowering fantasy to some working-class girls, may be read as sexist by their middle-class equivalents, arguing that these two positions were in constant play. What Walkerdine says implies that middle-class girls would reject these texts, something not borne out by my reader interviews (see chapters 4 & 5). Further, readers reported many stories as aspirational, or inspirational, in showing girls overcoming hardship and achieving educationally, elements absent from her analysis.

Similar discussions of approach focused on *Jackie*. The comparatively extensive academic coverage of *Jackie* shows how central this title has been considered to girls' culture and how it has been seen by commentators, readers and others to have had a pivotal role in the period between child and adult life. By far the most significant contributor of academic writing on *Jackie* is McRobbie, who returned to it at various points (1978a, 1978b, 1981, 1984, 1991, 1997), finally comparing its contents to that of the new girls' magazines when it was about to cease publication. In this final account she asserted that work on women's and girls' magazines (a category in which she included *Jackie*), as exemplified by Winship's research (1987), was a central 'part of the history of the development of feminism in the academy' (McRobbie, 1997, p.190). Here then, the continuity of *Jackie* with women's magazines is emphasized over that of its relationship with girls' and other, comics.

Given the extensive period during which *Jackie* was the focus of McRobbie's research, it is inevitable that her arguments about the text shifted, particularly as the same period shows a number of changes in the text itself. Her early position had been that, 'Within the world of *Jackie* what we find is a cloyingly claustrophobic environment where the dominant emotions are fear, insecurity, competitiveness and even panic' (McRobbie, 1991, p.84). In summarizing her extensive body of work, which assigns *Jackie* considerable ideological power, it is important to note that the earlier work specifically analyses the texts using a semiotic approach. This is used initially to identify the main codes in the stories and other aspects of the periodical. McRobbie (1991) characterized these as, '1. the code of romance; 2. the code of personal/domestic life; 3. the code of fashion and beauty; 4. the code of pop music' (p.93). In establishing these codes, McRobbie worked through each aspect of the text, from stories to the problem page. Through this analysis, McRobbie (1991) argued, the intention was to create; 'A systematic critique of *Jackie* as a system of messages...an ideology which deals with the construction of teenage femininity' (p.82).

The comic strip stories were seen as focussing on several main themes. Primary amongst them was the need to get and keep a man, fighting for him if necessary. In these stories, McRobbie suggests, the saddest ending is seen as being a single girl. The message that is offered, she argues (1991), is that 'Girls can take humiliation and be all the more attractive for it, as long as they are pretty and unassertive' (p.107). Another major theme McRobbie identified was about not trusting other women, who will, it seems, stab the heroine, and by extension, the reader, in the back. The final, contradictory, theme was that being a girl is fun.

McRobbie (1991) argues that in presenting a generalized girlhood where romance and distrust are central '*Jackie* asserts a class-less, race-less sameness, a kind of false unity which assumes a common experience of womanhood or girlhood' (p.84). For McRobbie the continuing problem for these young women readers was one of isolation in real life, which was further exacerbated by the supposed unity on the page. This isolation was compounded by the fact that there was no emphasis on working together in the stories and by the problem page which both 'depends upon, exploits and offers a solution to the isolation of women' (McRobbie, 1997, p.195). McRobbie characterized the problem pages as saying that problems are to do with the behaviour of individuals. The solutions they offered were, according to McRobbie, ones that ensured that the reader would take on a traditional female role. To McRobbie, although *Jackie* was presented as a fun free-time choice, it was nonetheless conventional and centred on consumerism, especially self-improvement through purchase and beauty. McRobbie argued that, 'Adolescence comes to be synonymous with *Jackie*'s definition of it. The consensual totality of feminine adolescence means that all girls want to know how to catch a boy, lose weight, look their best and be able to cook' (1991, p.84). In her accounts of changes in girls' magazines in the late 1980s and 1990s (1991, 1997), McRobbie continued to use *Jackie* as a starting off point, charting shifts from acceptance to assertive girlhood, from romance and boys to friendship and to oneself. She also suggests, however, that the cost of equality is being an even better consumer, offering continuity with her earlier arguments.

Barker (1989) agreed with McRobbie that Jackie offered 'exclusive attention to an already powerless group' (McRobbie, 1981, p.128), but also suggested that a lack of power does not mean that girls were more open to media influence. Whilst McRobbie spoke about how the publisher 'attempts to win consent to the dominant order- in terms of femininity, leisure and consumption' (McRobbie, 1991, p.87), Barker argued that one could see readers as a community, using the texts, rather than being manipulated by messages within them. In support of this argument, he refers to McRobbie's (1978b) article 'The culture of working class girls' where *Jackie* was identified as the focus of communal activity. Far from encouraging competition between girls, it was used to signal boredom at school and was central to their resistance to boys and authority. Thus, it can be argued, the way that readers used the text undermined that text's possible ideological implications.

In addition to flagging up the possibility that readers may use the texts in resistant ways, Barker also offered extensive textual analysis. His reading of the problem pages, for instance, was that they offered an alternative standpoint in each issue, in that they 'have always stressed the importance of female friendships and have encouraged girls not to give up female friends because of a romance' (Barker, 1989, p.157). In a close study of the whole run of *Jackie* stories, he identifies variations in tone and outlook that also apply to the letter columns. His argument is that the stories reflect shifts within the period of publication and that this indicates that *Jackie* did not offer a consistent ideology of femininity. Barker summarized these variations by saying that the earlier stories were more conservative, emphasizing 'self-sacrifice and self-diminution by the woman' (1989, p.169). By 1969, this is on the wane, he argues, although the aim remains passivity and the theme shifts to facing up to emotions rather than self-sacrifice, in an acknowledgement of the right to choose. The next change Barker identifies, in the early 1970s, is understood as a backlash against the comparative liberalism of the stories in *Jackie* in the late 1960s. Here the emphasis is on the need to fit in and constitutes a narrowing of horizons. By 1975, there was a decline in confidence regarding romance and stories about death emerge. The final phase Barker identified was tied to the technological changes of the late 1970s when titles began to use photo-strips. *Jackie* followed the trend. In summary, Barker argued that there is no monolithic ideological bloc and that the use by readers may further undermine such an assertion.

Barker also suggested that research into the way that readers interpret texts should be further developed. Both he and McRobbie, in relation to work with audiences, acknowledged the importance of an article by Elizabeth Frazer on readers of *Jackie*. In relation to Frazer, McRobbie states that:

> Frazer (1987) demonstrated that my own earlier work on *Jackie* magazine wrongly assumed that ideology actually worked in a mechanical, even automatic kind of way. By carrying out interviews with groups of *Jackie* readers, Frazer showed that instead of accepting the meanings, the girls actually negotiated them, arguing with the magazines and taking issue with what they were saying. (McRobbie, 1997, p.195)

Frazer further opened the debate by looking at the ways in which it was used and talked about by readers. Her work employed the notion of the discourse register, described as 'an institutionalized, situationally specific, culturally familiar, public way of talking' (Frazer, 1987, p.421). The idea of a contract between text and reader was central; a dialogue where the contents were used in a particular way. Readers' discussions of a particular story in *Jackie* and problem pages in general, revealed that they used more than one way of discussing a topic, hence Frazer's assertion that 'We should not take it that people are unselfconscious about these registers [of discourse]' (1987, p.424). The research was concerned with current readers of the form, a radical departure from earlier surveys of children's reading that acted predominantly as a vehicle for adults' fears about children's reading.

In conclusion, the majority of work on comics in Britain in the past has emerged from the discipline of Education, and has addressed concerns about mass media and particularly 'media effects' against a paradigm of high versus 'low' or popular culture. The cultural climate in which children and adults have read and analysed comics has meant that they have consistently understood the form as problematic. In this climate, control of the text has often represented control of the child. This is not to say that children are the passive victims of a ruling-class plot, but to reinforce the view that children's lives, and particularly those of female children, are, as in Nikolas Rose's words 'the most intensively governed sector of personal existence' (1989, p.87). Further, as Walkerdine suggested, control of the text may be part of an effort to produce girlhood in particular ways. As Jenks argues: '[Childhood] is not a natural phenomenon and cannot be properly understood as such' (1996, p.7). Girlhood is both social construct and interpretive frame.

These concerns about mass media and children have been, as I have described, dominant in writing on comics in both 'common sense' and educational accounts of these texts. My training courses on developing collections in libraries and schools, (see p.3) in illustrating both official and personal discourses about comics, give an indication of the complexity of women's relationship to the comic and that these discourses had an impact on these readers as girls. Whilst disapproving as professionals, they may have also been enthusiastic readers of what they now condemn.

In looking at writing about the comic across a number of other academic disciplines, it is clear that most begin from similar roots in considering comics in relation to a paradigm of high versus 'low' or popular culture. However, the impact of changes in the academy that resulted in the development of Media and Cultural Studies obviously made an impression elsewhere. The emergence, through the work of Walkerdine, McRobbie, Frazer and Barker, of a very different set of discourses about comics offers a range of complex and comparatively non-judgmental approaches to comics. Walkerdine (1997), in particular, in drawing on her personal memories (although not of comics), as well as pointing to the power of these texts elsewhere, offers, through the exploration of her own subjectivity and position as researcher, a potential bridge between memory and the comic form. Rather than one way of reading the text, in the work of these writers many are embraced and debated, suggesting the richness of both the texts and the academic and personal responses to them. It is to readers' responses, to their memories of the girls' comic that I now turn.

Notes

1   See Barker (1984) for a full account of this campaign.

Chapter Four

The Readers' Tale: Girls Reading Girls' Comics

In this chapter I explore how reading comics had an impact on how the reader was perceived and how reading choices were part of social and cultural positions of class and femininity. Thus, looking at reading practices engages one with definitions of girlhood and issues of class, aspiration and escapism from the perspective of the reader.

In the following chapters on the girl reader of comics for girls and comics for boys and mixed gender audiences, the focus is on how academic and other writing about these readers link, or not, with the actual practices expressed through personal accounts, juxtaposing 'real' readers against an implied reader. In engaging with the ways in which, in the course of interviews, autobiography is written and re-written these chapters are, in some ways, about the problem of who the 'real' reader is. Working with readers' memories may produce a new reader in relation to public history, no less a discursive construct perhaps than that created through textual analysis, but one which is produced through a double dialogue: between reader and researcher, and between the remembering and the remembered self of the reader. As Elspeth Probyn (1994) argued, the 'imaged self' which emerges is both a discursive and an experiential construction, both 'real' and a 'working image of the self' (1994, p.171) which will shift according to the context in which it is spoken. The self, she writes is an 'active articulation of the discursive and the lived' (1994, p.92). Thus, textual analysis may tell us one story about the meaning of any given comic, but readers tell another. Their stories are about who they felt they were at a specific time. They are also about the place of the comic in the culture of girlhood.

These links and differences between 'real' and implied reader are explored here through responses from readers, allowing me to question received knowledge about girls' comics and girl readers of comics. In addition, in exploring how comics were seen and used by girl readers, the tensions between medium and audience that served to dislocate the comic from girls' lives are apparent. The readers' letters and interviews offered in these final chapters are, therefore, valuable in questioning academic and industry-generated versions of girls' reading, enabling new understandings of the changing relationship between girls and comics to emerge, but also serve as a map of conflicting and conflicted accounts of girlhood.

This chapter particularly focuses on those readers who read the girls' comic. Comics specifically for girls have been seen as representing the worst and weakest that the form offers. Further, whether from a feminist viewpoint, or in the writing of educationalists like Alderson (1968), girls' comics have been seen as limiting girls' achievements or ambitions. Assumptions about the audience are also evident in *Mum's Own Annual* (1993). The writing, although it is meant to address the mother, actually often slips into lines like 'In Mum's day' (p.13) suggesting that there is a second audience, the daughter. The reader is automatically cast in the role of a mother with daughters of her own with whom she will share the book. Constant harking back to 'a whole generation of future mums' (p.13) suggests a definition of readers as having followed a trajectory that leads solely to motherhood. These perspectives, then, inform both academic and popular accounts, acting as the norms against which girls' comic reading has been contextualized.

I begin with a long extract from an interview, one that sets up some of the major issues that emerge in this and the final chapter. The long extract is from an interview that took place with Pru, a Literature Promotion Officer from Bedfordshire whom I originally met at a training event. In talking about herself she described her work with readers as having become very important to her, but also as a role she felt she had 'drifted' into, having previously worked in a number of sectors. She used comics in her professional life and so had an interest in current titles, which was why she had attended the training event, but this had recently turned into reading comics for pleasure.

Mel: What comics did you read as a child?

Pru: I used to get *Bunty* and *Judy* every week ...I really looked forward to getting them. I also had some of the older ones, the annuals ... *School Friend* and *Girls' Crystal*. I read them all over and over again. I haven't got them now. They were thrown out by my parents.

M: Where did you get the annuals?

P: Some were given to me and some I bought at jumble sales. The covers [of the annuals] were fab. They always seemed to feature girls doing sports.

M: Can you remember what you liked about *Bunty* and *Judy*?

P: The stories ... they were quite edgy and the heroines were usually hard done by. Sometimes the stories were supernatural ... although not 'The Four Marys' [Laughs]. I went to a lot of different schools as we moved around a lot. I finally ended up at a boarding school. It *wasn't* like 'The Four Marys'... [Pause] ... I didn't enjoy school, but dealt with it by being very quiet and reading a lot, hiding, or running away. I really didn't settle, with moving so much... it was always difficult. [Long pause] The stories [in the comics] weren't cosy like lots of the picture books you see now. Not cosy and suburban and middle-class like Shirley Hughes. If I see one more harassed looking but loving mum in a picture book ... I like picture books to be more humorous ... more out there.

M: Anyone in particular?

P: Colin McNaughton. I started to read his books when my kids were small. I like the fact that his books are like comics. The stories are funny and he has such an ironic take on things. The artwork is great. He obviously likes *The Beano*. He uses speech balloons and panels and really bright colours. Not like *Bunty*. It was printed on dreadful paper that had a serrated edge. It was really soft and sort of beige ... off white ... grey. The ink smelt as well. It's funny how books smell. When I first took graphic novels to one of my reading groups the blokes took them out of the box and smelt them [Laughs]. They stood there smelling the books rather than reading them [Shakes head]. *Bunty* had those cut-out dolls. Really difficult to do because of the paper. [Makes angular cutting movement and pulls a face]. Especially around the tabs.

M: You use comics and graphic novels in your work now. Is this linked to your own reading of comics?

P: No, I don't think so. It was because I was working with young adult males, getting them to read. Comics seemed one of the obvious things to do. Working with librarians is sometimes a problem. They don't seem to value male readers or books with pictures, or lateral thinking. I like graphic novels myself now because of my work. I've discovered lots of authors and artists. I started by reading classics like *Watchmen* and *Sandman*. I share my books. I'm not anal about them. I've learnt that from the blokes I work with, they don't keep books. They pass them on to someone who they think would like them. The real hit with me was *The Tale of One Bad Rat*. I enjoy books that look sideways at things... using Beatrix Potter like that. I thought the issue [of abuse] was handled well. It wasn't a saccharine ending even though it was happy. It reminded me of parts of my childhood ... and *Bunty*... and I like the artwork, with him being both writer and artist ... it's like Colin McNaughton, the writing and the art both appeal. [Long pause]. Actually, I think it [her interest in using comics and graphic novels in her working life] is because of comics I read as a child. 'Dan Dare' I loved. My brother read the *Eagle*. He got it every week. He's younger than me ... well, he didn't *read* the *Eagle* ... he couldn't read it. So it was mine really. I only liked 'Dan Dare', because of the colour as well as the stories, not the helpful hints and history. They were boring. No, I only liked 'Dan Dare'.

M: What else did you read?

P: I also read paperbacks, Fontana and suchlike, in my teens. Mostly horror. I remember reading Poe. Reading comics faded out. The house is full of books now ...

What becomes immediately apparent from Pru's account is that girl readers are difficult to pigeonhole. Even dividing readers into those reading girls' comics and those reading 'other' comics, those for male or mixed gender audiences, is problematic. Although Pru initially positions herself purely in relation to the girls' comics, she later discusses the *Eagle* as well. Thus, her reading, as a girl, included comics that were aimed at middle-class boys as well as titles that were aimed at working-class girls. In addition, the second-hand annuals she reports having read were aimed at middle-class girls of earlier generations. This suggests a blurring of identity and girlhood across time, as well as class, in that reading any given title or story was rarely limited to a single generation. Comments recurred across generation throughout the interviews and other accounts, meaning that there is no clear breakdown by age or title in looking at readership.

To return to class, whilst it is not directly mentioned, the reading choices Pru (who described herself as being middle-class) made as a girl nonetheless upset the assumption that girls read only those titles which are aimed at the class to which they 'belong'. Her reading also challenges the idea that comics are specifically a working-class concern, which, as we saw in Chapter 3, has long been a common assumption about the medium. Consequently, Pru's choice of reading as a girl serves to blur producers' and commentators' notions of class in relation to comics. In addition, her choices also destabilize the similarly widespread impression that all girls only read girls' comics.

The notion of individual identity in this interview, like the girl reader, is difficult to pigeonhole. This account offers shifting and blurred identities rather than a unified self. Pru moves in and out of various child, professional and adult selves (with the latter including both parent and new reader of comics) during the interview. The detailing of age and work offered at the start of the section, which anchors and labels the reader in certain ways, detracts, in a sense, from the shifting, slippery sense of girlhood and self that emerged in this and many of the other accounts. However, the constant hesitations, pauses, breaks and shifts and the slipperiness of the interview, is evident here, suggesting a complex and less than unified sense of identity.

In addition, like many of the other interviews, this one was punctuated by laughter. This represented both genuine amusement (as when Pru describes readers smelling their books) and tension, in her reference to 'The Four Marys'. Some of the hesitations and the nervous laughter can therefore be seen as pointing to Pru's desire and simultaneous unwillingness to discuss on record some aspects of why, as a girl, she had found *Bunty* and *Judy* so personally meaningful. Hesitation, a feature of many of the interviews, can, then, also flag up moments of self-protection, both of current and previous selves. A number of interviews followed similar patterns, with a discussion of comics proving more revelatory than would have been expected in that it touched on issues far beyond what popular culture is often seen as evoking. This, in turn, implies how important comics could be in individuals' lives and in the culture of girlhood in Britain.

Another theme that emerges from Pru's interview is the way that the comic functions as a marker of identity and change in relation to girls' culture. In this case, Pru demonstrates how parental disposal of her comics acted as a marker of their perception that she was no longer a child. The final discarding of a comic collection by a parent is something that appeared frequently in readers' accounts. Such accounts contradict the dealer's interview in Chapter 1 in which he asserts that women keep their comics. This symbolic, as well as actual, disposal could also mark a break in girls' sense of self.

In addition to the use of comic as marker, the titles Pru read and the pleasures she says they offered, create an image of the girl reader of girls' comics that is recognisable from writing on the comic. However, what Pru describes as her next stage in reading does not follow the feminine trajectory from girls' comics through to women's magazines, which, in the literature, is often assumed to occur. In contrast, she moves on from comics to classic horror. In doing so, Pru breaks with the model of the feminine reading career. Her account indicates that readers may have resisted, been unresponsive to, or simply been unaware of, girls' comics' supposed role as a training text for 'proper' femininity, a role that would have been realised through readers transferring from them to women's magazines and romance.

Despite Pru's later shift into reading horror, there is, in the interview, a strong sense of girls' comics being a pleasure, again a later focus in this chapter. Here, however, they can be identified primarily as appealing because of their tone, their lack of cosiness, something that clearly chimed with her personal experience. A similar response is apparent in her attraction to *The Tale of One Bad Rat* and in her linking of that book with what appealed to her about *Bunty*. In both this and other accounts, comics offered further pleasures as well. For instance, getting a comic every week was a source of security and continuity for Pru. Whilst many of the pleasures of the comic are communal, as we shall see, what Pru describes is another important aspect of how comics functioned in many girls' lives. The emphasis here is on creating personal time and space, resisting peer and other pressures. Thus reading as a personal rather than shared activity and the comic as serial publication are important aspects of how the comic is understood and enjoyed.

Other pleasures of the comic, as recalled by Pru, focus on narrative and characters, a frequent theme in interviews, as I explore later. Pru mentions few specific stories in rela-

tion to girls' comics except 'The Four Marys' and that one ironically. However, she identifies the 'hard done by' characters as part of the attraction of the girls' comics she read.
Here, again returning us to issues of class, a girl who in having experienced boarding
school would probably be considered middle-class, found the stories of struggle aimed at
and featuring working-class girls relevant to her situation. In addition, she also mentions
the attraction certain images held for her as a girl, in this case those on the covers of annuals featuring girls doing sporting activities, although whether it was the activity or the
artwork that attracted her is unclear.

These pleasures in comics do not preclude being critical of them, suggesting that these
are not memories that should be understood entirely in the light of nostalgia. Pru's use of
'The Four Marys', for instance, juxtaposes her actual experience of school with their fictional one in a way that shows both her knowledge of the strip and her disagreement with
the image of boarding school that it offered. Respondents usually had strong opinions on
girls' comics, often related to narrative or to issues of education, class or gender - resisting
or accepting the models of female behaviour that stories or titles offered. In addition, Pru
is critical of one comic, *Bunty*, as an object, describing the quality, texture and colour of
the paper it was made from in negative terms. Referring to the comic as a physical object - an object experienced - was frequent in both interviews and letters, although often
more positively than in this account. Academic writing on comics, in contrast, typically
addresses only the narratives and images contained within comics, although Ian Hague's
(2014) work on comics and the senses is an exception.

In locating girls' comics as offering security and continuity, there is little space in Pru's
account of her girlhood reading for a theme which was frequent in other interviews, that of
rebellion. It is, however, worth noting that her response to *Eagle* could be read in that way, or
as a rejection of a limiting notion of girlhood. Pru's possessiveness about this title was quite
fierce when it emerged in interview and surprising given that the comic was something
of an afterthought. Whilst I discuss swapping as a practice in the next chapter, what Pru
describes is rather different, in that it is an assertion of ownership. Yet this is ownership of
a text positioned as properly belonging to a boy, having been bought for her brother. Her
account suggests that as a girl she knew she was the secondary audience for the *Eagle* because it was bought for him *and* because she was a girl. Her use of seniority and reading skill
as counter-arguments to gender, whether that reflects a justification for reading *Eagle* that
she developed as a child or one created in interview, work to re-position her as part of the
primary audience. This argument allows her to appropriate the text, but also acknowledges
that being a girl would, on its own, not be enough to claim ownership. This appropriation
suggests a rather complex relationship with girlhood, one marked by tensions rather than
a simple acceptance of a position as 'girl'. That the memories of 'other' reading emerged
later in this interview, as they did elsewhere, hints at the existence of partial and provisional
'unfeminine' and rebellious selves that are later forgotten, discarded and perhaps buried.

Pru's interview is also illuminating in relation to the differences between public, approved definitions of what comics are and whom they are for, and personal definitions, expanding and confirming what emerges on this theme in Chapter 3. Firstly, in a professional sense Pru sees younger male readers as forming the audience for comics. That Pru has, simultaneously, been (and has once more become) a reader of 'boys' comics is an indication of her holding conflicting definitions of the comic. Secondly, the interview also contains a definition of the comic as properly 'funny'. Yet many of the narratives Pru mentions are serious in tone, focusing on adventure, issues or melodrama. So again, Pru's interview reveals tensions around definitions of what comics are and contain. Thirdly, Pru does not see reading *Bunty* as feeding into her current practice, but does see reading the *Eagle* as doing so. This is partly because she deals with adult male readers and so sees reading girls' comics as irrelevant. In making this distinction she separates off one group of texts as addressing a male audience and another as addressing a female audience. Whilst the former group of texts represent a continuous line of reading into adulthood, girls' comics appear to be an isolated past experience. Such a division also serves to isolate a girlhood self. Many interviews showed this kind of dislocation between woman and girl selves.

To conclude this brief analysis, much of what is described here is about how comics were remembered, a topic to which I return in the next section. Pru's interview encompasses memories of comics as physical objects, as a contested space, in relation to the narratives they offered, in terms of a community or an individual reader, and as having a number of functions, personal, emotional and social. However, a final conclusion can be drawn from the way that the interview floats in and out of focus on comics, making links to places, events and other reading both past and present. It was clear from both interviews and written accounts that the comic acted as a trigger for other memories about place, time, friends and family. There is a network of associations here, rather than a simple and clear picture of childhood reading.

Remembering Girls' Comics

Most discussions, although not Pru's, started with the interviewee saying that their memories of comics were relatively unexplored. This was the case with Melissa, a manager in local government from Northumberland whose responsibility was mostly for personnel. She did not read comics herself, but became involved with contributing to this book when she brought her two nephews to an event that I ran. She began by saying that, 'I haven't thought about this [her comic reading] for years'. Typically, interviews would then move onto the subject of favourite titles or stories. Melissa, for example, having initially asked me for a list of what titles were available, seized upon one with a sigh of pleasure,

> Oh … *Judy*! I had forgotten how important this was for me. I've kept a copy for years, [because] my name is in it. I'll send you a photocopy.

Figure 7 Corinne Pearlman, 'Girl Annuals', *The GirlFrenzy Millennial*, Slab-o-Concrete Publications, 1998, p. 20.

Her memory of comic reading, having been vague, leapt into sharp focus here and remained so for the rest of the interview.

Potentially this vagueness could be seen as related to a nostalgic understanding of comics, yet this rarely occurred, even amongst those who described their memories of reading comics as nostalgic. For instance, Fiona, a teacher from Sunderland, began her letter with the statement that,

> After reading the article about your work I felt compelled to respond. The fond feelings of nostalgia conjured up by the mention of *The Bunty* need to be shared.

However, she then offered a largely unsentimental account of the impact of *Bunty* on her life, including how it influenced her future career, which is mentioned later in this chapter. The complexities of tone in this remembering – however labelled as 'nostalgia' it might be – are summed up in a rather different 'memory text' about comics, the comic strip 'Girl Annuals' by Corinne Pearlman, which appeared in *The GirlFrenzy Millennial* (1998) edited by Erica Smith. Here too, the assertion of nostalgia is tempered by flashes of dry humour, for instance in the reference to light shades, a typical *Girl* craft activity (Fig.7).

I initially assumed that readers had forgotten things about the comics when confronted with vagueness in interviews. However, I began to question whether fading memory was the only cause when I realized that memories of *Bunty* and *Jackie* dominated the early part of most interviews. Later in interviews, other titles, often described as the reader's favourites, came to the fore and some aspect of them might be described in detail, as occurred in Pru's interview with regard to *Eagle*. I would suggest that this initial focus on the two most popular girls' titles occurred because of several factors. Forgetting and re-writing personal history has an impact, as does the importance that *Bunty* and *Jackie* have assumed as part of a generalized history of girlhood, being seen as shorthand for the whole genre (particularly in popular accounts of the 1960s and 1970s).

It is also in part due to institutional factors in that these titles benefited from a definite sense of identity, unlike most titles, which were absorbed, amalgamated, or otherwise combined by publishers, something which might explain why the genre collapsed. Although the respondents were not aware of the publishing practices involved, readers from different generations had read some of the same stories in different comics, so recycling of stories blurred generational distinctions, linking girlhood experience across reading generations, geography and class.

Which titles readers remembered varied. In addition to those above, older readers regularly mentioned *Girl*, *Girl's Crystal* and *School Friend*. According to Chapman, research into girls' reading in the early 1950s revealed that '94 per cent of fourteen- and fifteen-year-olds read one or more of these papers' (Chapman, 2011, p.108). This group of five titles was the most cited, but these were not the only titles readers discussed. In some cases, interviews and letters produced lists of childhood reading. Judy, whose letter shone with her pride in her children and grandchildren, took this a step further. She began by detailing her own childhood reading, including *Film Fun* (Amalgamated Press/Fleetway Publications, 1920-1962) which Judy says she only got it 'now and then, as at the price of 2d. they were considered expensive', and her regular title *Rainbow* (AP, 1914-1956), a pioneer nursery comic selling one million copies week at one point (Gifford, 1975, p.136), but then went on to describe her four children's comics as well:

> My eldest child was fortunate in having *Mickey Mouse* and *Topper* (DC Thomson, 1953-1990) sent to him…as my children were spread out over seventeen years I was still buying *Topper* 31 years later. I got to the stage where I read it first along with *Bunty* and *Mandy*. The girls swapped two of their comics for *The Beezer* –I loved 'Mr Magoo'- and *Dandy*. It was a household with a comic in every room. My youngest loved *Twinkle* and reading of the 'Doll's Hospital'. From 13-14 years of age she progressed to *Smash Hits*, and…then it was *Jackie* for teen girls- [which] explained girls' problems, also how to kiss a boy.

In addition to readers mentioning a wide range of titles, there was also variation in how readers remembered comics. Readers used a number of strategies, some about other aspects of their lives, some about the comics themselves. Whilst most interviews established early on which titles were to be discussed, as is the case with Pru, in others readers were more confident about characters or stories than titles. Readers also used titles as shorthand for a particular period, which works with *Girl* (1951-1964), but less well with *Bunty* (1958-2001). Another way of remembering publications for girls was through technical change. For instance, the transitional period between the story-paper and the comic appeared in both reader accounts and in a collection of memoirs about girlhood in the 1950s, edited by Liz Heron (1985). Other technical aspects of the comic book which also made decisive breaks with past practice were noted by readers, including the introduction of the photo stories in the late 1970s and early 1980s.

Another strategy in remembering comics was to associate specific stories with a specific period: for instance, Linnette, a retired teacher from Durham, had read 'The Silent Three', the story about three schoolgirl detectives featured in *School Friend*. Linette wrote a brief but evocative description of the story filled with ironic asides and obvious affection, a dual tone that was frequent in accounts. It distances the adult from the topic, whilst simultaneously allowing them to acknowledge how important such reading was to their girl selves. Linette said that 'The Silent Three' attended a girl's boarding school (where else), wore long, green- hooded cloaks for their secret meetings and solved mysteries, unmasked shady characters and had an amazing amount of free time unhindered by a school timetable. They wore wonderful school uniforms including skiwear (where they held their winter sports I can't imagine).

All of those mentioning the story in interview had read 'The Silent Three' during the 1950s, although both story and title had continued until 1965. The readers identified the title as very much a part of the 1950s and were surprised that it survived into the 1960s. No readers younger than this group mentioned the story at all. Conversely, some stories appeared in nearly all accounts, having occurred in various forms throughout the entire period that the girls' comic existed. The various incarnations of 'The Four Marys' in *Bunty*, for instance, had an 'old-fashioned' look to many readers, having started in 1958 (created by Bill Holroyd) and stayed the same into the 1980s. Yet this was a very popular story and was possibly made *more* memorable by the distinctive visual style.

Another aspect of the interviews was that readers often asked for information about specific titles or characters, hoping for confirmation that their memories were correct, which, for the most part, they were. Such questions are possibly a product of the amalgamation of titles and the lack of distinct identity that titles could have as a result. Readers' questions proved to be a form of barter, asking for something in return for the interview or letter, as well as a reflection of their assumption that I was an 'expert'. Olive, for instance, who sent a letter from Sunderland, but offered very little information about herself except her age, concluded by saying,

> Just another couple of points. I'm grateful to finally see the fourth Mary's surname
> – I could remember the other three but not Mary Field.

Also was it *Bunty* that featured the pie-eating headmistress? She was a bit of a favourite.

Interviews often centred on which stories appeared in which pre-teen comics. A comic rather than a story could also be the subject of a request. Maureen, a teacher from Newcastle, for instance, wanted more information about a comic called *Seven*:

> I wonder if you can shed a little light on a comic mystery that's plagued me a little over the years? When I was aged seven a glossy weekly comic full of fairytales was published, called *Seven*. It was, as I remember it, a very lovely and high quality magazine. After only a few issues, however, it changed its format to a smaller size with thinner paper and changed its name from *Seven* to *Esmeralda*, which was the name of a witch character in the comic. Then it completely went off the market and I was rather heartbroken at the time! No one I know remembers this comic.

She wanted to check that it had existed and that she 'hadn't made it up'. Maureen's request shows a very detailed memory of the comic as object (something common to many accounts). There is also a mildly apologetic tone (which appeared in many interviews), perhaps indicated by the repeated use of the word 'little' in the first sentence. Finally, the detail of her description, and the fact that she describes herself as 'plagued' by the mystery, suggests that the question and memory are important to her, no matter how much she plays it down.

In researching a response to Maureen's question, I found confirmation of the existence of *Seven* and of how short a period these publications could exist for. The first version, by publishers Gresham (Wells Gardner Darton), appeared from February to June 1971 and the latter version from June 1971 to January 1972. These memories of short-lived titles such as *Seven*, *Pixie* from IPC which only lasted from June 1972 to January 1973, or *Emma* (DC Thomson, 1978-79) also had a secondary function useful to the researcher in that they confirmed which generation of readers an interviewee belonged to.

Remembering comics encompassed non-narrative aspects of comics as well as favourite stories, which I look at more closely shortly. Discussion might encompass the physical text (as we saw above) or the context of consumption, or other aspects of the comics. For instance, Xena, a mature student from Surrey, sent an e-mail that joked about the adverts and letters page in *Jackie*:

> Do you remember the 'Cathy and Claire' problem page (strictly no sex) and the constant adverts for Anne French Cleansing Milk (good for blackheads!)

However, one non-narrative aspect of a single comic dominated accounts above all others, that being the cut-out doll from *Bunty*. Fiona said, 'For me the very best of *Bunty* was the cut-out doll and clothes on the back page, but I could not get it until all members of the household had had their read'. Maureen recounted how she 'had a box full of those grubby, thin cut-out dolls and wardrobes' and that because of the doll, '*Mandy* and *Judy* never had quite the same appeal as *Bunty*'. Olive said that she was 'Such a poor cutter-outer that the little tabs to keep her clothes on would always get chopped off'. Pru and many others also mentioned their tendency to cut off the tabs. This theme ran through *On These Days* (BBC Radio 4, 17/1/98) as well. Kate Saunders, the narrator, describes her own reading of *Bunty* in the 1960s as 'For your money you got thrilling stories, practical hints and a cut-out doll you could dress in slightly bizarre versions of the latest fashions'. This is also interesting in that destruction of the comics signifies pleasure here (as was described as the case for boys), unlike the dealer's assertion in Chapter 1 that girls' looked after their comics.

Finally, in terms of tone, these accounts of childhood and reading were often mildly self- ironizing, as many of the comments above confirm. They revealed a shared laughter about child selves that counterbalanced how strongly readers felt about their comics and, as I suggest earlier, allowed the adult interviewee to distance themselves from the girl reader that they had been. The tone of much of the discussion and letters was along these lines, in some ways both defensive and apologetic (as is the case in Maureen's account) about a passion for 'trivia' in girlhood. Interviews sometimes ended with an 'admission' that the interviewee still had one comic, which she had kept because she had won a prize or, as Melissa suggests, because her name was in it. For instance, Gill, an arts manager from the South Midlands who was not a current comic reader (although her partner was) said, with a tone that was both serious *and* tongue-in cheek, that,

> I had a letter in 'Cathy and Claire' [in *Jackie*]. It was about a teacher and it almost got me suspended ... I prize it almost as much as my Blue Peter badges!

Whilst suggesting that these were in some ways guilty pleasures, these interviews revealed immense amounts about the speaker's younger self. The self-mocking tone employed often functioned as protection in case of criticism in making public private information. The interviews could be seen as confirming the anxieties and assumptions around reading comics analysed in the previous chapter.

Remembering Narratives

Readers' memories of narratives in comics took many forms. In some cases they offered detailed description of plots, in others, illustrations, as we shall see, and, in a few cases readers, whilst not remembering specific stories, recalled responses to the serial form of the narrative. Frances, a P.A. from South Shields, for example, said 'I don't remember the stories, just wanting to know what happened next'. Similarly, Rosemarie, a civil servant from Belfast, sent an e-mail in which she incorporated stories, comics and, for her, the main reason for reading comics. She wrote,

> This brings me back to when I used to read the *Bunty/Mandy/Jinty* and *Lindy* (IPC, 1975) magazines, but in particular the one with 'The Four Marys', because the endings were so good that I could hardly wait for the next week's publication.

As mentioned earlier in relation to Pru's account, comics could be a source of continuity and security, but these accounts also suggest that the serial format could offer excitement. What happened next was always a driving force in the serial story: having to wait until the next week simply increased the tension, inviting involvement and engaging readers.

The range of stories discussed was very wide. Readers' accounts give a much broader picture of the genre from horror to humour, from fantasy to non-fiction, than is often the case in writing on the girls' comics. Elizabeth, a dealer in 'collectibles' from Leeds, who has been very much involved in British grass-roots feminism, offered a long list of stories she had liked. She described the stories in these titles as including ones about,

> Princess Di types creeping around in hoods at night and giving money to the poor. I saw no charm in ballet or horse stories, but was a softy for the school story and ones where girls performed heroic feats.

She saw no contradiction between her adult feminism and her favourite girlhood titles having been *Girl* and *School Friend*, and argued that some of the active heroines were proto-feminist. Alongside the stories, she remembered liking the non-fiction illustrations of costumes, flags of the world and kings and queens. Specific stories, rather than types of story, featured in some accounts. Maureen, for instance, recalled,

> My favourites were a cartoon character who was mad about fashion- 'Up-to-Date-Kate' and another about three witches who lived on Hampstead Heath. I also remember giving myself nightmares over a 'Man in Black' ghost story - which would probably seem very tame today.

Similarly, Fiona's account mentioned specific stories. She said that, "'The Four Marys' were great, but for some reason I remember 'On to Oregon'- it definitely fuelled my imagination'.

Pre-teen comics dominated accounts regarding narratives. Readers were not dismissive of the teen papers, but tended to see the anonymous romances as repetitive and discussion was more likely to be of the problem page. Charlotte, originally from South Shields but now living in America, was one of the exceptions in focusing upon the stories. She found out about the research because she was sent copies of *The Journal* and *The Shields Gazette* on a regular basis to enable her to keep up with the local news. She said that,

> *Jackie* of course interested me more when I was older, and could really get into all the love stories which typically featured heroes by the names of Steve, Mick and Dave, and Terry. The female names seemed to change more often, but the guys were almost always named one of these! I wonder why!

Charlotte's account shows that romance comics offered few specific heroes and heroines. Maureen confirms this with a generic description of romance heroines: 'And, no, I never attained the heights of beauty reached by those long-legged, mane-haired, doe-eyed cartoon girls with their square-chinned boyfriends!' Romances, the readers felt, demanded the most ironic and self-reflexive comments. As Wallace, a lecturer from High

Wycombe, asserted in an e-mail, 'Happy thoughts of *Jackie* and being socialized into the socio-physical, non-attainable, ideal of modern female beauty has kept me going through this last half hour! [Of boring paperwork].' Whilst they might comment on how a certain romance strip was drawn, what readers tended to focus on, in terms of narrative, were the stories and heroines of the pre-teen comics.

In titles for the pre-teen three story strands emerged as important, each serving to undermine the image of these papers as offering only one kind of story, that involving the suffering heroine. The first was the group story where friendships and helping each other were vital, such as 'The Four Marys', already mentioned numerous times in this chapter. The second was the solo story, emphasizing independence and physical competence on the part of a single, often isolated, central character. Such characters led Maureen, for instance, to say that,

> I think, looking back, the heroines of the *Bunty*-style comics were quite feminist in that they often did things which girls traditionally did not do- however, the goodies were ALWAYS blonde!

Such heroines are not usually understood as feminist, but it is worth noting that they had adventures rather than romances and, in addition, that the group stories emphasized female co-operation. The final important strand was that of the suffering heroine. These stories focused on the individual overcoming difficulties, whether moral, physical, or based on class position.

Some stories in girls' comics do focus on suffering and passivity as leading to reward, as Walkerdine suggests, although in the following case, as in others, it is an outside influence and the heroine's actions that lead to resolution, as Barker (1989) stated. The importance of these stories to some readers is indicated by Olive's account of her reading, which centred on a description of one *Bunty* story. This story

> [c]oncerned a very poor family with two children, the older one a daughter. They were so poor that the younger child had no cot but slept in a drawer. There was a mysterious lady benefactor who somehow gave the older child some money, or the older child was given money from some source. The child was faced with the difficult choice of spending the money on the bicycle that she really wanted or buying a cot/bed for her younger sister/brother. After much soul searching, she bought the bed. Then the mysterious lady benefactor stepped in and bought her the bike she dreamed of! I know this will sound really naff but this was a tremendous influence on me to do the right thing whatever the circumstance.

One can see such stories as training texts designed by adults to moderate the expectations of the female child in a very effective way, and this story had a considerable impact on Olive, imparting lessons on how to live in a certain way. This impact may be linked to the nature of serial publication in that it offers the reader opportunities for thought and reflection on a theme over a period of time. However, as I have suggested, the comics also show female protagonists who are *active* in the face of suffering, as overcoming through their efforts rather than their passivity. Thus, there are two types of heroine in these stories, one who depicts passive strength in suffering and one linked with attributes usually typified as male (through being active).

Writers on girls' comics have emphasized their role in introducing girls to a female world of pain and restriction through the stories, but interviews suggest that this was not how readers understood them. Elizabeth's list of favourite stories, given above, for instance, emphasizes independent heroine and group stories, and Maureen's focuses on horror and humour. Frances, despite having read '*Judy*, *Bunty* and *Mandy*. My gran bought them' asserted '*I don't remember them being miserable*'. In addition, as Heron states, 'In our games we borrowed lives...from the hardy and hard-done-by heroines of *Bunty*, *Girls' Crystal* or *School Friend*. We shared their dreams of escape and vindication' (Heron, 1985, p.161). In girls' play, the emphasis is on overcoming difficulties and achieving ambitions, rather than suffering and self-sacrifice. Further, terms such as 'escape' and 'vindication' suggest that the readership already had an awareness of the pain and restriction that such comics, it is suggested, introduce. This quotation also illustrates that collective activity went on around the comics, undermining the notion of the comic as addressing isolated girls reading about girls in similar circumstances, although this was sometimes the case.

Overall, it was the school story that was the most frequently mentioned type of narrative, linking the comic with the school story tradition in children's books. The image of the girls' comic is bound up with the school story to the extent that it has become a generic marker. This genre could encompass group, independent and suffering heroine stories, but it is the group story, 'The Four Marys' that dominated memories. For instance, Rosie Waller (1999), in an editorial in *The Journal* written in response to an article about my research, reported:

> top of the reading list had to be 'The Four Marys', those goody-goody boarding school prefects who stamped out bullying, befriended the spotty and defended the merits of neat handwriting at St. Elmo's. They had adventures and were the human equivalent of a well brought up Lassie, all of them, and when I was a child I wanted to go to boarding school in the hope that I would meet three Rosies and be part of a group just like theirs. (p.8)

Waller outlines very well the key appeal of the stories: the desire to be part of a group of like-minded and active friends. She uses active verbs like 'stamped out', 'befriended' and 'defended', which contrast with the qualifications, like 'goody-goody' and 'well brought up', that surround her description of 'The Four Marys'. The combination of the two again suggests ambivalence as well as pleasure. The representation of the boarding school as an ideal community of girls who do things together also appears in *On These Days*. In her interview for the show, McRobbie described the appeal of stories such as 'The Four Marys' as an escape from the family, reprising her comments about school stories in all formats:

> It's the family that is more claustrophobic for the young girl and it is the family who are putting all the pressures on in terms of sexual stereotyping.
> In these different worlds, outside the family, the characters, and by extension, the readers, are free to explore a wider range of possibilities than would otherwise be the case. So I think that the freedom was really what was so appealing. (BBC Radio 4 17/1/98)

Comics, in this reading, allow a fantasy exploration of being outside the family, a way of resisting the 'real' world. Many of the stories in *Bunty* and other comics that are not school based could also be seen as offering a similar escape from the family.

However, whilst what McRobbie says may be the case, it is also possible that the competence of these characters, their understanding and movement within their worlds is what appeals, particularly to an isolated child who finds school and growing up bewildering. In interviews, a number of discussions focused on the comics as offering positive role models in their use of images of independent women and girls. Iris, a dance tutor from Durham and Claire, a lecturer from Manchester, for instance, had both aspired to being 'Valda' as girls, a character that gained power through use of a crystal that absorbed sunlight. Claire ended her e-mail 'Long live Valda!' and Iris said,

> I liked *Mandy* best and my favourite story was about an independent woman warrior called Velda ... no, *Valda*. She defended herself, had adventures and did not need others to look after her. She was an inspiration.

Such independent characters regularly featured in the pre-teen titles. Curiously, this was the story mentioned most by those interviewees who had as adults gone into teaching or lecturing. Although their backgrounds varied enormously, they all described a sense of recognition in reading the story about this powerful outsider and heroine. Reading 'Valda' as an 'outsider' text opens it to appropriation by anyone bullied, bright or otherwise different.

Other characters were also remembered as having appealed to readers because, like 'Valda', they focused on notions of female strength. Many characters exhibited physical strength or were involved in a range of activities. Kate, for instance, who was a retired secretary from Sunderland, wrote that, 'I went on to the *Bunty* [from the *Beano*] and loved reading about girls doing ballet or ice-skating'. Maureen, similarly, had been impressed by "Gelda from the Glacier' [who] sticks in my mind for some reason! (She'd been frozen for 100 years in a glacier and emerged in the twentieth century as a wonderful skier!).' Linette expanded on this theme in outlining the impact these stories had upon the games she played with friends in emulation of the detective schoolgirl heroes: 'We certainly used our initiative and imagination and had the freedom to roam about and have adventures which children unfortunately cannot do anymore.' It is possible to see this physicality as radical: as a statement that girls can be active rather than conforming to a notion of fragile femininity, although, as I discuss later, this positive viewpoint on the active heroine was also contested in some reader accounts.

In addition, the independent heroine narratives involved a different kind of investment by the reader. Most school stories and suffering heroine narratives laid emphasis on eventual conformity to the group, or on the notion that good girls get their just reward. In contrast, independent heroine narratives seemed, from my research, to have involved considerable investment by readers in the notion of rebellion, as Iris's comment about 'Valda' implies. Hilary, a lecturer in her early thirties from Sheffield, argued that many of the characters could be seen as rebelling. She included both rich girls 'fighting against stuffy families to follow their dream' and those 'overcoming poverty to achieve their ambitions'. I return to how readers used comics as part of their own rebellion and resistance later.

To conclude, pre-teen titles dominated readers' memories of narratives in comics. Whilst romance comics appeared, as we shall see, in relation to adverts, problem pages and products, few readers discussed specific stories. Three key story strands appeared in relation to pre-teen titles, which consisted of group stories and those featuring independent and suffering heroines. A huge number of stories were mentioned and a number of genres, including horror, but 'The Four Marys' was the most consistent reference, cutting across age, location and class. The suffering heroine stories, surprisingly, given the critical attention to those specific narratives, were reported as having been less important to many readers than those featuring groups and independent heroines.

Contextualising Girls' Comics

Comics were contextualised in a number of ways in interviews. One important approach was in balancing them against other kinds of reading and media (as Gill, above, suggests in her reference to the BBC children's television programme Blue Peter). For instance, there were many comments on the serial nature of comics in comparison to books. Noreen, an educational advisor from Sunderland, touched on what she saw as the differences between the relationships the reader might have with comics and with books:

> Books are more important, in that they stay with you and have wider significance … Comics were throwaway, yet very important to who you were at the time.

Here books are permanent (and described in the present tense) and comics, as serial, weekly publications, are ephemeral (and described in the past tense) and therefore tied to specific times and activities. Whilst ephemeral, or perhaps *because* of their ephemeral nature, the memories they evoked were identified as very directly of experience at a certain age, and especially of points of transition. The serial form, then, is connected more tightly to a shifting sense of self. For instance, Noreen suggested that the romance comics, unlike most books, offered ways of dealing with the possibility of relationships at an age 'when you are looking for clues'. Noreen linked this notion of the comic and magazine as information to the sensation, particularly for those women who formed the first generation of teenagers, stating that 'you had to work out where you fitted in'.

Comics were often compared to other reading in other ways as well. That accounts frequently incorporated both books and comics shows that the educationalists' fear that comic readers only read comics is, in general, an error. As Gemma Moss states in her account of reading histories, written in response to teachers' concerns about reading, 'Any reader, no matter how committed or obsessional, is unlikely to restrict themselves to one kind of text' (in Buckingham, 1993, p.122). Typically interviewees discussed other reading; even Norah from Billingham, who described herself as 'having a career in science', who was an *extremely* avid current comic fan, offered an account that included non-comic reading:

> I read my first book when I was fourteen (*The Hobbit*) my second at fifteen (*Lord of the Rings*) then I discovered science fiction. Despite this and my mother's fears I got to grammar school, got 'O' levels, 'A' levels and a degree without reading a word of Charles Dickens and Thomas Hardy.

The emphasis laid on academic achievement was common to many accounts: for instance Maureen asserted that '*Bimbo* (DC Thomson, 1961-1972) has a lot to answer for, but as I now have an MA, I suppose at least it didn't turn me into one'. Many interviewees were at pains to emphasize that reading comics had not done them any harm, suggesting how aware they were of suggestions that comics were harmful. These ironic claims show an awareness of the negative and anxious public discourses on comics discussed earlier, yet often real readers cut through that public attitude.

Interviewees usually saw comics as giving positive pleasure, but a few respondents were in conflict over some aspects of their comic reading. For example, Charlotte was comfortable with girls' comics,

> I started out on feminine fare such as the *Bunty* and *Jackie*, and when I was younger, I enjoyed all the schooldays stories of people like 'The Four Marys' etc.

However, she saw reading many other comics, including British mixed gender comics, as addictive or otherwise dangerous. For instance, she described superhero comics as filled,

> with supernatural groups of creatures saving the world with their powers received usually by some cosmic interaction with someone bent on world destruction.

Despite her concerns about the cult and occult nature of these texts, she did see comics as making her a keen reader. Yet these sentiments were couched in terms that revealed a discomfort about comics, with perspectives that once more echo the debates about comics and literacy outlined in Chapter 3:

> On a higher level, I do feel that comics helped me in my growing years, to become more proficient in reading. It did not seem like hard work at all, but I believe it helped me quicken my reading pace, and that comics made reading such fun (now I'm talking like one) that they helped inspire me to other reading heights in 'real' reading. A change is as good as a rest, and after chewing the bubble gum of comics, I was happy to get back to some 'proper' stuff!

Readers' accounts also contextualised girlhood comic reading in relation to their current situations and selves. Fiona, for instance, linked her enthusiasm for cutting out the dolls in *Bunty*, with her first choice of career: 'Perhaps the cut out doll, more than anything, inspired my initial career as a designer after studying Fashion at Trent Poly'. At least two respondents, Iris and Noreen, 'blamed' their early careers in dance on ballet stories in comics, particularly 'Belle of the Ballet'. They were of very different ages, having read the story at opposite ends of its run. However, they were both quite sure that this first love of ballet was inspired by comics, as were the many readers that went (or were desperate to go) to dance classes. Such links between reading and aspired to career also applied to some readers of comics aimed at primarily male audiences. For instance, Norah said 'I still blame Jack Kirby for my choice of a career in science'. The theme of career and education, then, ran through the accounts, linking later life with early reading and defining the present in relation to the past.

In conclusion, comics were contextualised in accounts in a number of different ways. In this section, I have discussed two of those ways, the first being in terms of other kinds of reading material and the second being in terms of the later careers that interviewees chose. Yet, as I suggested earlier, the most common way to contextualise comic reading was as part of a network, a web of associations with other people: with family, especially siblings, and friends. They were also tied up with social position and used to reinforce a sense of both personal and group identity. Given that comics exist in a nexus of relationships, I now move on to exploring how publications might be remembered in relation to other people, beginning with the readers' parents.

Parents and Comics

Interview material from readers indicates a wide range of responses to the girls' comic and the comic in general on the part of readers' parents. Whilst the focus of this monograph is those who read comics as children, in some homes, comics were simply forbidden and a common response when I asked people at training courses about their childhood comic reading, was to say, 'I wasn't allowed them'. Such a statement was nearly always followed up with the reasons why (usually given as the cost or parental concerns about class, literacy, or gender). Within many families, even the girls' comic was not acceptable. For those forbidden the comic, the relationship with comics could be characterized as either wanting them and feeling excluded, or rejecting them because of the feelings of exclusion they engendered. In addition, the vast majority of accounts from those who were allowed comics emphasized the role that parents had in the control and direction of childhood reading. This becomes particularly pertinent in relation to reading as rebellion.

This is not to say that comics were considered problematic in all homes, as comics *were* indicated as having been acceptable family entertainment in some accounts. Charlotte, for instance, despite her concerns about some comics, nonetheless described a home in which comics were welcome:

> Friday nights were like my pizza delivery night of reading material, when my Dad would come home from work at his job as a bus driver … and from his pay packet he would spend quite a chunk of money on my comics.

In her letter, as we have seen, she mentions *Bunty* and *Jackie* and superhero comics. She ended her letter with a list of the other material she could recall having read. This was clearly less important to her than the girls' comics, but was included in an attempt to offer as complete an account as possible. Her reading included,

> 'Rupert the Bear', where everything happened in rhyme. 'Lady Penelope' where the characters were mostly taken from the 'Thunderbirds' TV show. And let us not forget the comics each Sunday in *The Sunday Post* newspaper, where even today we can read about 'Oor Wullie' and 'The Broons', who never age a day and are forever frozen in their timeless appearance and activities, screaming "Help ma, Boab!" at every strange occurrence.

Her account also suggests how saturated in comic strip materials British culture was when she read all these titles in the 1960s. Another example was offered by Elizabeth, who shared an enthusiasm for comics with several generations of family. Her granddad bought *Beano* and *Dandy* alongside *Film Fun* and *Knockabout* and shared them with her (I have not been able to trace a title for children called *Knockabout*. It may be that the title was confused with *Knockout* (Amalgamated Press/Fleetway, 1939-1963)). In many households the comic linked readers across generation and gender, with shared reading being a norm. When adults saw these as desirable and acceptable texts sent a distinctly positive message to the child reader.

However, this was only one of the two subgroups of readers who did have access to comics. The first, as we have seen, had access, with permission, from the adults in their lives. Comics were also sometimes used as rewards. As Maureen noted, 'buying the comics was a regular part of our Sunday morning routine when we would be taken to the newsagents by my Dad (possibly as a reward for sitting through church)'. In contrast, the second group, those who did not have parental permission, organized access via borrowing and reading outside of the home. Parental regulation applies, then, to readers as well as non-readers of comics. For this second group of readers in particular, the lack of parental approval for girls' comics (as well as other kinds) made them attractive, but also reinforced their 'outlaw' status as not 'proper' reading in relation to class and gender.

Most typically, interviews revealed intervention in comic reading that ranged from simply buying on behalf of a child through to vetting reading, or actively banning titles and substituting others. At the least interventionist end was the example given by Crystal, a teacher. She said that her father was the main source of comics and magazines, but that he took particular pleasure in buying *Valentine* and *Boyfriend* on her behalf as it meant he could ask whoever was working in the newsagents that week, 'Do you have a *Boyfriend?*' Other types of parental intervention included simply insisting that their child asked their permission to get a specific title. Waller speaks of seeking parental permission: 'Youngsters ...in my day wanted nothing more than permission to get *Mandy* as well as *Bunty*, or *Jackie* if their parents were modern...' (1999, p.8). Alternatively, Pru's account suggests another kind of intervention, where comics are acceptable, but are purchased for the children along gendered lines. Many interviews focused on the difficulty of getting access to the comics readers wanted when pocket money had to be spent on approved reading. Even if a reader had the freedom to spend their pocket money as they wished, parents still had preferences about what their children bought.

Intervention by one parent in a child's reading, if not supported by the other parent (assuming they were present) meant that comics could also become points of tension between adults. Such accounts also give a sense of the comic as a tool of resistance. For instance, Kate explained that her father disapproved of comics, although it did not stop her from getting them:

> There was a little newsagent's shop on the corner...and I would not pass this shop unless I could buy either *The Dandy* or *The Beano*. My dad would say to my mam, 'Do not buy any more of those 'comic cuts' for Kate'. He insisted I would not be able to read, he would say that they were 'just pictures'. My mam did still buy these comics for me, and I would hide them from my dad.

His fear that Kate would rely on the pictures and so be a weaker reader is one that continues to be a concern for some parents and professionals, as already outlined. Her father's opposition to comics served to make mother and daughter closer, in that Kate's mother persisted in getting her daughter forbidden reading, so quietly rebelling against her husband.

It is clear, from the accounts above, that children's culture is not sealed off from that of adults and that the intentions of adults inevitably form part of the child's relationship with culture. Parental perspectives on the comic were wide ranging, running from approval to complete disgust and they expressed their views through what they allowed their children to read. Comics had to be gender appropriate in many homes, with girls often being directed to girls' comics, a theme that is considered more fully in the next chapter. Parental perspectives were also, as I will discuss, expressed in class terms, with many parents from both middle and working class defining the comic as a 'lower class' form.

Class, Aspiration, Rebellion and Comics

The tendency to see comics in the light of class is illustrated by an anecdote in Heron's (1985) collection of memories about girlhood in the 1950s. Ursula Huws describes how her father, in trying to get her to keep her knowledge of Welsh, bought her all the comics he could find in that language and describes how these comics were received. She says they were 'banal comic books, illustrated in a style that I had already learned from Mother to call vulgar' (Heron, 1985, p.177). The medium represents a despised cultural 'other', Welshness, from which Huws' mother sets herself and her daughter apart. Huws also implies a correlation of masculinity and comics in specifying that these views of the comic as 'vulgar' were her mother's. Most importantly, however, Huws' mother sees Welsh language comics as the antithesis of the middle-class-ness, femininity, and Englishness that she aspires to for herself and her daughter, and she defends these values from what comics connote.

Huws' mother, in seeing the comic as the antithesis of middle-class-ness, expresses views expressed by other adults regarding the medium. The comic has been seen by some as predominantly 'lower' class and unfeminine and so could potentially be problematic for girl readers, in that reading comics could undermine their status as 'proper' girls. The term 'proper' is loaded with connotations of middle-class-ness and respectability, even if readers did not use such terms (few described their relationship to comics specifically in relation to class, but rather in relation to this mediating notion of 'proper' girlhood). The women I interviewed had rarely spoken of their comic reading as young people, particularly if that reading was in genres categorized as not for girls. This is not surprising if reading any comics at all could be seen as an admission of being, or of having been, somehow deviant and 'other'. What one chooses to read in girlhood, then, may have an impact on whether one is perceived as respectable and thus has implications in terms of class and, as Skeggs (1995, 1997) illustrates, femininity.

Looking beyond parental perceptions of the comic in general, a few specific girls' titles were seen by parents and readers as representing middle-class interests. One exception to the parental perception of the comic as 'unsuitable' reading was *Girl* in the 1950s and 1960s, which was considered a 'nice' comic and 'bought for' some girls on this basis by their parents. Thus, to be 'respectable' a comic had to be middle-class and gender specific. Of course, that does not mean that the child chose to read that comic. Noreen, for instance, was bought *Girl*, but also

> read *Valentine*, *Romeo* and *Roxy* down the road at my friend's house. I wasn't allowed to read them at home because they were considered 'common and vulgar'.

In addition to being 'common', then, these titles were, as romance comics, also considered unsuitable by Noreen's parents because they considered them to encourage an interest in sexual relationships.

Parents', and readers', identification of specific comics as connoting class was partly a result of content. For instance, despite the increasing numbers taking part in ballet by the 1970s it was still seen (critically by some) as a middle-class activity that limited and confined girls. Negative comments about a given activity were often related to generation; an activity characterizing girlhood in one era, like ballet, being typically replaced by another, for instance gymnastics, in the next. Class was marked in other ways as well. *Girl*, for example, had a higher cost than many other titles. Further, that *Girl* was broadsheet to *Bunty*'s tabloid was also important, in that both formats have class connotations in a British context.

Overall, however, it was another aspect of the physical nature of the comic, paper quality, which was seen as the key class indicator. Readers often contrasted *Girl*'s high quality paper with that used for *Bunty*. This contrast was not necessarily flattering to *Girl*. Although the paper used for *Bunty* and other DC Thomson publications was very poor quality newsprint, memorably described by Frances as 'like toilet roll', she and many others associated that paper with their childhood and recalled seeing it as preferable to the shiny pages of better made publications. Frances did not like the new publications printed on better paper that came out as a consequence of the updating of the presses at DC Thomson, arguing that

> It was upsetting when story comics started to go and they replaced them with things with glossy paper. I didn't like the pop star stuff.

She associated shiny paper with coldness and fuzzy paper with warmth. Susan, who worked in computing in London, echoed this sentiment. Here memory, as Bergson (2004) suggested, is linked with senses other than sight. She said,

> I just wish I'd kept the copies I bought every week. I do have the annuals but somehow they are just not the same as the weeklies printed on that dreadfully poor quality paper.

Thus, even the paper a comic is made of becomes part of a reader's identity, with readers' preferences for different types of paper becoming a marker of class identification and position.

Class, respectability and femininity were linked with what one read, which might be seen as representing to others what kind of girl the reader was (although few mentioned titles in relation to class, this was an implicit part of their assessment of titles). When I mentioned *Girl* to Frances, who identified herself as 'working-class girl made good', and as someone who had read *Bunty* and *Judy*, for instance, she humphed, sniffed and rolled her eyes. This, it became apparent, was an expression of her contempt for the comic and its readers, whom she characterized as 'snobs'. In addition, when I told someone else that I had read *Girl* her rejoinder was to say that I was more posh than I seemed. This suggests that the comics one read might have class implications. What Frances's response suggests is that readers positioned themselves and their reading against other sets of readers and texts. Positioning yourself in relation to girlhood reading also meant positioning yourself in relation to class.

What Frances's response to *Girl* also illustrates is that for many working-class readers of later generations, *Girl* represented the 'enemy', the 'posh girl', reflecting how it became part of a number of different social and ideological contexts. Frances was not alone in her view of *Girl*. Ursula, a university student from South Shields who had entered university as an older adult, for instance, described *Girl*, which she was actually too young to have read when it first came out, as it had finished publication around the time of her birth, as 'conformist, twee and do-goody'. Her rejection of that comic was framed as a rejection of a previous generation's notion of 'respectable' girlhood, of a middle-class-ness that had connotations of negativity and exclusion. In effect, it functioned as the 'other' to a positive working-class identity. Generally, interviewees like Frances and Ursula saw *Girl* as what *Bunty* was reacting to, despite some very similar story threads running through the two.

However, whilst some saw *Bunty* as expressing a positive working-class identity, other readers saw it as offering middle-class ideology, something some interviewees and others saw in a positive light. The most typical response is illustrated by Waller's account of

'The Four Marys' (p.190) where she suggests that she wanted to go to boarding school as a result of reading that particular strip. Similarly, when Maureen Rice, who subsequently became the editor of *Mizz* and *19*, was interviewed on *On These Days*, she saw aspiration as central to *Bunty*'s appeal, a total contrast to Ursula's interpretation of the title:

> I loved the fact that it was terribly middle-class. I loved the fact that everyone went to ballet school, boarding school and had ponies and glamorous mothers who wore hats and posh teachers with mortar boards. I loved all that...*Bunty* taught me to aspire actually...I came from a very working class family in a very nowheresville place and I thought it was a fabulous, glamorous escapist read. Yet when I look at it now, it wasn't at all glamorous, it was on newsprint, it wasn't glossy...and yet it seemed to open up a world to me. (BBC Radio 4, 17/1/98)

Like Waller and Rice, many interviewees saw these comics as offering aspirational images that they were inspired by. Girls' comics, it seems, indicated class and class mobility throughout the existence of the genre.

The aspirational aspect of girls' comics can be interpreted in two ways. Firstly, these titles could be seen as offering images of strength and competence not necessarily offered elsewhere: in career, in goals in life, dreams of being a ballerina, or having special abilities. *On These Days* argued that *Bunty* 'was born at a time when barriers for women were being broken down rapidly'. As such, it was seen as part of a rejection, not a confirmation, of established notions of class and a celebration of a new mobility. Walkerdine's notion of these texts as potentially empowering fantasy for some working- class girls is part of how participants of *On These Days* (and some of my interviewees) understood their reading. Walkerdine further argued that middle class readers would be unlikely to see these texts in a similar light (1997, p.50). However, many of those interviewed who identified themselves as middle-class also saw the images as empowering rather than sexist or limiting.

In contrast, it can be argued that girls' comics, irrespective of actual intent and content, have the function of making the middle-class world accessible to a wider audience. This could be seen as particularly the case in the late 1950s and 1960s, when comics like *Bunty*, *Judy* and *Mandy*, which were designed and aimed at working class children, were launched. In this context, the story comics are about encouraging class mobility, and so could be seen as 'improving texts' or training for working-class girls so that they would want to fit in to middle-class models of girlhood and womanhood.

It could also be argued that the texts reinforced the social positions of actual readers, serving to emphasize a sense of exclusion, something perhaps suggested by Ursula's account of *Girl*. In *Truth, Dare or Promise*, for instance, Harriett Gilbert's reading in the 1950s led her to conclude that, 'Not in *The Famous Five*...not even in *Eagle*, or in *Girl*, did any family behave itself like mine' (in Heron, 1985, p.52). This comment reflects a feeling amongst some of those interviewed that the stories told you about another more privileged world. Such perspectives, applied by a previous generation to *Girl*, began to be applied to *Bunty*, despite the fact that the producers aimed it at a more 'working-class' readership. Linda, who worked in local government in London, for instance, identified *Bunty* as 'for posh girls ... all those ballerinas, ponies, tennis clubs and private schools ... who else could it be for?' As she put it: 'I felt out of it'.

Those reading *Bunty* before the middle of the 1970s seemed to see it as expanding their horizons. After this point, readers tended to see it as constricting. *Bunty* became, in effect, the accepted text against which to rebel, being reinscribed as middle-class in comparison to horror, or to the new magazines that incorporated photo-stories of everyday life. As Norah suggested of her reading before she turned to the superhero comic, 'I read *Bunty* and remember *Judy*'s debut and those dreadful plastic flower bracelets on useless elastic. I remember preferring *Judy* and thinking that *Bunty* seemed a bit dated'. By the late 1970s, some of those interviewed preferred *Jinty*, *Misty* or the new wave of teenage magazines that were emerging, like *My Guy*. The only exceptions were girls who saw *Bunty* et al as part of genre reading. Hilary, for instance, located *Bunty* in the genre of the school story and asserted that 'everyone read them'. Such readers accepted all school stories as working similarly, not only in comics, but also in novels for children such as those by Enid Blyton.

Parents' and readers' perception of the comic as connoting class also suggests that these texts were potentially tools for rebellion. Why parents were hostile towards these comics was not necessarily clear to young readers, but they identified this hostility and acted accordingly. Such a rebellion might involve reading any comic at all, or, more likely, it might involve reading the 'wrong' girls' comic. For instance, Noreen's reading of romances at a friend's house when these titles were considered 'common' by her parents suggests that their disapproval made these titles attractive to her. They became, as Noreen put it, 'illicit, it was considered naughty to read them'. In reading them elsewhere, with a friend, she sets up an identity that is very much separate from that of her family, and emphasizes friendship over familial ties.

In some way, girls' comics create a space, characterized as resistant, for the reader. With regard to comics, the space is that of an independent girlhood and teenage, separate from womanhood and from adulthood. With regard to the comic format, there is an additional level to how the comic works in that the *medium* connotes resistance. That the comic itself is problematic, rather than the content, shows it to have a symbolic function as representing rebellion.

To return to romance comics, they were often reported in interview as having been a point of tension within families, as Noreen's comments suggest. Janice Winship, introducing her work on women's magazines confirms this, saying 'I would never have dared to ask my parents if I could take one of those comics-they were much too risqué' (1987, p.1). What is problematic here is the active female sexuality that romance might imply.

Analysed alongside Noreen's comments it is apparent that some parents' definitions of romance comics as problematic conflated active female sexuality and working-class-ness. In their eyes, one can speculate, for Noreen to read these titles undermined her 'proper' middle-class femininity and put her future at stake.

Jackie, in its turn, had a similar impact on parents, in that many adults saw *Jackie* as conflating sexuality and class in much the way that the romance comics had done. Where it differed from the earlier romance comics, of course was in the practical advice it gave: something likely to be seen as even more problematic by parents, even if the advice, as Olive reports, was somewhat limited:

> My favourite bit of advice on teenage matters concerned learning to kiss by practic-
> ing on the back of your hand! Perhaps that explains a lot!

That *Jackie* could seem a potent weapon of rebellion is illustrated by Sarah's account. Sarah, a mature student from Hexham who had previously been a secretary, told me that comics had been forbidden in her parents' house. In particular, her father described the title critically as 'working-class'. Consequently, her sister began reading *Jackie* specifically to offend their father. As Sarah said, 'She would shake it out in front of him, and sit facing him, reading it'. Although 'in awe of my sister's daring', Sarah did not have the confidence to follow her example and read crime novels as a teenager instead.

Jackie is also very significant as a marker of rebellion, and later, of hostility across class and ethnicity, in Meera Syal's (1997) *Anita and me*, a novel uses comic reading as an indicator of class and of shifts in class position. Set in the 1970s, the book follows Meena (the main character) from the age of nine, ending shortly after the results of her 11-plus examination. The Anita of the title is one of Meena's friends, a slightly older girl who is at secondary modern school. Meena's family sees Anita as 'rough' and out of control, assessing her in the light of their assumption of middle-class identity. Anita is signalled as working class through their disapproval (as well as in terms of family background and education), Anita's choice of fiction is also seen as indicating class position. She brings to the club that the local children form 'a pile of back copies of *Jackie*, a teenage magazine which formed the basis of my sex education for the next few years' (Syal, 1997, p.137). Anita and *Jackie* thus represent forbidden knowledge, dangerous sexuality, and are both seen as working-class. The connection between Anita and *Jackie* is maintained throughout the book, later as a symbol of the changing relationship between the girls, and of the limits of British conceptions of girlhood.

The realization of 'otherness' is also apparent in terms of race, as Meena realizes that *Jackie* excludes her from British girlhood because of her Punjabi family, and in terms of education, as Meena is expected to pass the 11-plus examination that Anita has failed. *Jackie* finally becomes a weapon as Meena, now revising for the approaching 11-plus, becomes the butt of attacks from Anita. Although Meena now gets her own copy of *Jackie*, she finds it often arrives with insulting notes from Anita inside. Thus girlhood, specific texts, race and class are intertwined in the novel. The comic functions similarly in this novel to the way it functioned in the lives of interviewees, in that it frequently linked the reader to a specific community. The use of the comic in the novel also suggests that race, as well as class and gender can be negotiated via the 'appropriation' of comics. Syal also describes very well the limits that some identified in the texts, and how rejecting them might mean exclusion from certain identities.

Alternatively, accepting the texts might mean embracing those identities, or as in Meena's case, being both attracted to and distanced from the messages offered.

Whilst romance comics often became an attractive option for readers who wanted to show opposition in terms of reading, they also stirred contradictory feelings of both pleasure and guilt in the readers. Such feelings also applied to those later readers who started reading after *Jackie* had largely replaced the romance comics. Theresa, for instance, described the passionate kissing in *Boyfriend* as 'quite smutty', acknowledging that she read the title and showing her discomfort at some aspects of the content. In addition, Maureen said,

> I still have some clippings from the *Jackie* of the mid-seventies and a 1975 *Jackie* annual and in one way it makes me wince- it's so girly (and downright sexist and unreconstructed!) but in another I love re-reading it because its innocence seems so appealing.

Mixed feelings like those that Maureen describes were very apparent in those accounts from women who as adults saw themselves as feminists. Although they recognized that their girl selves had used these texts as resistance, as adults they felt compromised by the femininity that they contained.

The use of the comic as rebellion and resistance was not limited to relationships with parents. Teachers' responses to the comic, as Chapter 3 discusses, were also usually linked to issues of class, either in relation to the medium as a whole or in relation to girls' comics in particular. In the following account the format of the comic, rather than the subject, again acts as the primary concern, as was the case with the romance titles. Zelda from Sunderland, who had recently retired from her work in local government, read *Girl's Crystal* as a girl, but reported that:

> [w]e were banned from reading them at school. If they saw us reading they would be confiscated. It was a grammar school, you see. We also read the little square ones [text-only]; we were allowed to keep them. Myself and another girl were great fans, we'd read all our books and these comics were new stories. The teachers noticed

them and when they did they made a fuss and banned them. We didn't see what
the problem was.

The teachers made judgements about who constituted the audience for comics (clearly not grammar school girls). In this example, those who read comics are labelled as working class, as not aspiring, as going to secondary modern schools. In choosing to read comics, Zelda and her friends chose what was seen as inappropriate or improper literature.

Many of those who had been enthusiastic readers of these comics talked about the difficulties of trying to sneak what they wanted to read past parents or teachers. Their enthusiasm was possibly due to the opposition they encountered. However, in seeking out comics, there was often collusion with an adult, usually a grandparent or aunt, or, as in Kate's case, her mother, in response to the strictness of her father. In a number of accounts, as a result, comics were not kept in the parental home. Frances, for instance, explained that all her comics were read 'at Gran's house. One evening a week me and my cousins all stayed at Gran's. We went straight around from school and started reading'. Whilst some adults were supportive, the disapproval of other adults meant that the comic became forbidden fruit for readers.

In conclusion, comics are very much bound up with both parents' and readers' perceptions of class, identity, girlhood and femininity. Because of this, they play a part in the contradictory urges of aspiration and rebellion. The use of the comic as rebellion in schools, children's leisure choices and the family reinforces that these are sites of confrontation between adults and children over popular culture. Girls' comics, despite being seen as conformist by some readers, were used by others in the context of building a girl identity that was not adult, not parent, not teacher. Such a reading enhances the potential of the girls' comic as a weapon against authority figures, a use of the comic at odds with its equally important function as marker.

These texts represented rebellion to readers, whether indicating growing up too soon, or a refusal to grow up. However, in choosing to read inappropriately yet within the confines of publishing for girls, rebellion through these texts can also be seen as representing conformity. Rebellion, then, may be seen as maintaining the gender and class status quo rather than questioning it. Parental disapproval and intervention in girlhood reading was largely based around issues of class and 'proper' femininity, which meant that for some middle-class readers in particular, the comic might allow an expression of a self that did not conform to standards of middle-class girlhood. Such rebellion is based on an understanding of these texts as 'other', in a sense reinforcing the notion of the comic as a form primarily addressing working-class readers. However, many working-class readers used comics as rebellion in a similar way if their parents insisted that the comic addressed 'lower' class readers, showing that it is always a problematic 'someone else' who reads the comic.

Pleasure and Comics

In many accounts of the girls' comic pleasure hardly features, such is the concern with the ways in which the reader is drawn into the value system the texts offered. However, pleasure was a central theme in readers' accounts. For those that enjoyed the British girls' comic there were a number of distinct pleasures remembered by readers relating to both the actual texts and the context in which they were consumed. These included using the comic as a rebellion and being able to make private space through reading, as we have seen. Pleasure was also linked in their accounts with the serial nature of the publication as Pru's interview demonstrates, or with specific stories, as the section on remembering narrative shows.

The greatest pleasure of all, according to readers' accounts, seems to have been having owned a text aimed at you and your peers alone. If parents did not actively disapprove of comics, they appeared to be uninterested. One interviewee in *On These Days* said,

> You looked forward to coming home from school and going to the newsagent to pick up your comic and you'd carry it all the way home in your satchel virtuously not reading it. It was a great thrill because you knew the grown-ups wouldn't be faintly interested, it was just yours.

The comic was often delivered to the house, or kept to one side for the reader. For a young person this too marked out the comic as special and for some simply getting a comic was enough. In my interviews one reader, Theresa, a youth worker from South Shields, who now preferred to read non-fiction, reported, 'I remember the thrill of getting my comic, but I wasn't bothered about reading it'. It was having something of her own that mattered, not what was in it. Getting these comics was part of girlhood, as either rebellion (within acceptable parameters) or conformity and so they confirmed the reader's identity as girl, defining girlhood as a separate space from adulthood. Whether read or unread, comics functioned to create and support a notion of girlhood and to establish peer groups of readers.

Another source of pleasure was often the reader's knowledge of comics. As this knowledge increased, it became possible to become an expert, expressing a competency that was a source of pride. Zelda, for instance, said, 'I'm an expert on them'. In doing so, she did not speak as an adult who had not seen any girls' comics for years, which was the case, but as an enthusiastic girl reader, such was her passion. Being an expert could be a private pleasure or a public one, as the member of the group who knew the most about a subject. Thus, this pleasure in the comic also has implications in terms of the group, emphasizing the importance of these texts in creating and maintaining a community of girls.

There were exceptions to these accounts of all-girl reader communities. As I describe in the section about parental intervention in comic reading, in some families the comic was a shared and approved of text. Consequently, the readers' community could have a radically different form in that it would include adults. Fiona, for instance, who described herself as an 'avid reader', said that her father also read *Bunty*:

> The youngest of three sisters, we had to vie with each other and my father, who worked a night shift, to get to *Bunty* first. It was delivered on a Monday and dad claimed it helped him get to sleep! Needless to say the man of the house came first and the youngest last more often than not.

This also demonstrates that men did read girls' comics: something usually seen as very unlikely by commentators on the comic.

Unlike Theresa, who did not read her comics, the majority of those interviewed reported that one pleasure of the comic was reading and re-reading their comics many times. Corinne Pearlman's cartoon demonstrates this through a caption which says, '100th reading' (see Fig.7). Comics might be flicked through once, on another occasion read thoroughly, on yet another read to isolate the reader, offering the girl a place to herself. Pearlman's cartoon demonstrates several of these different reading patterns. In addition, it shows how comics were passed on in a caption that explains that whilst *Girl* was her favourite 'My sister's *Schoolfriend's Picture Library* collection ran a close second'. Pearlman emphasizes comic reading as a largely private activity, but these aspects of reading could become incorporated into a more public space through the sharing of comics and discussion of stories amongst peers. These pleasures of the comic centred in their role as shared texts. As Maureen recalled:

> I remember in particular one story, which must have been typical of [*Bunty*'s] content: two young friends who were adopted from an orphanage by a rich woman who believed that one of them was her natural daughter. The serial concerned the fight to find out which was the real daughter. This story really gripped me and another classmate for weeks and we were sure we knew the answer- it had to be the dark-haired one, because the mother had dark hair too. We were pretty disgusted when the blonde girl won the day- but isn't that always the way with blondes?! Actually in true moral fashion, the blonde destroyed the evidence so that she would always be able to stay with her friend.

Maureen's comments flag up the fact that comics were discussed intensively at home or school to emphasize solidarity (and shared values) with friends and female siblings, if they were close in age. Reading titles together was common, as was swapping. She also indicates her understanding of the genre as a girl, and how female friendship was an important element of the stories, as well as important to the readers.

In addition, a title might function as a reminder of a friend who was not present, as well as those who were there to share the comic. Dot, a college lecturer from Liverpool, for instance, had been '[v]ery fond of *Mandy* because my cousin read it. Whenever I saw it I thought of her'. Knowing that what you were reading was read by another person of whom you were fond, whether friend or relative, at much the same time as you were reading it, was part of the pleasure comics offered. Throughout the interviews, the comic was characterized as a symbolic form of communication with other girls, a tool that helped the reader to create links.

The all-girl communities that developed around comics did involve conflict at times, however. For example, the comic could simultaneously become implicated in rivalry as well as cohesion between siblings. Illustrating the latter, Waller describes with amused detachment:

> It was a Thursday morning tradition, and every week we would prepare to fight. The footsteps down the front garden path brought us sharp to attention... It was a case of guarding the doormat, any alliance between the three of us long forgotten; pushing, pulling clothes if it came to it. Like a victorious rugby player emerging from the scrum, the lucky one would then pull free the object of our longing and it was straight to the bathroom, the only room in the house with a lock, to pore over every detail in peace. We were big fans of *Bunty* in our house. (1999, p.8)

Although some of these conflicts seem light-hearted, as the one that Waller describes does, others were more serious in asserting that comic reading might also be governed by peer pressure, a point I return to in relation to the comic as marker. The use of peer pressure, or bullying, also suggests that such publications might act as a symbol of group identity and status for the girl reader, although in a very different way to the communal pleasures of the comic.

Accounts also suggested that these texts, particularly comics aimed at younger readers, offered pleasure through the stimulation of creative play. As Linnette said, in relation to her shared reading of the *School Friend*,

> Naturally we too had a 'Silent Three'. My two friends and I wore little green velvet capes, which I made from an oddment of velvet belonging to my grandmother. We met in a "den" – an old outhouse in my friend's garden every Tuesday after school where we made rules and goodness knows what.

These games involved performing girlhood, and show other ways in which the comics allowed readers to explore possibilities. Stories like the 'Silent Three' focus on the importance of female friendship, and in playing out the comic strip readers cemented and explored their own friendships.

It was not only stories in comics for younger girls that were shared and communal - other aspects of the comics reinforced group and individual identity. Free gifts became part of a whole culture based around a specific title, the basis of a sense of girl community. For instance, Maureen recounted that 'Every girl at school had the same (freebie) eye make up from *Jackie* at one time!' Wallace also mentioned the make-up, but rather than touch on community, she offered a memory that was both tongue-in-cheek and simultaneously heartfelt:

> I haven't thought about this for ages, but I loved *Jackie* when I was a young (ish!) teenager - I read it avidly, and desperately wanted to be Twiggy - I seem to remember the predominant colour being purple and it once had a freebie of some stick-on eye-liner strips, which were dreadful, nearly took your eyes out.

In addition, *Jackie* and other titles aimed at older readers contained posters, usually of pop stars. Maureen recounted how her walls were 'festooned' with them and Kate said,

> Then in teenage years it was the *Valentine* and, I think, the *Roxy* [that I bought]. Of course this was for the Cliff Richard posters which were in the middle and were great for putting on the bedroom wall.

The quizzes in *Jackie* also featured as part of a shared culture (and could be seen as reinforcing both heterosexuality and consumerism). Comics had an economic role in developing new markets. These gifts, and the memories readers have of them, also suggest how detached girlhood consumerism increasingly became from the comic, as the magazine, with less emphasis on narrative, acted as a more cost-effective vehicle for new products.

A final feature of most comics that encouraged a sense of pleasure was writing to the editors. Writing in was encouraged although there seem to have been few comments upon the narratives themselves and more about readers sharing aspects of their lives, again showing the communal nature of comic reading. *Bunty* in particular was regularly inundated during its forty-year existence because the editors offered prizes of a scarf or pen and pencil sets. Maureen recalls 'I also remember writing dozens of letters to the *Bunty* letters page but never won more than a paperback Enid Blyton book!' Interaction was clearly something that readers wanted, although the office itself was seen as distant, exotic and slightly daunting. The role as advisor, through the teen papers problem pages, helped to emphasize that the staff were people in the know, but also to isolate the reader from them. With regard to *Jackie*, for instance, Maureen said 'I genuinely imagined that in the *Jackie* office, the Bay City Rollers and David Cassidy regularly dropped in for a cup of tea and a chat'. Similarly, Rice in *On These Days* stated:

I don't know if I ever imagined the people working at *Bunty*. I suppose I imagined someone incredibly glamorous and amazingly fabulous and girls full of daring-do and adventure. I didn't think for a minute I could just write in and join them.

Sharing through writing in to the comic had a counterpart in the shared reading of the letters, especially in teen magazines. Discussing the answers given on the problem pages with friends and seeing how far they agreed with them was an aspect of readers' interrogation of and conforming to the models of girlhood offered in these comics.

In conclusion, despite what is generally seen as their conservative content, these texts assert the reader's difference and independence from adults, whether as a girl or as a teenager, something which itself offered readers a great deal of pleasure. However, the role comics played in cementing friendships or developing a sense of a girl community was just as important as that of creating personal space. Looking at the context in which comics were consumed, then, allows the centrality of the comic in girls' lives to be more clearly understood. Reading did not only take place in a certain period, with the impact that attitudes of a period might have, or not, upon the comic, but also in a nexus of relationships with peers.

The Comic as Marker

As I indicate above, some of the pleasures of the comic are tied to their serial format. I have shown that any given publication would be read for several years and that some titles were tied to distinct phases in girlhood and to a sense of identity. This linking is clear from the accounts of those readers who offered extensive personal reading histories. I have also suggested that the comic acted as a way of cementing girls' relationships with each other. Combining all of these factors implies is that such reading acted as a marker of points of transition within girls' culture.

This process of moving from one title to another to none was part of a number of reading histories. The texts formed part of the question, and a partial answer of what it meant to be a girl, fixing identity temporarily. Kate, for instance, charted her reading from *The Beano* and *The Dandy*, to *The Beezer* (DC Thomson, 1956-1990), *The Topper*, to *Bunty* and *Judy*, and then to *Valentine*. Fiona, in contrast, described her reading pattern as follows,

My comic reading started with *Robin* and the *Bunty* before we progressed to *Jackie, Petticoat, Honey, 19* (IPC, 1968- 1986) and the dreaded *Over 21* (MS Publishing, 1972-1988).

Whilst the readers are quite close in age these two histories include rather different titles. Where they are similar, on the other hand, is in describing a feminine trajectory into women's magazines.

What older siblings read was very influential. Maureen recounts following the same line of titles as her sister:

> I would get *Twinkle* and my sister, five years older, bought the *Princess* and then *Diana*. I remember that to me, *Diana* always seemed a very grown-up and sophisticated comic and I would 'sneak' a read without my sister's knowledge.

Maureen then followed a pattern from *Bimbo* to *Twinkle* to her sister's *Princess* and *Diana* to her own *Bunty* to her sister's *Jackie* and then her *Cosmopolitan* (Hearst Corporation 1965-date). Maureen recounted how she became disillusioned with *Jackie* at thirteen and moved on to *Cosmopolitan*. It was partly because her older sister was by that time reading it, but also because:

> [m]y new sister-in-law told me that the very young and trendy-sounding 'Cathy and Claire' had been in *Jackie* when she used to read it...and I guessed that this pair must be actually aged around (shudder!) forty. It never, ever occurred to me- until about now, I guess- that there may not have been a 'Cathy' or a 'Claire'!

Such moments are important markers both at the time and afterwards in adulthood. The comic can locate the reader within girlhood and as the reader moves from one 'stage' of girlhood to another this is marked by a change of title.

When a title became described as 'boring', it was usually because the reader had outgrown it. The choice of the next title usually acted as a statement of who the reader intended to be, as Maureen's account demonstrates: another way in which the reading of girls' comics could be seen as aspirational. Changing to a new title lagged behind the reader's realization that they had moved on, grown older. Changing titles was not necessarily wholly welcome in emotional terms and was also a nuisance in practical terms. Typically, those who read the girls' comic followed a specific trajectory linking texts with points of personal transition, either into puberty, changing schools, or into adulthood.

The majority of respondents followed a trail of comics that led into reading women's magazines, conforming to the pattern that is suggested by Walkerdine and McRobbie. *Bunty* and *Jackie* segued into each other, to these writers, in terms of ideology as well as biography. However, these titles were not necessarily the only reading someone did. For instance, Fiona adds that her reading: '[w]as interspersed with *Look & Learn* at my mother's insistence'. The choice of *Look & Learn* (Fleetway Publications, 1962-1982) in particular suggests parents trying to engage their child with educational and academic pursuits rather than popular culture. Other readers similarly traced a central line of reading, whilst identifying other texts that had been part of their overall reading experience. Some were chosen, some not. These other comics were, at times, not comics intended for girl readers at all. Further, other reads moved on to music magazines linked with specific types of music.

Whilst the motive for changing titles was largely positive, representing changes in the individual, there were readers who reported that the transition might not be so welcome. In some cases, the peer pressure to read specific titles, to read what your friends did and move on when they did, was intense. These were forced shifts that often become very important memories. The forced shift also necessitated pretending to like what the group liked. Diane who had recently become a mature student, having stayed at home when her children were young, said that, '[t]here was terrible peer pressure to read what your group did', yet she also emphasized how communal the activity of reading was. She was unwilling to speak further about peer pressure. Whilst it was generally accepted that girls' 'grew out of' the comic sooner than boys, peer pressure to 'grow up' and conform to the thirteen plus scene usually meant dropping all comics.

Bullying might, therefore, enforce the standards of the group that the reader became part of. As Gosling reports:

> They did, though, go on to deprive me of one pleasure, that of reading girls' comics. Initially I spent all of my pocket money on buying these to read on the train - *Bunty, Judy, Mandy, Tammy*, to name but a few - as choosing them also occupied some of my time before arriving at the station. This habit was viewed as extremely "babyish" by the girls I travelled with, and on my thirteenth birthday I promised them that I would renounce reading comics forever. (It was only in my twenties that I rediscovered the comics world, going on to study at the London Cartoon Centre and becoming a member of the Comics Creators Guild.) In retrospect, perhaps they (rightly) regarded me as being queer, and felt that if I stopped reading comics and started wearing makeup, this would change - an attitude which my mother continues to possess at the time of writing. (Gosling, 1998, Section: My Own Schooldays)

Gosling's comments tie in with some of the reader's accounts. Peers tended to accuse readers who continued reading after the time seen as appropriate for a specific title was over of being 'a baby', implying that an attachment to *Bunty* or the later pre-teen magazines was simply immature. Why readers might resist changing titles varied. For instance, several interviewees who identified themselves as lesbian reported resisting reading heterosexual romance titles like *Jackie* and *My Guy*. Elsa, for instance, a rights activist from London who worked in computing, said by e-mail, '*Misty* was my very first comic, and my introduction to horror/occult/general weird shit writing *and* I fancied Misty like mad'. The pressure to read romance titles was described as defining. Readers felt titles aimed at younger readers, such as *Misty*, offered, in contrast, possibilities for re-reading, reading against the grain, in ways that tallied with their emerging sense of sexuality.

The vast majority of readers, as well as following a typical pattern of readership, moved beyond comics altogether in adulthood, although they usually kept the older material if possible. Personal history was partly maintained through holding onto physical texts. Being considered too old for comics altogether was another important marker. Parents were cited as having put readers under pressure to dispose of their collections. Zelda said, 'I threw them away when I got married…They would all sit in the wardrobe in piles and my mother would ask when I was going to get rid of them'. More usual was that parents threw out comics on their child's behalf. Scott in her article on *Jinty* begins, 'Sadly, I lost my *Jinty*s some time ago; as usually happens with these things, my mum gave them away (though she says that I agreed to this – bah!)' (in Smith, 1998, p.95). This can be contrasted with one correspondent, Tanya, a student, who asserted

> I've kept all my *Buntys* and *Mandys* and *Judys* and I'm never going to let anyone make me get rid of them. I've heard so many sob stories about people being persuaded or deciding to get rid of their books and things, its not going to happen to me!

Many male collectors also report parents disposing of comics. But whilst female respondents might have thought about the material but had usually never gone back to them, men had gone back either to buy the issues that they had lost or to find new titles. For women, reading comics into adulthood, like reading children's books, was seen as acceptable if you had children, but childish if you did not. This does not mean that comics lost their appeal. As Waller states, 'A colleague of mine, who I have promised not to name … admitted the other day that a copy of *Bunty* fell through her letterbox every week until she was 21. Wow' (1999, p.8). However, there are few women actively seeking out comics as collectors. The dealer cited in Chapter 1 reported having been outbid for some *School Friends* at a recent auction but could be no more specific. In contrast, a London antiquarian bookshop (where I found some comics in the basement) reported not having had anyone ask about girls' comics in recent memory. Few of the women I interviewed or had letters from continued reading girls' comics into adulthood, although Judy was an exception: 'Even now if I go to the dentist's and there are old comics in the waiting room, I always read them rather than women's mags'.

The comic as marker was, in part, one of the pleasures of the girls' comic. Titles acted a private recognition or public display of your position in girlhood, in relation to mothers, perhaps, but more likely in relation to siblings or peers. However, the use of the publication as marker contradicts the use of the text as rebellion. Using the comic as rebellion is about being different from one's parents and, sometimes, from other readers. In contrast, the use of comic as marker is about conformity. Aspiring to 'proper' womanhood meant aspiring to read similar texts to those read by older female readers. As magazines began to target ever-younger readers, the comic became less relevant to girls, losing its symbolic power as a marker on the way to womanhood and femininity. In this reading, the reason the comic for girls disappeared could be that it was increasingly seen as something to be left behind in a 'correct' progression onto magazines.

In conclusion, women's accounts of their childhood reading of girls' comics included a range of texts and reading patterns unaccounted for by academic writing. Whilst negative perceptions of the comic were reflected in the accounts that readers gave of their memories, there was not a monolithic set of experiences of the girls' comic. In addition, the ways that girls used comics counters current assumptions about comics and gender that are presented as 'natural'. What they read, and how they read, differed hugely from the image of the passive girl reader blindly obeying the dictates of patriarchal publishers. Readers also referred to a range of comics that were *not* for girls, or were for a mixed audience and which they read with varied levels of parental approval. This too runs against the grain of assumed knowledge about comics and their audience.

How readers remembered was also important. The audience can be seen as in negotiation with the texts, both at the time and in memory. Texts were rarely remembered without a range of other associations, often relationships. Each generation recalled a range of overlapping, but changing titles. Issues around the production of the comics also affected the responses that readers gave (particularly the practice of recycling stories). This had a substantial impact in blurring the sense of separate reading generations.

The actual texts, whilst important, often seemed most significant in terms of their social use. Work with readers opens up this aspect of the texts. In the accounts, themes included parental intervention, class, peer group pressure and community. Class rather than generation was the most important variable in accounts. Generation did have an impact on other themes, particularly aspiration, which was rejected by younger respondents in favour of the use of comics as resistance to conformity. It was also apparent that pleasurable reading for one generation usually became problematic for the next. This was particularly the case after the introduction of titles like *Bunty*, where the question of generations of readers became yet more tightly bound up with issues around class. Comics were seen as aspirational and largely positive, stretching the reader, yet also locating readers in relation to certain norms in ways that can be characterized as entrapping. This pattern appeared both in relation to specific generations of readers and across generations, cross cut by class. The models of girlhood that emerge for each generation of readers in the texts, as used by real girls, could be both supportive and potentially constricting. Sharing, whilst it establishes a notion of community, is also open to pressure around conformity.

Comics act as important markers of transitions on a path through girlhood, both at the time and in memory. Memory and meaning are not only tied to the stories that the comics contained, but to the texts as a whole. Respondents used this idea to make sense of their enthusiasm for texts even if they could not remember reading them, or remembered having bought them, but then never actually reading them. I initially thought that this

enthusiasm for ownership, but lack of engagement with the text, might be about collecting, but as no one characterized themselves as collectors, the idea of the comic as signpost
emerged. The readers positioned themselves now in relation to both childhood and texts
that were part of that childhood, creating another set of networks or formations, this time
in the re-writing of autobiography.

There are similarities across generation, predominantly in the ways in which the
texts re- work what it means to be a girl and the way in which the readers responded to
that reinterpretation, emphasizing that girlhood is a condition continually in flux. Relationships with adults are articulated through these comics, right through to the parent
throwing away the comics as part of the reader growing up. It seems to have been a common practice, across several generations of readers, to see comics as part of a resistance
to authority. This resistance took a number of contradictory forms. It could be against
previous titles (and the models of girlhood they offered). Alternatively, one type of story
could be used to comment on another (for instance preferring the horror of *Misty* to the
romance of *Jackie*). It could also count as a rebellion against the middle-class ideals of both
school and parents, or against the aspirations of parents, (a rebellion signalled by reading
those titles adults labelled unacceptable or working-class). Finally it could be a rebellion
in staying a girl (reading titles seen as too young), or *not* staying a girl (reading romance at
a younger than appropriate age), both of which also raise issues about the reader positioning themselves in relation to heterosexuality.

All of these possibilities, however, take place within the bounds of a genre that is
about girlhood and for girls. Children's texts are generally provided and produced by the
adults that they are subsequently used against. This was a very real rebellion to readers, as
their accounts suggest, particularly in the way parents responded by limiting reading, and
trying to ensure it was age suitable. The interviews, in my interpretation, show evidence
of readers having negotiated community, individuality and conformity within patriarchy
through their relationship with these texts. Yet, this was also in many ways an 'acceptable'
rebellion in that these titles also performed the function of allowing girls to rebel in ways
that still served to contain them within acceptable bounds of female behaviour. Choosing
comics, as the association of the form with the male became more explicit in the 1970s
and 1980s, eventually ruled them out as too extreme a way of expressing individuality.
Magazines became, in their turn, the acceptable version of rebellion in girlhood, for girls.

Chapter Five

You Can't Read Them, They're For Boys! Girls Reading Boys' and Mixed Gender Comics

In much of the critical writing about girls and comics, there is evidence of a largely un-explored assumption that historically girls read only one type of comic book, those aimed at girls, if they read them at all. For instance, Alderson (1968) focused on only three titles, including *Jackie*, although her statistics on girls' wider reading (p.81-85) incorporate titles seen as for boys or mixed audiences. Thus, actual reading practices are lost in the face of making points about the ideology of specific texts.

The general assumption that there is only one pattern of female comic reading suggests that something may have been at stake for those adults determining what 'appropriate' media for girls might be. In part, then, adult perceptions of childhood and adult roles in the 'correct' upbringing of the child are involved. This can be seen in the way that in the 1970s and 1980s, some feminists saw comics for girls as oppressive and non-representative. This begged a question about what alternatives existed creating a call for non-sexist or explicitly feminist content. Such concerns suggested that choices were constrained by gender boundaries, presenting a worst case scenario that was politically strategic in campaigning for overall change. Unfortunately, they may also actually have served to silence or negate the experiences of readers. Further, saying that girls selecting comics aimed at boys will only be exposed to messages that negate them as people suggests that there are no 'suitable' texts for girls at all.

One aim of this chapter is to show the limits of such assumptions and explore the diversity that existed in girls' reading practices. I focus here on girl readers who chose to read texts that were not seen as solely for girls, or indeed, not originally intended for girls. This includes readers who also read the girls' comic, but focuses primarily on a group who rejected those titles. I explore what comics they read and why they chose to read them. I also look at the practice of swapping comics. Girls' comic reading embraces titles aimed at a specifically child audience (rather than boy or girl) and titles aimed at boys. Whilst girl readers throughout the period of the 1950s to 1980s read titles for boys, the meaning of this practice changes as the 1970s progress. This is because of the way that the magazine becomes more associated with female readers and the comic with male readers. Girls choosing to read comics, then, were increasingly engaged with a medium seen as for boys and men.

I also, in the later stages of this chapter, draw on a different body of theory in discussing readers' accounts. These interviews with readers of boys' comics address very different issues and move discussion into new territory. For instance, the readers of this kind of comic are often part of fandom. As fans, they claim cognitive mastery of their subject. Readers of boys' comics, as we shall see, rarely mentioned the issues that emerged in Chapter 4 about class, girlhood and respectability directly, although they clearly work with those notions in constructing their reading selves. In this chapter, these accounts of actively claimed fan selves offer a set of breaks with the previous chapter.

As in Chapter 4, I begin with a longer section of interview. This sets up some of the main themes that are discussed later, particularly in relation to American comics. The interview was with Robyn, an English teacher from Cornwall, who was interested in myth and legend, both in the context of teaching and on a personal level. I interviewed her when I ran some activities for students at the school where she worked. As part of these activities, I brought along an extensive collection of current comics. Some of the teachers, including Robyn, took time to read and comment on these titles during the day. Where the interview took place had an impact on the nature of the interview. Our discussion was shaped by Robyn's professional concerns and by so many comics being to hand.

Mel: Have you always read comics?

Robyn: I was always a reader. I used to buy two comics every morning from our newsagents across from where I waited for the bus to school. I bought two of those little square ones … the war comics.

M: *Commando* comics.

R: [Nods] So all of my money went on comics and books. I read a lot of Science Fiction. [Picks up comic] This *Kingdom Come* isn't based on a novel is it? There was a Science Fiction novel of that name. I've been looking for it for years, but it's out of print.

M: No, I think it is a different book entirely. Was it *Commando* comics that you liked best?

R: Really I liked Marvel comics best … [Laughs] … although they weren't for girls … Now what did I like? [Pause] There was a man who fought 'Hydra' … [Pause] he had white highlights … what was his name? It was just like the myth, if you cut one of the Hydra's heads off several others grew.

M: 'Nick Fury'.

R: [Screams] Yes, yes, 'Nick Fury'. How could I forget him? I wanted to be him.

M: I wanted to be Tom Baker.

R: Yes, you would, wouldn't you? So did I. He was my hero, but then I met him and I wasn't impressed. I've got lots of friends who like Dr. Who and Star Trek and comics.

M: Male or female?

R: Mostly male. Now, who else did I like? … I liked the 'Inhumans' … there was one who couldn't speak … or rather, shouldn't speak because he could destroy the world if he did. [Pause] What was he called? [Pause] 'Black Rod' … [Both: Laughter]

M: I don't think that was it. [Both: Laughter]

R: He had a kind of tuning fork thing on his head. And I liked the 'Silver Surfer' … and the man with the cabinet …

M: 'Dr. Strange'?

R: Yes, I was going to say 'Dr. Caligari' [Giggles] … Yes 'Stephen Strange'. But talking about comics has got me thinking … I could use some for teaching. There was a woman in the 'Inhumans' too. 'Medusa'. Myths again … We could use the comics to teach myth.

M: I know someone who uses Kafka and 'The Incredible Hulk' together.

R: Yes, that would work. I must phone my mother and ask her if any of them are still at home.

M: You don't have them?

R: No, I gave them to my brother when I left home and he sold most of them and made a fortune ... I wish he hadn't, they were still mine really. I didn't think I should take them with me.

M: So did you stop reading comics when you left home?

R: Yes, except that when I went home I read the ones my brother bought, so I kept up that way for a long time. [Pause] Are there any I'd like, do you think?
[Long pause while R flicks through about ten books]
I like the look of these two ... though that one [*Sandman*] is rather strong. The cover art is really good. You can tell this one is for adults. It is isn't it?

M: Yes. [Gives brief outline of *Sandman*]

R: Oh, myth and legend again. [Nods] I like the idea of a library for books that haven't been written yet. And I think the school should use this one for PSE [*The Tale of One Bad Rat*]. I love the way this one looks ... and the men look so nasty ... lecherous ... [Tails off and starts reading]

M: Did you read girls' comics?

R: [Dismissive] Oh no, why would I do that? They weren't proper comics like Marvel. Marvel comics were for adults ... they had complicated stories. They [Pause] ... 'Black Bolt'. He was called 'Black Bolt'. He went missing in one story and had amnesia and so he didn't know he could kill everyone by speaking. There was constant tension, because you knew who he was and what he could do, and he didn't ... and one of the other characters [in the 'Inhumans'] had a monster dog. No, girls' comics were not for me.

M: When did you start reading comics?

R: I was about nine. There was a shop where we lived that sold all sorts, bits of radios, things like that. And the man who ran it wore fingerless gloves, yes, and grey cardigans, and amongst everything else he had a big box of comics.

M: Did you have trouble getting comics in sequence?

R: [Nods.] You were never sure what you would get. I had to piece stories together over time. With my brother reading Marvel too both of us were trying to find things, which helped.

M: Were there any other stories you liked?

R: 'Thor'. Myths again. I think that the comics fed into my wanting to do archaeology ... [Pause] Its difficult teaching English Literature 'A' level today because they don't understand half of the references. Haven't read the Bible or myth, so Shakespeare is really difficult. You've really got me thinking. I loved those comics. I was so upset when my brother sold them. He made a fortune. They weren't reprints ... [Pause] And you think I'd like this one? [Waves *Sandman* and is then called away to deal with some pupils].

Firstly, certain aspects of this brief interview support points made with regard to Pru's comments. Robyn's choice of reading, for instance, further undermines the notion that girl readers are limited to one set of texts. Both interviews reveal a network of associations around comics that includes people and texts rather than a simple linear memory of reading that moves from one title to another. Also, Robyn's interview, as was the case with Pru's, offers little evidence of a feminine trajectory in reading. In addition, in both interviews gender rather than class is central to the perception of text and self. Further, the interviews have similar structures. There are a series of breaks, hesitations and abrupt changes of direction accompanied by a marked set of shifts between professional, adult and child selves. These could be seen as reflecting the context in which Robyn's interview took place, a busy school, except for the fact that Pru's interview, which took place in non-work setting, had a similar pattern.

I would argue, then, that the breaks suggest points where the interview gets too close to uncomfortable feelings and memories for interviewees. Robyn, for example, having moved away from discussing her anger and regret about the loss of her comics to a safer topic, returns to those feelings later in the interview. This means that the overall tone of the interview varies considerably, moving from humour to professionalism to discomfort and back again very swiftly. As I noted with regard to Pru, laughter and hesitation often seemed related to self-protection in interview. This theme of loss and anger in Robyn's interview again emphasizes how these supposedly ephemeral texts are often intimately connected with formative moments.

For Robyn, reading comics was largely a memory - again, like Pru. The loss of her collection (a marker of movement into adulthood, as I have suggested) had been, as her interview suggests, rather traumatic and she had not returned to collecting, unlike many of the readers of these other kinds of comics that I spoke to. Her assertion that, having left her parents' home, she felt she should not own comics any more, connects femininity and maturity with rejecting comics. The interview implies that as an adult female she felt she had no claim on such material.

Her description of reading her brother's comics in her parents' home, rather than buying her own, confirms that one of her definitions of the comic is that it is properly male, and belongs to childhood, although, contradictorily, she also says that Marvel comics were for adults. In one definition, discarding one's comic collection marks of the end of childhood; in the other, they are adult texts. Further, the latter definition incorporates the notion of the comic as non-British, a point I focus on later with regard to readers of superhero comics. Thus, the interview incorporates a number of definitions and uses of comics, much as Pru's did, and shows them, similarly, to conflict with each other.

Robyn's reading of her brother's comics, as well as signalling what I describe above, could be interpreted as an unwillingness to entirely relinquish her love of the medium (and as a sense of thwarted ownership). Through reading her brother's comics after she left home, she becomes part of a secondary audience, a 'pass-along' reader. Robyn's acceptance of this role can be interpreted in several contradictory ways. On the one hand, it could be seen as allowing a tentative link to be maintained with a child self. It could also act as confirmation of Robyn's other definition of the comic, in which adulthood and comics are not mutually exclusive. On the other hand, it allows her to maintain a distance from comics and childhood. Taken together, these interpretations imply that buying comics for oneself might destabilize adult femininity but also that this might be, in some way, an attractive option.

How comics might destabilize femininity is suggested by the way that they were bound up, in Robyn's interview, with a rejection of girlhood, evinced through her dismissal of the girls' comic. Her assertion that girls' comics were not 'proper' comics means that she defines comics as for boys, as was the case with Pru, who also felt that not all comics were of equal value. In addition, however, Robyn clearly defines herself as part of that boy audience, even if isolated within it by her gender, not as part of a community of female readers. She positions herself as a transgressive reader of 'male' texts rather than a reader of 'female' texts. Her interview suggests that as a girl, she would have seen reading girls' comics as compromising her identity. Comics, then, are part of an important 'not-girl' identity, which could be seen as threatening her adult, feminine, self. Her reading reflects, perhaps, a sense of identity in which girlhood is a difficult or unpleasant position to inhabit.

The interview, then, shows Robyn negotiating several selves and various definitions of comics. Finally, however, it is her professional self, and the possibility of using comics in relation to that self that allow her to let comics, and her 'not-girl' childhood and teenage self, have a place in her present. Robyn recognizes that comics might be useful in the classroom and the interview shows her willingness to use her own knowledge of the medium, once she has, through the training day and the interview itself, discovered ways in which it might be practical. Later in that day, she arranged for a number of titles to be sent to the school to form a permanent collection. She also ordered a number of books for herself. This chimes with her perception of the comics she read as a child being for adults.

Whilst there are similarities between Pru's and Robyn's interviews there are some differences between them as well. Firstly, Robyn focuses more on the comic in relation to a sense of place. It is where comics were experienced, on the bus, at home, and in the comic shop, rather than comics as physical objects, that is the important aspect in her account.

Robyn's interview also offers evidence of cross-gender identification, undermining the notion of girls needing to see female characters to engage with a text, a point I return to later. In addition, my role as interviewer is rather different. Whilst I had begun the interview with the same strategy that I had in relation to Pru, Robyn continually forced me into the position of 'expert', asking for information about past and present reading in almost every exchange. Although it was informal, the frame of the interview became that we were both 'professionals'. My role and so the context in which I met most of these readers, could have resulted in my 'expertise' being a feature of every interview. However, whilst the readers of girls' comics often wanted a question answering about their reading, multiple questions were a dominant feature in interviews with readers of other titles.

What Robyn's interview also demonstrates is the tendency of readers of comics other than girls' comics to list titles and characters. That she does not specify which artists or writers she is interested in, as some of the other interviewees did, acts as a confirmation that she had not followed this interest as an older reader. Whilst comic fans tend to start by following various characters or titles, continuing this interest into later life is often marked by an awareness of, and enthusiasm for, the work of specific creators. Nonetheless, Robyn exhibits very typical fan behaviour. The listing and questions are ways, perhaps, of building links. It could also serve as a test, demanding I show my 'mastery' of the form. As I explain later, proving oneself to be a 'proper' fan through exhibiting the correct kind of knowledge was a feature of some accounts. Further, my familiarity with the titles she mentions gives her permission to continue with and expand on her themes of myth and teaching.

To conclude this brief analysis, much of what is described here is about how comics were remembered and defined, a topic to which I shortly return. Robyn's interview, like Pru's, encompasses memories of comics in relation to the titles, narratives and characters they offered. It also incorporates memories of comics as a contested space, as marker, and as rebellion. In addition, the comic is remembered as part of a network of associations, a community or an individual reader, and as having a number of personal, emotional and social functions. So in many ways the girls' comic and the other comics, although very different, were remembered similarly. Where Robyn's interview differs from Pru's is in her association of comics and place, her rejection of the girls' comic and girlhood, and the centrality of collecting and losing comics. However, what is most important is that the interview suggests that readers related to these other texts in ways that call into question many of the assumptions about girls as readers evident in both general and feminist histories of the form.

Rejecting the Girls' Comic

Many of those I spoke to remembered being 'desperate' to find a reading option other than the girls' comic. Linda, for instance, said that what was upsetting for her was that there was 'no choice'. She could remember reacting to girls' comics by trying her brother's superhero comics and reading them for quite some time, before giving up on comics entirely.

The interviewees who had read girls' comics negatively felt restricted to specific kinds of story and behaviour, as if they needed to be very tightly directed and had no say in who they were to be in later life. What was at stake to them was whether one performed girlhood according to the girls' comic, or tried to find some other more productive option. Anna, for instance, a mature student from Leicester who had formerly been in local government, said, 'I hated cut out dolls and *Twinkle*. My parents bought it for me'. Her initial response was to choose to read comics for mixed audiences and, finally, she ended up reading comics aimed at a male audience, a total rejection of a feminine reading trajectory. Her parents, Linda said, [e]ventually … got me *The Beano* instead, which I was fond of, but not wild about. Later I began to nick my brother's *2000AD*, got into 'Judge Dredd' and never looked back. In cases like Anna's, the choice of other comics marked the reader's opposition to those aimed at girls and the models of girlhood those comics offered.

Interviewees' association of the girls' comic with pressures about gender roles was also tied up with their relationship with their parents, as Anna's account suggests. Similarly, Norah wrote that: 'My mother started buying me *Bunty* when I was little, an attempt I think to encourage a daughter who was more interested in newts and toads into more ladylike pursuits'. In this context, the girls' comic was seen as a tool for directing the child towards traditional feminine role models. The women who had disliked these titles as children often saw them as training tales on how to be a good girl, how to fit in. These readers, rather than recognizing that publishers wanted to create fiction to attract and amuse them, saw instruction and constraint as the primary, or only, aims of such comics.

Many of the accounts revealed an understanding of reading otherwise as being seen as problematic by parents. Sheila Rowbotham, in describing her own childhood, mentions comics only twice, but suggests through them, as well as other texts, changes in her family and herself:

> Next thing *Dandy* and *Beano* were banned. I was learning bad language. Three years went past…I wore shorts, read about Queen Margaret of Scotland and a missionary heroine in *Girl*, listened to 'Dan Dare' on Radio Luxemburg. (in Heron, 1985, p.193)

Here she states what comic her parents saw as suitable and why they preferred it, whilst also hinting at her own resistance to what was on offer. *Girl*, as I suggested earlier, was seen as appropriate reading for middle-class girls. The slapstick comedy of *The Beano* and *The Dandy* was not, something perhaps linked to criticisms regarding linking humour and violence in those comics, something which lasted into the 1980s (Dellino, 1981, Gale, 1971). Whilst resistance was a characteristic of the way that many of these readers used comics, I am not assuming the existence of a resistant girls' culture, but a complex relationship with comics on the part of individual readers. Here too, as is the case with readers of girls' comics, texts are used in support of the definition of identity.

Self-determination, then, (in the face of age and gender) was a common thread in accounts of the rejection of the girls' comic. For many girls like Linda, the answer to their problems with the girls' comic was to choose not to read them, or even not to read any comics at all (this was a separate group from those banned from reading comics by parents and teachers). This rejection had a number of sources, but may, in part, have been linked with feminism. Although not necessarily identifying the impulse to reject the girls' comic as feminist, the rebellion against restrictions that readers discussed has much in common with feminist inflected research on publications for girls. In their conjectures about the meaning and aim of the stories in the girls' comic, many have seen them as offering a trap of one form or another. I remember feeling, as a girl, that girls' comics were unremittingly bleak and felt that they rewarded you for being a victim. In describing the girls' comic in this light, commentators identify the reasons why some girls chose to reject these titles, although their readers saw girls' comics as a force for personal change, as the previous chapter suggests.

Those who had rejected the girls' comic as restrictive but had chosen to continue reading other kinds of comic reacted to subject matter as well as to parental intent. They rejected characters that they saw as representing certain qualities associated with girlhood. For instance, Fran, a librarian from Wales, used language more in keeping with girls' comics than most other kinds, in that she described such characters as 'wet'. A similar tone can be found in academic accounts of comics. For instance, Cadogan identified *Twinkle* as a repository of 'characters who convey cosy domesticity' (1999, p.58). Both comments summarize what some saw as the lack of appeal of girls' titles. To these interviewees, reading a comic of any other kind could be seen as an act of rebellion against the constraints girls' comics offered.

Irrespective of what generation the reader belonged to, those readers who rejected the girls' comic refused to enter a 'contract' related to any aspect of their social lives with those texts. Through their rejection, they insisted that the position of the implied reader in girls' comics offered them nothing, and they chose to enter into 'contracts' with other texts which they felt somehow related to their lives as girls more directly than those that were supposedly designed to do so.

Swapping Comics

Most girls read boys' comics and mixed gender comics even if they were girls' comic readers. As the reading histories in Chapter 4 indicate, girls managed to get access to boys' and mixed gender audience comics by various means. Gaining access could be very straightforward, in that some parents were comfortable about their daughters reading and buying a wide range of comics. However, most female readers swapped their girls' comics for others, rather than actually purchasing boys' or mixed audience comics. In addition, those who did reject the girls' comic came to the decision to do so through the practice of swapping, which gave them experience of other kinds of comic.

Buying and swapping could be seen as complementary practices with regard to comics. The former, as part of adult culture and so the official space of child-adult, and especially parent interaction, became a point of tension in battles over identity whatever kind of comic was involved. The latter was 'underground' in being part of child culture, allowing the reader to try out different reading identities whilst secure in the knowledge of what one was meant to read. Of all the reading practices that surround comics, swapping offers most evidence of a pattern of reading that undermines notions of the girls' comic as the only reading matter that girls engaged with. Swapping comics, a more formal practice than being a pass-along reader, is a significant aspect of reading practice, yet is often omitted from critical commentary. Perhaps, as many female readers said, they did not tell adults about this other reading in case it was seen as 'wrong' and got them into trouble. It is also a practice that is largely invisible and unreachable except through talking to readers.

In most cases, readers' accounts focused on swapping with male relatives, whether brothers or cousins. Swapping was a feature of all female comic readers' practice, whether they rejected the girls' comic or not. For instance, Fran said that the comic reading ritual in her home was that she and her brothers used to read comics aimed at their own gender first, then swap, then read the ones aimed 'at all of us'. Another reader, Bunty, a charity volunteer from Surrey, an avid reader of *Jinty*, *Tammy* and *Judy*, also swapped with her brother to read his copy of *The Dandy*. Frances had swapped girls' comics for *Hotspur* and *Victor* (DC Thomson, 1961-1992) with a male cousin when reading comics at her grandparents' house, where all the cousins went one evening a week. Finally, Elizabeth had a similar ritual, which she described as following a specific pattern. She said, 'We each read our own comics, then the ones for both of us and then each others'.

Other readers, however, gained access to a range of comics through less direct means, swapping at school with friends, or with the children of neighbouring families. Even those who read a great many comics added more titles to those that they knew through this practice. Norah, for instance, signed off her letter by saying, 'I'll stop now, realising I haven't mentioned [various comic artists] or 'Kelly's Eye' or the 'Steel Claw', which I borrowed from the boy next door'.

A clear understanding of which reading belonged 'properly' to which reader is present in most of these accounts, although Norah, who read superhero comics, is an exception in refusing to accept that as a girl she should begin by reading specific girls' titles. Yet, at the same time as showing an understanding of who the intended audience for specific texts was, accounts of swapping also undermine ownership patterns across gender. In addition, these patterns are further undermined across age and generation in Elizabeth's account because she swapped comics with her grandfather. Thus, despite buying patterns suggesting that gender determined readership, the actual social practices based around swapping, as a clandestine arrangement of which parents were often unaware, meant that all comic readers were much more flexible.

Swapping also implies that boys read girls' comics, yet there is little mention of such practices in critical accounts of comics. The idea of reading across gender was, it seems, yet more problematic for adults when boys read girls' comics. The small numbers of girls who admit to having read comics for boys is large in comparison to those boys who will admit to reading comics for girls. Female accounts of swapping often included boys as readers of *Bunty* et al, but there are comparatively few accounts by men of what male readers found attractive about girls' comics. In this context, perhaps, there is more at stake for the adult male reader in becoming associated with femininity.

There are, however, a few exceptions to the silence on this subject. Neil Gaiman (1997), for instance, says 'When I was a boy, in England, I tended to prefer my cousin's and sisters' girls' comics to the blander fare that boys got, because the stories were better. (They may have tended to be about virtuous young ladies being ill-treated by vicious step-families, their only friend the cheerful young stable-boy, but they were stories, dammit. They were going somewhere)'. He asserts that the attraction was good plotting and well-rounded characters.

Several male interviewees mentioned reading girls' comics, including Ed, a freelance trainer from Leeds, who reported that 'We had *Bunty* in our house and everyone read it'. Another respondent said that the events in girls' comics chimed much more with his own experience of life than those found in comics for boys. Graham, a builder from South Shields, who got in touch after reading about my research, recalled reading *Bunty* but only after reading *Victor*, *Hotspur* and *Wizard* first, which he had seen change from text to strip format. He recalled that he had thought that 'some of the *Bunty* stories were good, although I didn't read the soppy ones'. Finally, he and Ed admitted both to having read problem pages and entering competitions as well. Several interviewees in Chapter 4 mention fathers, brothers and male cousins taking their turn reading girls' titles. Although limited in number these male readers confirm the existence of a routine crossover audience of boys reading girls' comics.

In conclusion, that swapping could continue throughout a reader's youth suggests an alternative model of girls' relationship to childhood. Far from being a single generic childhood, there was a distinct model of girlhood that was recognized and responded to by girl readers as well. In addition, for readers of around eight or above there were also separate titles for boys. Such a division suggests that there was a triad within reading of girlhood, boyhood and childhood from the age of around seven, in which both boys and girls were still sharing some comics. This shows how one might engage in different modes of experience simultaneously.

Girls' relationship to childhood, then, based on reading comics across gender, could be seen as an oscillation between several sets of texts. Of these, one was associated with a female audience and one with a mixed audience that had a larger number of male participants, whilst the third consisted of what were considered boys' texts.

The pattern of readership that emerges in looking at swapping suggests that girlhood, and indeed boyhood, can be seen as unstable categories that continually shift and may be shored up by various texts and practices. For many interviewees, there was an oscillation between several types of comic and the attendant forms of childhood they represented, from any or all of these sets, not a simple shift from one thing to another. As the reader ages, they may follow a preferred path through reading whereby the oscillation is limited to mixed audience and girls' comics until the reader is 'fixed' on texts for girls. Some of these forms of comic were weighted more heavily according to gender, class etc., and thus more likely to be read by girl readers or chosen for them, as I have suggested, but readers negotiated a range of types of comic and identity simultaneously.

Finally, there is a tension between a notion of childhood that definitely includes boys, but which girls may participate in, and a distinct and separate girlhood. This tension is linked to the shift to the magazine format at around eleven for girls. The shift suggests both that the comic medium itself was seen as related to childhood, but also that it was linked most strongly to boyhood. Thus, childhood, boyhood and comics are intertwined in a more straightforward way than childhood, girlhood and comics. Consciousness of that tension might well result in choosing to read texts that offered what might be seen as more freedom from what they saw as an oppressive girlhood for at least some of the readers.

Comics for Mixed Gender Audiences

Comics aimed at mixed audiences were mentioned frequently in interview. These were titles for which some readers swapped girls' comics and which others bought. As we saw in Chapter 4, a number of reading histories, including Charlotte and Elizabeth's included comics not usually seen as being aimed at a female audience. Mixed audience comics drew in both readers of girls' comic and those girls who predominantly read comics aimed at boys. Everyone interviewed remembered reading at least one mixed audience comic, usually *The Beano* and *The Dandy*, the market leaders, and a thread of continuity through the childhood of British girls and boys. Beyond British titles, the subsequent stop for most British readers was to look to America. The only real exceptions were *Tintin*, *Lucky Luke* and *Asterix*, which were staples of many school libraries by the 1970s.

The comics aimed at a mixed audience can be divided into two types. The first includes educational titles such as *Look & Learn* and the second, humorous titles. By definition, such comics engage female as well as male readers and like the horror comics and penny dreadfuls, the 'funnies' and educational comics did succeed in drawing fairly even numbers of male and female readers for most of their history. The balance began to shift in the 1970s, with a clear change by 1981, at which point the female readership ran at around 25% (Barker, 1989, p.93). That these titles appealed to both boys and girls is illustrated by Kate's letter, for instance, in which she offers a recollection of sharing humour comics with her male cousin:

> I remember one day saying to him, "What are you laughing at?" He said "Look at this, it's 'Desperate Dan', and look at his dinner". The way he started to describe the picture was hilarious and we both couldn't stop laughing.

Of course, there were assumptions that these titles will also influence children for the bad, for instance as argued by George Gale (1971) in the article 'Violent & Deformed-the prosecution case' the title of which captures the argument very well. Gale focused on violence, incitement to laugh at those who are different, slang and anti-authoritarian messages in *The Beano* and other comics.

Such shared reading, and practices such as swapping, as we have seen, raise questions about the total dominance of the girls' comic amongst female readers. At the very least, they imply a dilution of the negative influence that texts for girls have been assumed to exert throughout the period. Logically, female readers should not be seen as out of the ordinary or in any way problematic in the context of educational and humour comics aimed by publishers at both boys and girls.

Who are Humour Comics for? Remembering the 'Funnies'

I suggest above that the question of who mixed gender comics address should not arise. However, in looking at readers' memories of humour comics and adults' responses to girls' reading them, it becomes apparent that these were seen by many adults as inappropriate for girls. Readers reported being irritated beyond measure that they had to have girls' comics when the humour titles looked much more fun. For instance, Wilma, who was from Liverpool and training in arts management, said she 'got bought' *Mandy*. Wilma 'didn't like *Mandy*', she insisted, because 'it wasn't *The Beano*, which my brothers got' and was totally put off comics by the experience of reading it. She had only just begun to rediscover comics via her children at the time of interview and was 'careful not to restrict their reading'.

Vera, a museum curator from Nottingham, described a different version of the parental ban on girls reading humour comics. She reported that she recalled having envied her brothers because 'we were told 'comics are not for girls' by our parents' and so the entire medium was forbidden to her on gendered grounds. This led to her brothers teasing her because of her difference in not being allowed comics. In other homes, comics for a mixed audience were seen as suitable up to a certain age, but beyond that became 'unladylike', which may have been the case with Rowbotham, above. That humour comics might be seen as 'unladylike' was a good reason for reading these unacceptable 'others' to some (again linking with notions of respectability and class).

As I understand it, those who felt coerced by their parents into reading only girls' comics, typically rejected both those comics and the model of girlhood they felt it represented. Sometimes, this became part of a much later rebellion, in reading comics seen as for a specifically male audience. This was the case with Vera, for instance, who 'got into' comics through a boyfriend's interest in them. Initially, she said, 'He read the The X-Men and I did girly stuff. Then I decided to go to the comic shop with him. I saw some of the covers and thought, WOW'. Vera's rebellion in reading, then, was not based around parental fears about class and education, as was often the case, but was primarily about reading in gender-appropriate or inappropriate ways, based on having been forbidden to read comics earlier in life because she was a girl.

Parental responses to humour titles, when negative, mostly involved comments about gender-appropriateness, revealing a tendency to consider humour comics as for boys or as 'unladylike' entertainment. I would suggest that these judgements about humour comics not being for girls were underpinned by three assumptions. Firstly, there is an assumption that there are not enough female characters for girls to identify with in humour comics. The link between female characters and female readers is drawn frequently in accounts of girls' comic reading as well. Sabin, in contrast to these 'common-sense' accounts, suggests that courting a female audience by including female characters is evident in titles as early as *Ally Sloper's Half Holiday*. He also notes that a significant female readership has existed throughout the publication of *The Beano* and *The Dandy*, accounting for up to fifty per cent of the total, again seen as related to the number of female characters. Secondly, parents seemed to assume from the comments above that there should not be any female readers because the narrative content of those comics is unsuitable for them. Consequently, actual female audiences are dismissed as insignificant or problematic. Third is an assertion that these are comics for children, not specifically for either girls or boys, but that girls should 'grow out of them' sooner. The final two assumptions imply that any girl reading such comics, either at all, or at an unsuitable age, is not a 'proper' girl, but whilst the first sees comics and girls as entirely incompatible, the second sees them as appropriate partners within a specific time frame.

In all three cases, the reader accounts both set up, and then undermine, these assumptions. Readers' memories, for the most part, are of reading and enjoying these comics, as Kate's comments earlier in this chapter suggest. However, the actual audience and the audience that parents felt these texts should have are at odds suggesting that these comics were a source of tension in some parent-child relationships. These tensions are suggested by the way that some readers had internalized messages about humour comics as being properly for boys, whilst still reading them.

The first assumption about humour comics having little appeal for girls since there were few female characters is in part confirmed by there being a comparatively small number of strips with female protagonists. Those that existed included 'Beryl the Peril' and 'Keyhole Kate'. This does suggest that publishers might have thought female characters would attract girls. Further, interviews confirm that some readers of humour and other comics were looking for more convincing female characters. Linda, for instance, stopped reading her brother's superhero comics, because she felt that 'none of the female characters were worth the bother'. This might imply that female characters had to appear to ensure female readership in other kinds of comic.

However, Linda was rare amongst readers of other titles in dropping them for not containing particularly good female characters. Generally, readers who mentioned mixed gender comics and those primarily aimed at boys cited both male and female characters as favourites in interview. Hence, Kate records that, 'I was in a different world when I read these comics. I loved 'Corky the Cat' and 'Desperate Dan' ... 'Keyhole Kate' and 'Dennis the Menace' were also favourites'. This suggests that the appearance, or the absence, of female protagonists does not automatically mean that more girls are likely to read a text.

The assumption that a comic needs female characters to appeal to girls, then, is debatable. However, female characters in these comics stimulated other concerns. Accounts by adults describe the few existing female characters in such a way as to emphasize that how they look and the narratives they appear in are unacceptable. This means, of course, unacceptable to parents. Readers, in contrast, often saw these characters as positive. Kate, for instance, said: 'There was a 'Pansy Potter', she was the strong man's daughter and I was really impressed with her. She had a spiked hat or hair'. Whilst Kate found much to admire in humour comics, to many adults, these comics were not considered middle-class. Thus, parents and others saw these female characters as 'unsuitable' for girls, returning us to notions of 'proper' girlhood and of class.

Other objections were about role models. Returning to Kate's comment, above, it is clear that 'Pansy Potter' was read as an image of female strength. Some commentators, and parents, read them in very different ways. For instance, Cadogan (1999), in a slightly despairing tone, articulates apprehensions about comics, about what and whom they are for, as well as questioning how female characters are depicted in comics. 'Pansy Potter the Strong Man's Daughter' and 'Keyhole Kate' come in for particular criticism from her. Cadogan asks, 'Were these comic but unappealing girls simply designed to give boy readers a good giggle and a sense of superiority? They could hardly be seen as good role models for girls' (Cadogan, 1999, p.58). In proposing that comics encourage boys to laugh at girls we may feel differently about them, but it does not change the relationships, often positive, that readers had with humour comics. In addition, Cadogan sees in the comic only inadequate role models or texts that make victims of their readers. In such a reading, readers who saw themselves as rebelling against a norm of girlhood would be compromised as much as those that conformed. Another view of female characters is seen in *Mum's Own Annual*, which asserts that any claims by publishers to have a female readership for mixed gender comics must be wrong, as they did not contain convincing female characters (Anon, 1993, p.48).

The reader accounts throughout this and the previous chapter prove that a girl audience for these texts did exist. *The Beano* appeared repeatedly in reading histories. Yet the second assumption by adults was that the female audience for these humour titles did not (or should not) exist. Accounts that deny or dismiss the existence of a female audience for comics often serve, paradoxically, to confirm that it does exist. In Judith O'Connell's (1982) dissertation on sexism in comics and television, discussed in Barker (1989), for instance, she characterizes girls as non-readers of comics because they are excluded by the lack of female characters. In making this assertion she dismisses the 15% of female characters in *The Beano* et al that did exist in 1982, and the 25% of girls who read the titles that her own samples identify. Further,

> Whitehead et al (1977) expressed some surprise that humour titles continue to appear in the girls' tables, 'because their rather crude humour does seem, on the face of things, to be directed towards boys rather than towards girls' (p.159).

That these comics were seen as inappropriate by female readers was also expressed in a few accounts. Humour comics troubled Charlotte, as her description suggests,

> But I was also a bit of a tomboy, and I had to have two or three of the dreadful comics featuring strips about the 'Bash Street Mob'…The strips were all about distorted, fat ugly creatures in patched raggy clothes getting into some kind of trouble, often with whole frames of the cartoon stating only 'Pow!' or 'Boom!' or some other sound effect. I remember wondering why these awful things were something I wanted to read, but they were like a drug I guess, no rhyme or reason, but I had to have my fix.

Her perspective on comic reading links in with Hoggart's comments about disease, addiction and the comic, as seen in Chapter 3. Charlotte, in using the language of addiction, denies that reading these texts was a willing choice and associates certain titles, supposedly seen as for a mixed audience, with a male one. In seeing her child self as an inappropriate tomboy, not a 'proper' girl, she concurs with adult perceptions of the humour comic. However, she also announces their fascination, simultaneously confirming and denying that she was a willing part of the readership. Whitehead et al (1977) record an account of a girl reader, which treads very similar ground to Charlotte's comments. This girl is described as spending:

most of her leisure time dressed in trousers, playing football, or engaged in other tomboyish activities, with her brother and his friends. Her comics include a number of boys' comics, as well as the obligatory *Judy*, *Mandy* and *Bunty*. It seems clear that the drives which govern her living do not at present lead her to attach much value to reading, though this is not to say that they could not be channeled in this direction by a percipient teacher. (p.166)

The tone corresponds to that of Charlotte's interview in depicting some reading as a cause for concern. Such comments about children who read a wide range of comics reveal that Whitehead et al consider this reading to represent those children's unresolved problems. It is implied that whilst books ('proper' reading) are the ideal, texts that are appropriate from the researcher's point of view in terms of age and gender are indicative of 'correct' development and that those children who choose to read otherwise are troubled. Such comments suggest what a loaded subject reading was amongst teachers at the time and how it was seen as linked to development in the child. To read outside the limits that Whitehead et al suggest is automatically to be considered a problem. Given this context that parents should forbid their daughters to read humour comics is not surprising.

Alternatively, female memories of the 'funnies' might actually focus on the girl reader as part of a secondary audience, distancing girls from the humour comic, but indicating that they had had contact with it. For example, Heron's (1985) account includes a chapter by Julia Pascal, where she talks of being taught to read by her father using *The Beezer*. She says, 'He sat with me and showed me David's comics and the first line I read was "Little Plum Your Redskin Chum"' (in Heron, 1985, p.39). Note that this was David's comic, but was, in this family, seen as acceptable for a girl as a secondary audience. Similarly, Pru's account, (p.173-179) addresses this notion of girls as a secondary audience in her reading, and appropriation of, the *Eagle*.

The third assumption underlying parental beliefs that humour comics were not for girls was that girls grew out of comics for children (as opposed to those for girls) more quickly than boys did. As I suggest above, this assumption is different from the other two in that it does envisage a girl audience for humour comics, if only for a short period. This shift away from humour comics does appear in accounts. For instance, Kate says that she moved from humour to girls' comics, 'Then came *The Beezer* and *The Topper*, they often gave a free gift with these comics. I went on to the *Bunty*...'. Maureen, similarly, moved from a comic for boys and girls to one for girls' alone:

The first comic I remember my dad buying for me was called *Bimbo* and it was for toddlers, I suppose - I can't even remember exactly what the main character was but I think he was either a little bear or a penguin ... From there I progressed to *Twinkle*.

Readers in the girls' comic reading majority tended, as Maureen did, to assign reading mixed readership titles to an earlier period, recognizing that they associated reading comics (and later magazines) which had specifically feminine concerns with maturing, learning their 'proper' place.

This assumption that girls grow out of children's comics quicker than boys presupposes that there is a childhood that boys and girls share, but which girls pass through more swiftly. Given that humour comics have been seen as aimed at readers up to the age of ten or eleven, this would imply that girls move on at that point onto a separate set of texts. However, such an assumption does not consider the implications of the existence of nursery age comics specifically aimed at girls. In terms of production a separate structure of publishing for girls ran alongside the humour titles, maximizing potential sales and also suggesting that girlhood was somehow at one remove from childhood from the very start. There was no male equivalent for *Twinkle*, for instance. In addition, Maureen's experience locates a shift from child to girlhood as taking place at five or six not ten or eleven. In this reading, interviewees' emphasis on the comic for girls as their primary contact with the form acts as a counterbalance to the notion of an all-embracing childhood that girls leave earlier.

Finally, some of these underlying assumptions about girls and humour are also apparent in readers' memories of reading adult humour comics such as *Viz*. Readers reported having read *Viz* from about thirteen and into adulthood, including Olive, who had moved to it as an adult after *Bunty*, *Jackie* and magazines. Again, this rather undermines the notion of a standard feminine trajectory in reading. *Viz* had a female audience of around 15%, according to the *Viz* readership survey cited by Sabin (1993, p.122). Women chose to read it even though female characters such as 'Millie Tant' and 'The Fat Slags' could be seen as grotesque. However, male characters were similarly depicted and the 'Fat Slags' along with 'Sid the Sexist' were often women readers' favourite characters. 'Sid the Sexist', although read by some young male readers as an almost heroic figure, was read ironically by female readers. The same was not always the case with 'The Fat Slags', who some of those I interviewed felt were meant as an insult but whom others, including Jackie, who described herself as a housewife and was originally from Sheffield, chose to celebrate as 'females behaving badly'.

That *Viz* is based on the older humour comics as well as referring to other British titles, makes it a text that some women readers feel they understand and have a stake in. However, readers persisted in seeing it as being predominantly a text for boys. Jackie was one of those readers. When we discussed which comics she bought, Jackie said, 'I don't buy my own *Viz*, I 'borrow' it from my sons'. Her comment suggests that somehow the pleasure of reading it, and keeping knowledge of having read it to oneself, felt more transgressive than ownership would. The pleasure of reading *Viz* was equalled by that of seeing oneself as appropriating it from the 'real', male, audience.

In looking at the British humour comic, and reader accounts, both of their reading experience and of their parents' responses to reading, it becomes apparent that whilst most girls read and enjoyed these comics, some adults (and some readers) found this enjoyment worrying. In seeing reading of mixed audience or boys' comics by girls as inappropriate, whether viewed from a conformist or a feminist inflected perspective, commentators on the comic share this perspective. Critics such as Pumphrey (1956) or Whitehead et al (1977) identify the mixed audience comic as primarily for boys and, frequently, as addressing a specifically working-class audience. They question what a mixed audience comic offers girls, or say that it represents a troubling attachment to childhood. These were perceptions of the comic that readers understood and responded to, whether through inner conflict about reading, or overt rebellion.

Comics as a medium are again, through the humour titles, implicated in the maintaining of a 'correct' progression through childhood. Thus, the dominant media for children in a given era reflect, support and direct notions of gender and childhood. However, girls' relationships with humour titles also suggest the problematic and complex nature of girlhood. What the comments from Charlotte and the other readers suggest is that reading might be used by girls to make statements about who they felt they were, but also that there was a lot at stake for the girl reader in choosing to read otherwise. Whilst humour comics might be acceptable for all up until a certain age, continued enthusiasm on the part of readers is characterized as childish, being a tomboy, or being unladylike. Similarly, in reading *Viz*, adult women readers were making a conscious choice to read something controversial. Who humour comics are for, then, proves to have a rather different answer to the one than we might expect from the label 'mixed gender'.

Other Issues of Ownership: Educational Comics and Girls

The ambiguity about the readership of supposedly mixed audience comics is also clear in relation to the few information titles available in Britain. Readers' accounts imply that girls' saw themselves as the secondary audience for such titles, with the exception of *Classics Illustrated* (Elliot Publishing Co. 1941–1942, Gilberton Company, Inc. 1942–1967, Frawley Corporation (Twin Circle), 1967–1971) actually an American series, which Noreen mentioned, recalling that they were 'a good way to cheat at English Literature exams'. Because of their educational brief, these titles were often seen as acceptable by parents, but there is evidence to suggest that some adults and readers saw them as more suitable for boys. For example, *Look & Learn*, seen as boring by many female readers, was an inspiration to an enthusiastic few. Polly, a lecturer from Durham, for instance, declared that 'I wanted to be a hero like those in the "Trigan Empire"'. The strip, like the comic, contained few female characters. She compared the title to girls' comics, and was scathing about the latter in her conclusion that '*Look & Learn* did not consist of

'Milly-Molly-Mandy' stories'. Like Robyn, she focused on reading material like science fiction which she saw as predominantly for boys. In establishing this pattern of reading as a girl, Polly, too, had been a 'not-girl' reader, establishing a problematic, but personally satisfying reading self.

There is a brief section in *Mum's Own Annual* on educational comics, particularly *Look & Learn*. The author argues that educational comics had no real appeal for girls, despite that fact that, 'half the staff were female'. The author also refutes the publisher's claims that the 'girl readership was at the same level as boy readership throughout its entire 21 year life, and that no one ever complained of gender bias' (p.52). Instead, *Mum's Own Annual* suggests that it couldn't appeal to girls because it was, 'injected five years after its launch with 'The Trigan Empire' and six other pages of picture strip stories' (p.52). Again, the comic strip appears to be antithetical to girls and the use of the term 'injected' suggests that the story was seen as very much an unwelcome intrusion. So whilst acknowledging that girls read educational comics the author argues that they didn't really enjoy them and that the publishers exaggerated the readership figures. The female readership of mixed audience comics for older readers is promptly declared, in reality, non-existent. *Look & Learn* also featured in *On These Days* (BBC Radio 4, 17/1/98), where an interviewee, bitterly rather than humorously, articulated another view of the title:

> I've always thought that the reason my brother got to Cambridge and I went to Birmingham Polytechnic was because he read *Look & Learn* and I read *Bunty*. There was quite definite discrimination here, I mean, obviously *Look & Learn* was available to me to read as well, but I read *Bunty* and he read *Look & Learn* and learnt lots of facts and all I ever learned was how to make a Christmas decoration or something equally useless.

Here parental intervention in reading ensured that children were given 'suitable' texts, those being clearly gender-specific. Comparing her experience with that of her brother, both of reading and of education, this interviewee saw the girls' comic as limiting girls' aspirations.

In relation to educational comics, whilst there were few comments about them from readers, there is evidence of a perspective similar to that held by parents and readers about humour comics. These titles were also, in the end, seen as for boys. These comics were also a contested space, and the memories of conflict with parents, and inner conflict over definitions of the comic and its readership, reflect that. In addition, as Polly's comments suggest, she used *Look & Learn*, as we shall see others use superhero comics, as a way of attempting to build a different kind of identity, one that attempts to escape aspects of girlhood. Such identity is founded on an acceptance of these texts as having a male audience, rather than being open to girls. In insisting that the text connotes 'boy', girl readers can position themselves as transgressive.

One Step Beyond! Remembering Reading Comics for Boys

In moving on to girls' reading of comics aimed predominantly at a male audience in preference to other titles, themes of gender and identity are even more evident. There is very little work on female readers of comics seen as for men, with Barker (1989, 1993) and Nyberg being amongst the very few offering some account of such readers. Nyberg (1995) focuses on American readers of superhero comics. In these final sections, I explore many of the themes that emerged from Robyn's comments at the start of this chapter. These themes include the way that past and present were often closely inter- linked in these readers' accounts, how such comics were remembered, issues about collecting and fandom, and the notion of 'not-girl' ness and identity.

Many readers, like Charlotte, tried comics aimed at predominantly male audiences and did not like them, but a few of those that I spoke to had not only been attracted to these titles, but had read these comics consistently for a long period, either as children or as adults. These readers included Robyn, Anna and Norah. Whilst the majority of inter-viewees were speaking of little discussed memories and saw their comic reading as situated in the past (and so separate from current reading) these readers often offered very different accounts. Norah, for instance, wrote

> When I was seven I discovered DC comics ... As I got older, Marvel comics came out and I thrilled to the adolescent problems of 'Peter Parker' and the 'X-Men'. My interest in comics waned when I was fifteen, overshadowed by an interest in music and boys (in that order) but the first 'Silver Surfer' stayed under my bed ... About eight years later I was in a secondhand bookshop buying old Ladybird books for my young daughter and whilst waiting to pay my eyes strayed to a 'Superman' comic in a box on the counter. I bought it and was hooked again ...My collection swelled and I started on *2000AD* as well, only stopping the American comics about three years ago when I realised the only title I was enjoying was *Sandman* ... I have around 10, 000 comics now (I think) plus quite a few pages of original artwork on the sitting room walls.

Norah's account is clearly very different from those given by readers of girls' comics. There is, for instance, minimal separation between how these texts had been used in childhood and how they are currently being used. There are, in addition, very clear links between the reading self of the past and the reading self now, and so Norah offers a narrative about continuity in reading from childhood. This notion of progression in comics with a majority male audience can be shown in the reading patterns of both male and female readers. Her account is also typical of these readers in that these texts are portrayed as consistently central in her writing and rewriting of her autobiography.

Further, these readers often saw comic reading as problematic, in relation both to girls and to other groups. Norah, for instance, saw her mother's insistence that she read girls' comics as expressing a concern about her daughter's 'difference' in being interested in science. Nonetheless, this group of readers' continued feelings of difference and isolation from a norm of British girlhood, and indeed, adult femininity, is very relevant to this dissertation, in that the texts they read continue to have a symbolic quality that focuses on their assertions of difference.

This group tended, as girls, to favour American superhero comics, as we saw in Robyn's and Norah's accounts. As adults, many had moved onto comics offering very different kinds of story, including fantasy, thriller and many others. Whilst some readers mentioned British boys' comics as part of their early reading these tended to be a stepping-stone to American titles and were usually later dropped, except for *2000AD*. Here Norah is an exception, as her reading history suggests, in that she had, according to her letter, recently refocused her buying onto *2000AD*. In contrast to girls' comics, many comics for boys have adult readers, address a number of audiences, have adult equivalents or become collectable. In choosing to read comics that had led the reader into adult texts with a majority male audience (even if female-friendly, as many of the Vertigo titles were), this group differentiated themselves from other female readers and often saw themselves as reading as fans.

The Appeal of the 'Other'

American comics predominantly aimed at a male audience, despite the compromises and concerns around them for female readers, appealed to these readers in childhood and continued to appeal into adulthood, as Norah's comments indicate. This appeal was, in childhood, partly founded upon how different these comics were from girls' comics and, indeed, how different they were from British comics generally. Readers' responses to these titles, then, often relied on a thorough knowledge of British comics, enabling readers to compare and contrast the 'other' with the familiar.

This difference between British and American comics, and so their attraction for readers, was explained in a number of ways. The much longer stories, the exoticism of these titles, and the use of colour were all significant. British reprints of American comics existed, but, for the most part, they were in black and white and readers preferred the American originals. The impact was such that the colour used in British titles like *Girl* was forgotten. For some readers, in memory, British comics were always in black and white. Another argument was put forward by Helen, a literacy consultant working for a charity, who was originally from Morecambe. She argued that readers like her had, as she put it, 'loved the glamour of it all', adding that 'they were very exciting comics … they felt very grown up'. Readers like Helen also remembered American titles as having been sophisticated cosmopolitan texts because they, in addition to being in colour, they had glossy covers. There was generally less focus on the comic as object in these accounts, except through the colour images and glossy covers, primarily because the format for all of these comics was essentially the same. Because of this standardization, format did not have the importance in differentiating readers that it did in relation to girls' comics.

The American comics and titles like *2000AD* were also different in that there was a second-hand trade in them, although readers identified swapping as the initial route into comics for boys. Those who chose to read comics for boys typically had access initially like Fran, via male siblings or cousins. With American comics and with some of the later British comics like *2000AD* and its predecessors, including *Action* (IPC, 1976-1977), borrowing, rather than the more permanent swapping, was a common activity as these were more collectable than most British texts.

Readers, typically, slowly began purchasing titles, depending on parental control of pocket money. Buying second-hand was common, in that it meant that money went further. Whilst old copies of most British comics tended to turn up at school jumble sales and nowhere else, the American comics, for most of the 1950s to 1980s, would turn up in bookshops and stalls. Helen, for instance, described buying comics in just this manner to me and to her friend.

Helen: I used to go to a market stall at lunchtime from school [digression about school with friend] ...and I used to swap.

Mel & Friend: Swap?

H: You could swap what you had for other comics on the stall.

M: How did that work?

H: Once you had read a comic you could either sell it to them or exchange it for another one. They stamped all their comics so that they knew which ones were theirs. If you wanted to *keep* them, you bought them, but otherwise you swapped.

F: How did they make a profit?

H: No idea.

What Helen's comments suggest is that in the 1970s, second-hand buying was more formal and more commercialized in relation to American comics, with a growing tendency to establish selective collections and sell on. This is indicative of an emerging fandom, a difference that also made these comics attractive.

Where swapping and borrowing were largely clandestine, choosing to buy first-hand titles aimed at boys was a much more public statement and usually seen by parents as totally out of the question (if they knew about it). This was compounded by the difficulties of getting these comics new. Several women from the USA who came to training events commented how disappointed they had been in not being able to follow their favourites when they began living in Britain, often as children with parents in the armed forces. This was because comics were sold to newsagents by the yard, irrespective of titles, which meant the reader was left with unfinished narratives, and a burning but largely unfulfilled desire to see them completed. Carol, a librarian from Coventry, for instance, recalled, '...searching for the next comic in a sequence, often with no luck at all. I eventually started to avoid Marvel because you could never find out what happened in the end.' The battle to find out what happened next served, in some cases, to cement relationships to the form. Mystery acted as a stimulus to an enthusiasm for collecting before specialist comic shops developed. Thus, the readers increasingly engaged with the form both emotionally and cognitively as collectors. My experience of searching for comics, for instance, involved my cycling around eighteen miles each weekend, going from newsagents to newsagents and looking through all they had in stock on the chance that they had a missing part of sequence.

Charting the ways in which American comics, in particular, were attractive, also tracks how they have been marked as 'other' in the past. Although mainstream productions in America, in a British context until the 1970s these were an alternative to home-produced comics, cult texts involving specialist knowledge rather than what everyone read. As they were foreign, what they offered seemed exotically different. British comics, in contrast, were identified as much more bound up in trying to ensure conformity to the status quo, especially in the young working class readership. American comics, whilst performing the same function for their home audience, could not work that way abroad, although their secondary function as propaganda about the attractiveness of America certainly could. Whilst not alternative in the sense of the adult underground and alternative comics, they offered an option divorced from the traditional British comic.

In choosing to ally themselves to American products, the girl reader, whilst not necessarily aware of the debates about how comics reflected societal concerns about reading, was rejecting not only perspectives on gender and class, but 'Britishness.' For many British teachers or parents throughout the period of the 1950s to 1980s, for example, in the writing of Pumphrey (1954, 1955, 1964), the American comic, as the 'mass cultural' other, was the most problematic reading of all. As such, it became an *exciting* 'other' to young readers. Thus, these comics, along with the allure of the exotic, had the merit of having both general adult and specifically middle-class disapproval.

Remembering Narratives

Carol, before she became disillusioned by rarely finding out the conclusions of stories, recalled searching for 'next editions and neglected Marvel comics' precisely because 'they had complex interweaving plots like soap operas that unwound over months or sometimes years of issues'. This is an interesting comparison which suggests she is 'appropriating' the form, or assimilating it to a 'female' narrative form. By the mid 1970s American comics tended to offer only one or two longer stories, the main one continuing for some time, whilst British comics tended to contain a larger number of shorter strips. There were few recollections of distinct types of story, given that the all comics mentioned were within the superhero genre.

Another important memory of narratives in these comics was that they did not engage the reader in British models of girlhood. Anna, for instance, argued that in contrast to British girls' comics they offered 'strong female characters and an alternative world view'. As the accounts above suggest, they were also seen as comparatively sophisticated and complex narratives, as Helen's comment about them seeming 'very grown up' implies. This was linked with the protagonists being mostly teenagers or adults rather than children. Escapism, for some readers, was about escaping from childhood into adulthood and so into independence and self-determination. These comics, in offering stories about older characters, had considerable appeal to younger readers. This was also aspirational reading, but in rather a different way from British girls' comics, in that these comics contained images of what readers saw as powerful, if troubled, independent working women and men.

As was the case with girls' comics, memories of which characters featured in a comic were important to readers. As Anna's comment confirms, there were, of course, American comics which had female central characters, although only a few. My own memories of comics, for instance, include my having had an enthusiasm for 'Ms Marvel', whom I recalled as being a strong, complex character. Other characters that were mentioned included 'Supergirl', whose comic was generally seen as dreadful, but who actually got some positive comments in interviews. Norah, for instance, said that 'I loved "Supergirl"'. British girls' comics would always offer more female protagonists in comparison, but fewer of the independent heroine type that appealed to these readers.

These readers also had memories of having read many titles that did not have central female characters. Female readers, including Norah, repeatedly named comics featuring groups such as 'The X-Men'. Helen, for example, began her interview with a reference to a group comic, and with a question, which, as I suggest with regard to Robyn, was very typical of those who read this kind of comic. Here the question was a direct challenge, questioning whether I was an 'expert' in Helen's terms:

Helen: If you're doing a history of comics, who was 'Lightning Lad'?

Mel: [Gives potted history].

Friend: She bloody knows!

H: [Nodding] I liked that character. The 'Legion of Superheroes' was one of my favourite stories.

Other teams from comics mentioned in interviews included 'The Justice League of America' and 'The Avengers'. American titles differ tremendously from British girls' comics in consistently offering mixed-sex groups of protagonists. One appeal of these comics for readers was that female characters were often part of teams, as in the British school stories, but teams that featured male participants as well.

Female readers' memories of narratives did, however, suggest that they did not necessarily read these stories in the same way as male readers. In many interviews, readers recalled ways of understanding these narratives that could be seen as reading against the grain of group superhero titles in several ways. One way was to see the female characters as powerful role models, so relating these comics to both soap opera and feminism. Another way in which the group narratives were remembered was as romance. Some titles lent themselves to this, explicitly having romantic themes, whilst others could be re-read in that way. Karen, a librarian from Bolton, for instance, had become enthusiastic about 'The Fantastic Four' and the 'Avengers' when reading them to her nephews. She had subsequently stopped reading comics, characterizing her interest as motivated by the children in her life, but nonetheless asked me questions about one character: 'Wanda the Scarlet Witch', 'What happened to her, who did she marry?' This suggests how interviewees read stories as being about friendship and heterosexual romance rather than, or as well as, adventure. Jenkins (1992) argues that, '... Women must often participate on an unequal footing with men within the narrative realm' (p.113) and some of the strategies in reading these 'other' texts reflect that. Jenkins identifies strategies of rewriting that focus on social relations, as I do above, whilst acknowledging that women have been taught to make sense of male- centered narratives:

This practice may also have taught girls from an early age how to find their own pleasures in stories that reflect the tastes and interests of others, how to shift attention away from the narrative centre and onto the periphery, how to reclaim their own interests from the margin and thus how to engage more freely in speculations that push aside the author's voice in favour of their own. Not all women will feel compelled to adopt such strategies... For many however, there will continue to be a tension between their socialized reading interests and the commercial texts they encounter. (Jenkins, 1992, p.114)

In conclusion, memories of narrative were typically of specific comics, characters, and broad story arcs. Reading histories, as is the case with the one offered by Norah usually mentioned a large number of titles and who the creators and producers were, unlike accounts of girls' comics. The narratives, again all within one genre, were described as adventures, but often read through the prisms of romance or feminism. Memories, then, tended to focus on the relationships between characters. Seeing group superhero titles as romances usually contrasted (although it sometimes co-existed) with an understanding that saw the female characters as equal partners with the male. The latter perspective typified those who had engaged with group superhero comics in the middle of the 1970s and after, the former earlier readers. The latter re-reading emphasized work and co- operation rather than romance and was more consciously feminist in intent.

Rebellion, Gender and Identity

Readers used these comics in a number of ways. American titles, along with British boys' titles, appealed to female readers because they were *not* seen as for girls, again emphasizing their role in identity formation. For example, Annabel, a librarian from London, one of the few older respondents who had maintained a comic reading habit, was currently reading *Ghost*. She had not read girls' comics, which she described as 'soppy stuff'. Instead, she had first read *Eagle*, *Hotspur* and *Wizard* with the former being her favourite, saying 'Dan Dare and the Mekon, that was the stuff'. It is evident from her assertion about girls' comics being 'soppy' that the girls' comic was the benchmark against which these other titles were judged. Whilst readers identified such comics as a more challenging option than the British girls' comics, or as offering more potential in representing a wider range of female activity, they came to these titles as a rejection of girls' comics.

Equally, or perhaps more important was the fact that these other comics were 'not nice', a term which implies a lower-class-ness connoting 'unrespectable' as well as subject matter (seen as unsuitable) and a primary male audience. Anna, for instance, recalls having taken particular glee in the more violent 'Judge Dredd' stories, precisely because they were 'not for girls'. Cross-gender reading was seen as transgressive, as expressing an identity which, (even if sometimes problematic) was a *positive* choice. It also offered an alternative to traditional femininity in representing a refusal to wholly accept a gendered binary. In this I agree with Barker's comments on *2000AD*, where he insisted that, 'what is remarkable about *2000AD* is the emergence of a strong minority of passionately committed female readers-whose pleasures in the texts cannot be understood as some kind of textual cross-dressing' (in Buckingham, 1993, p.161). I would, in addition, extend this to female readers of American comics as well.

For some, the appeal of reading comics aimed at boys was an act deliberately designed to shock and to challenge adults (particularly parents). Barbara, an environmental activist and goth from Coventry, one of the youngest people I interviewed, offered the most extreme manifestation of this use of comics. Comics had formed part of an ongoing rebellion against her family's values. The daughter of fundamentalist Christian parents, she said, with no irony intended at all, 'My parents think comics come from Satan'. Whilst comparatively low-key, Norah also recalled that rebellion was partly her aim in her choice of reading after *Bunty*. Such choices were a 'knowing' use by readers of certain texts, based on an understanding of adults' assessment of texts as gender appropriate. It was an understanding comparable to that around the attitudes to class with regard to the girls' comic.

In engaging with these texts, the reader was further distanced from the norm of the British girls' comic and so from British girlhood. One could really offend by reading 'unsuitable' girls' comics, but another way to assert independence was to read boys' comics. In Norah's account, for instance, reading and other activities that were not 'girlish' were seen as a problem by her parents and therefore she seized upon reading superhero comics as a way of expressing individuality. Here again, reading is tied in with identity in a literal and symbolic way. As with girls' comics, commitment to these texts was sometimes generated as a result of their forbidden nature. Nyberg, in discussing a similar reading pattern in some women readers of American comics, describes them as 'trespassing' in ways that gave them pleasure (in Rollins, 1995, p.216). If reading can be construed as rebellion, and for some readers it was certainly seen as that, then choosing to read across gender in the comic can be seen as transgressive.

For some young women this reading was a personal choice rather than a public statement. The choice to be silent concerning reading was a strategy often generated from fear of peer pressure. Where reading communities existed, the role of *Jackie*, for instance, was as important as discussing what had been seen on the television. The consensus on what was acceptable meant that some readers kept reading the girls' comic, largely without pleasure, as a cover. In effect, this was a form of 'passing'. I, for instance, was publicly a reader of *Fab 208* (Fleetway Publications, 1966-1982) and *Jackie*, but privately worked through my aspirations, fears and concerns through American comic book characters. I saw American comics as central to my life and periodically made forays into other reading, comparing British comics to them rather than the other way around. At the same time, I went through an intense phase of reading science fiction novels, partly thanks to my local librarian who allowed me to borrow from the adult library although I was not officially old enough to join it. This meant that I saw reading science fiction, which I linked with the superhero comics, as a high status, adult, or at least older, and predominantly male activity. Simultaneously, I felt that this interest was one I should not tell female peers about, fearing their disapproval and that I would not be considered a 'proper' girl. Reading 'otherwise', then, increased my awareness and self-consciousness about being untypical for my age and gender.

To use reading as overt rebellion implies, in some ways, self-confidence, and a lack of fear about social position. To read privately suggests feelings of difference, perhaps reinforced through bullying, in terms of sexual orientation, race, class or education that the content of the comic offers reassurance about. In an article on *The X-Men*, Eshun (2000) discusses what this comic meant to him as a black British child in the 1970s and 1980s. What he describes mirrors the accounts of some of the female readers of the same comics. The characters' self-knowledge and fortitude in the face of prejudice meant that, as he put it,

> ...being born a mutant meant growing up alienated. But there were also rewards. Mutants could fly...In the pages of the comic, being different offered far more than the security of sameness. Each day I hoped that this would also be true of real life. (Eshun, 2000, p.1)

It was reading that could act as a reassurance that the readers could be valued. Choosing to read very different comics helped readers find a space in which it was positive to define themselves as different. However, it could also serve to reinforce that difference.

Interviewees who characterized their reading as private often saw themselves as conforming to family or other reading patterns rather than those of peers, particularly if those families were seen as non-traditional. Fran, for instance, having a number of older brothers, chose to read all her brothers' *Commando* comics, and superhero comics. It also seems to have aligned these female readers with male readers and relatives, brothers, cousins, grandfathers and sometimes fathers. Some of these readers, like Fran, however, were at pains to insist that they had not been tomboys. In reading comics for boys, the readers felt they could be seen as trying to be men, or aligning themselves with patriarchy rather than fighting it. There was also tension in readers' concerns that they might be seen as getting 'above themselves' or being 'snobbish' in reading titles seen as better than girls' comics, in engaging with a higher status product in a low status medium. Given that adults generally disapproved of the medium, the shift of girls away from girls' comics into boys' comics can be read as an acknowledgement and acceptance of the perceived status of comics for girls. In addition, this perhaps suggests an alienation from the girls that read them. Boys' comics could be seen as aspirational reading for girls in ways that reject girlhood.

Readers came to understand themselves as reading transgressively, but often guiltily, and later, as many of those who read other kinds of comics continued to do so into adulthood, as having an identity within comic fandom that was simultaneously problematic and satisfying. Far from stopping in adulthood, the transgressive nature of comic reading continued to be an issue and many readers felt compromised. This compromise could be professional, or personal, as an exchange between Carol and Deborah, another librarian from Coventry, part of a group interview, illustrates.

Carol: I go to work by bus and I've had some funny looks from people when they realize I'm reading a comic. [Nodding from all.]

Deborah: You get stared at…

C: And sometimes you overhear comments about literacy … which is an odd experience for a librarian.

D: [Nodding] You can't believe anyone would question your reading ability … Do you want to explain why you're reading comics?

Where the two women's comments differed was in tone. Carol identified herself as a 'fan' and Deborah had only recently come to comics. Consequently, Deborah maintained a slightly cross tone throughout the exchange and was clearly still disconcerted to discover the impact comic reading could have on how she was seen. In contrast, Carol, as a long-term reader, was more familiar with the response to comics.

In conclusion, rebellion, or secretiveness, and identity were very much tied together in these readers' accounts. Conformity to feminine norms was an issue for many of these readers, and many worried that their choice of reading might be taken as representing hostility towards other women or their roles as women. This suggests an understanding of the complications of their position in interview as adult comic readers. As adults they too tended to divide into groups, one secretive and one very vociferous and usually part of fandom. The readers were very aware of these questions, especially as most of those reading boys' comics consistently labeled themselves as feminist. For this group of readers, the tensions around the comic were further exacerbated by a feminist inflected hostility to comics for mixed audiences and boys.

'Other' Comics and Feminism

One issue that emerged regularly in my interviews was the relationship between reading comics and feminism, which was characterized by tensions around what might be seen as sexist images of women. These female figures have been seen as making any female reader complicit in her own objectification. This singular characterization encompasses both 'bad girl' art intended as pornographic, and superhero titles, featuring (as they often do) characters with unfeasibly large breasts and skintight costumes. These are the dominant images of women in this most popular genre within the medium, which is also the one that most female readers have first contact with. In addressing this issue, with regard to girlhood reading, interviews kept turning from the kind of spaces that girls had been offered, to the space that women now had in relation to them. In many cases memory and current experience were seen as similar.

Nearly all of those interviewed mentioned the way that women were drawn in many superhero comics they had experience as girls and later as adults, and expressed an opinion on it. Those who had continued into adulthood as readers reported that those who criticized their reading did so on the basis of images of women, and so the issue remained one that they constantly had to revisit. There were also occasions when, as women or girls, they felt very defensive about their reading. Olwen, for instance, argued that '[a]s long as they are active and strong does it matter what they look like?' As a feminist and a worker in comics, she saw herself as part of two very separate groups.

Olwen's comment focuses on a key issue in relationship to images of women in comics, the contradiction between the way women appear and what they do. The storylines female characters appeared in, and so what they did, were remembered as rather different from the images and considerably less problematic. When these readers were children, as we have seen, they identified these characters as powerful and interpreted them as heroic images, asserting their right to read these comics, something Jenkins describes as colonizing through interest (1992, p.114). In doing so, they choose to focus on the activities of the characters. As I indicate above, readers saw these as depictions of adult workers, often part of teams, who actively save themselves and others rather than screaming and fainting, particularly in the 1970s. This focus on teamwork and independence also suggests the importance of narrative identification as opposed to visual identification.

Having chosen texts seen as excluding girls, girl readers, once committed, found, as I have suggested, a number of reasons to remain so. However, what had initially attracted them became something of a burden in that having found these comics could offer a space to the female reader did not mean that their image as boys' texts changed. They then found themselves in the position of seeing potential in the form that was continually denied on a number of fronts, particularly the case with superhero comics.

Reynolds (1992) is a particularly good example of the tendency to insist on the lack of a female audience. For instance, he asks in relation to the figure of the super heroine, 'How can women who dress up in the styles of 1940s pornography be anything other than the pawns and tools of male fantasy?' (1992, p.79). He also argues that all female figures in comics are the same in acting as the 'sign of pornography...[which] comes to stand for an entire pornographic subtext, a series of blanks which readers remain free to fill in for themselves' (1992, p.34). These comments reiterate that the superhero genre is exclusively for boys and men and so serve to play a double role as feminist statements, arguing that this material objectifies women, but also as assertions of justified male dominance in the medium.

To illustrate Reynolds' use of feminist argument further, he says that:

Any feminist critic could demonstrate that most of these characters fail to inscribe any specifically female qualities: they behave in battle like male heroes with thin waists and silicone breasts, and in repose are either smugly domestic…or brooding and remote - a slightly threatening male fantasy. (1992, p.80)

Here he both distances himself from the 'feminist critic' and uses the argument that he assumes one might make. The idea of the heroine as disguised male also begs a question about what 'specifically female qualities' are, as they clearly do not include strength or activity, which reveal a woman to be a man despite appearances. Thus, the female characters are either fantasy females for male consumption, or male, again establishing the space as exclusively male. Nowhere is there a suggestion that they might be appropriated, celebrated or changed by female readers, either child or adult. Such arguments negate both the female reader and the possibility of other readings. The strong woman only exists as a sadomasochistic fantasy, none of the images of women in these comics are accessible by women or girls, and they represent damaging stereotypes that should be left to the male readers to whom they properly belong.

It was in coming up against these issues that readers felt the need to claim these texts as a spur to feminism in their childhood through offering the readers wider horizons. A number of women who were girl readers in the 1970s, such as Norah, had read *Ms Marvel* and *The X-Men* and had learnt from them (they claimed) that women could be heroes too, and not always ultimately self-sacrificing. Similarly, I first came across feminism when arguments appeared in the letter columns of the *Lois Lane* comics of the early 1970s on that theme. In addition, many of these readers identified themselves as political in other ways. Elizabeth, for instance, described herself as left wing as well as feminist. Readers' insistence on rebelling in childhood was often maintained as an adult, transformed into a more political form of opposition. Hence, Olwen and Elizabeth were active feminists and Barbara had become an environmental activist. As Barker suggests in relation to *2000AD* in the 1990s: 'My hypothesis is that girls tend to participate in the comics world from some more oppositional political sense… This would then connect with males giving slightly greater weight to comics being a world of secret knowledge…whereas females emphasised subversiveness, sharing an enthusiasm and getting inside an art form' (in Buckingham, 1993, p.161). The readers' assertions that these comics do appeal to women in various ways (including reading them as potentially feminist texts) act as an expression of ownership.

Some of those I interviewed, especially Olwen and Elizabeth refused to accept the appropriation of female bodies by male readers. In a blunt statement, Elizabeth focused on the issue of who comics and the female characters within them belong to, asking, 'Whose tits are they, anyway?' In making this comment, Elizabeth asserted her right to be a reader, her right to intervene in the content of comics, and offered a rebuttal of the way the comic has been understood.

As I have suggested, female readers of comics aimed at male audiences were often women who saw themselves as feminist and their choices of reading as children as motivated partly by an awareness of limited roles for girls elsewhere. However, the fact that their choices were seen as compromised in much popular feminism or feminist inflected research meant that they were also a group who had become very sensitized to the problems and limits of that feminism as adults. In effect, the two sets of texts, popular feminist and comic had collided for these readers in ways that problematized both for them. Their feminist awareness, as (now adult) women readers of comics, was built on their understanding of images of women and their controversial nature. However, female readers had long since, they felt, come to terms with the implications of looking at and enjoying female characters. There was also an undercurrent of slightly patronizing amusement. Wilma, for instance, was entertained by the fact that the majority young male readership seemed largely unaware of the homoerotic undertones and fetishised bodies of male characters. Thus, one of the answers to the controversy around images of women was to focus on equally fetishised male images. In doing so, the female readers claimed knowledge and understanding of this genre within the medium for themselves and refused to see it as a space that they could not be part of.

Being a Fan

Some female adult readers did not describe themselves as comic readers, but instead described themselves as fans, for instance Anna, Deborah and Carol. Fandom, in these readers' eyes, was bound up with collecting. Jeffrey Brown (1997) suggests that within comic fandom, knowledge of the medium is symbolic capital and the comic book is physical currency, thus, as in official culture, 'Collecting is an important marker of status' (1997, p.23). The collection reflects knowledge of the industry. It was also about having a broad knowledge of the medium, hence questioning me, challenging my position as 'expert', appears in the interviews, as Robyn's illustrates. In taking on such a role, these readers demanded that they be treated as fans rather than as specifically female fans, a demand that was not necessarily respected by some male fans.

This may have been, in part, because the interviewees expressed their fandom through *informal* interaction, discussing comics with other readers at home or over the Internet as part of an interpretive community. Norah, for instance, said her daughters '[d]id have the embarrassment of their boyfriends spending the evening nose deep in my comics or getting into in depth discussions with me over Miller's *Batman*. They survived but neither will even look at a cartoon now'. Vera discussed comics with her partner. 'He tells me that I have to think about stories as well. I avoid some [titles] because I don't like the artists'. Elsa, in contrast, who had moved from girls' comics such as *Misty* to superhero and other comics, chiefly discussed them through Internet discussion groups about specific creators or titles and so was the only interviewee involved in more formal types of fandom. Those interviewed did not, typically, attend conferences or conventions. In not taking part in formal fandom, then, they could be seen as not being 'proper' fans by other, male fans.

Those interviewed, in addition, did not generally create comics, either as part of fandom or professionally except Olwen. Few of those interviewed remembered having done so as children. Creating comics was comparatively rare in regard to British women comic readers. One current adult reader, however, intended to become professional. Barbara, a lifelong reader, was also an aspiring independent comic writer. She was particularly enthusiastic about the titles involving those who had been *Sandman* writers and artists. She said 'I'm working on a comic with my boyfriend about my childhood'. She was immersed in titles from independent publishers as well as mainstream ones and was enthusiastic about lesbian and Riot Grrl orientated comics.

The use of independent, alternative comics (and comics fandom) as a signal of alternative lifestyles for adults was important to Barbara and some of the others interviewed. Nyberg's account of industry audience profiling suggests that reading alternative titles is typical of female casual readers (in Rollins, 1995, p.222). The interviews I conducted differed because these readers, far from being casual, often made comic reading a central aspect of an alternative lifestyle, or part of dramatic changes in their lives that allowed a return to experimentation with roles. Anna, for instance, saw alternative comics and alternative girlhood as one, saying 'I gave my 'My Little Pony' a Mohican and it painted black' and that she had hated 'boyfriend stuff and photostories'. She clearly associated comics with female experimentation around identity and had become a committed reader because of this.

What I outline above is fan activity amongst these readers as adults. In memory, however, the first inkling of a wider fandom, beyond collecting specific titles, came through the letter columns in American comics. Historically, like the British girls' comics, the American monthly titles involved readers. However, rather than problem pages, or competitions, these comics had letters pages filled with readers commenting directly upon the stories and the issues raised in the text. Readers also sent letters spotting continuity errors or demanding costume changes. The range of contributors was wider in age and gender than those contributing to letters pages in British comics, so readers like Helen felt they were part of a mature and expansive international community.

Readers described their identity as children (and as adults) as centered on being a fan, not being a girl, as we have seen, but, simultaneously, they also identified comic culture of all sorts as predominantly male, right down to comic shops when they first started appearing. Readers reported that as girls there would often be only be one female in the building; themselves. Several also reported having been put off by the nastiness of most comic shops, or as Vera put it, 'the SMELL'. In addition, interviewees reported that as children, and as adults, they had met with opposition, or derision, from male comic readers who saw their interest as improper, or as about 'fancying' the male characters and therefore, in those male readers' opinions, not based in 'true' expertise. The difference between these two types of knowledge can be illustrated by reference to Norah's letter. With regard to her early reading, for instance, she said

When I was seven I discovered DC comics. I loved *Supergirl* and *The Legion of Super-heroes*, but despised *Lois Lane* and *The Flash*, the latter mainly because of Infantino's artwork and the shrewish 'Iris West'.

Her letter, then, in moving between discussing comics via artist and via narrative and character, could be used to characterize her as both 'proper' fan and 'female' fan. The dual mode of reading used by Norah suggests that when male and female fans look at the same comic they may interpret them differently and seek different pleasures from their reading. It also suggests that female readers of these comics have two models of readership in mind when looking at these texts and apply both to what they read. As Nyberg states, 'women readers try alternately to fit into the role constructed for the predominantly male comic book reader and to resist that construction' (in Rollins, 1995, p.205).

The possibility that female readers might have faced some resistance from male readers as girls is linked to the way that, as I have suggested, superhero comics in particular have often been zealously guarded as a male preserve. In one relationship of my own, my conforming to feminine stereotypes, even in reading, was terribly important to my partner. Comics were 'inappropriate' he argued, and insisted that I should read women's magazines. Somehow he saw my reading comics as a comment on his masculinity. Possessiveness about certain forms of reading amongst both boys and girls indicates how personal activities can nonetheless have a profound public impact. In denying a female reader's knowledge, decrying it as non-industry based, some male readers maintain their own position by using assumptions about gender as a weapon.

Another aspect of the fan activity of the interviewees was that it was marked by breaks. Again, this is different from male fan activity. Many of those interviewed, mostly respondents in their mid thirties or younger, had stopped reading comics as children or young women and only returned to them as adults. Norah reported losing interest in comics at about fifteen but kept her old comics and rediscovered the form in her mid- twenties. She also offered an account of how her adult collecting developed:

I started off quite slowly but as our finances improved I started buying up old *Spiderman*, *X-Men*, *Superman* and *Legion of Superheroes*, plus new discoveries like *Green Arrow* and *Green Lantern*, who were a lot better than [in] the '60s.

In taking pleasure in the superhero (rather than independent comics) readers like Norah break with the industry perception of the female reader. This was also the case for Wilma who had been put off comics, but who had started to re-discover them via her children.

For some, what had drawn them back was their perception of certain titles as being more 'female-friendly', as was the case with Robyn, who, as we saw, was attracted to *Sandman* and *The Tale of One Bad Rat*. However, this did not necessarily mean that these readers sought out female characters and identified with them. As Norah's reading history suggests, a reader might return to familiar titles remembered from childhood. Alternatively, once beyond the title that triggered a renewed interest in comics, and as they became more committed, they bought titles that could be seen as linking them with more of a male reader profile.

In addition, several of the adult women readers interviewed had found their way back into comics via male contacts. Typically, in a heterosexual relationship where the male partner read comics, the female decided to give them a go again, which means they can be described as 'pass-along readers' (in Rollins, 1995, p.207), something seen as typically part of the female reader profile by the industry in America. Vera, for instance, had been teased about reading comics and stopped, but later got back into comics via a boyfriend. Having braved the comic shop, as she put it, she got into comics via Dave McKean's cover art and started buying her own comics based on her attraction to the art rather than the stories. The return to comics and thence to fandom was sometimes expressed in interview as being compromised (and compromising to personal feminism) by having come through men.

On the one hand, readers reported that as young people they were drawn into being fans through participation, yet on the other, as young female readers they were not part of fandom as Jenkins labels it. Being committed to reading these comics presented a number of problems, but also, as I have tried to suggest, pleasures. However, fandom, whilst seeming to offer another way of expressing identity, did not allow the female reader to 'escape' from girlhood, as interviewees had hoped. Being female in this field inherently meant that they could not be 'proper' fans, despite having amassed suitable knowledge, 'symbolic capital' and using appropriate language in talking about texts. All felt that being a female in fandom, whether as children or as adults, had changed them and that by reading comics they put themselves on the periphery of several female worlds, whilst as women they existed on the periphery of the comic book world. To conclude, then, these female readers of other comics could be described, perhaps, as fans without fandom. In recent years fandom has changed considerably and is largely female-friendly, but these readers had, in earlier years, found it sometimes inhospitable. Elizabeth, for instance, began to avoid attending events.

In this chapter, I have explored how these comics, both those aimed at men and those aimed at mixed audiences, offered readers different ways of building self-images. However, readers who rejected the girls' comic and turned to another form found themselves implicated as victims in other ways. The girl who reads girls' comics is liable to fall into one set of 'traps', as I have suggested, but the reader who looks to comics for a mixed audience will also be reading questionable material rather than finding a solution to the 'problem' of the girls' comic. Those readers' who looked for alternatives, often as a rebellion against the norms of the girls' comic, might find themselves disapproved of for buying into values offered by texts seen as inherently sexist, or for not conforming to appropriate gender roles. These readers invested in texts that gave them a sense of being different and special, or rebellious, as children, whilst also being aware that this might be a problem as well. Their practices of media consumption in relation to comics were very much part of their construction, and later re-construction of identity and gender identity. This is very much in line with what Nyberg insists on in relation to adult female readers of superhero comics. They 'treat the constructed gender boundaries as 'fluid' and trespass both in the text and in a more physical sense by their participation in the process of purchasing and reading comics' (in Rollins, 1995, p.207). Such an assertion also suggests how unstable that sense of identity is for both the child and the adult reader.

In texts aimed at girls as well as those that are aimed at other audiences, it becomes clear that all presuppose a unified whole or a unified other that could be described as 'girlhood' as well as one that could be described as 'womanhood'. The texts offer markers that readers chose, or not, to incorporate into their sense of their relationship to that whole. These media constructs around girlhood and womanhood vary across period and in terms of class which suggests that they are not continuous fields of experience shared by all women at all times. In mapping the various uses that female readers have made of comics we can come to an understanding of the diversity amongst readers. What is at stake then, is the reader's sense of self in relation to media texts and the dominant media discourses around gender. In relation to these problematic texts, they might find that discourses of feminism also come into play, although not necessarily in ways that support their engagement with those texts. Where there might also be a sense of continuity is in the types of understandings readers have made of these comics, whether seen as for male or for female audiences. The readers negotiate a series of interlocking texts and attitudes towards texts, all of which have implications for how that reader may be seen or how they might identify themselves.

In exploring the activities and memories of real people, one can only speculate about the possible interactions between popular culture, readers, pleasure and feminism. In the context of women and girls reading comics aimed at male audiences, although there are many different kinds of identifications involved, the main issue remains how gender is articulated in media consumption. Despite what could be seen as a subjectivity that, as Ang asserts, 'can thus be described in terms of the multiplicity of subject positions taken up by the person in question' (1996, p.119), the readers found dominant gender discourses difficult (although not impossible) to negotiate. As suggested, the assertion that girls read only the comics aimed at them reflects a wider set of arguments about girlhood in Britain.

In addition, the tensions around adult female readers of the comic reveal that these concerns are not easily moved beyond. That the comic form is problematic in relation to female readers is borne out in titles aimed at boys as well as those aimed at girls. These are fans who are rarely part of fandom and who exist in constant tension with this identity unless speaking to other women who identify themselves as fans and who might understand the problems and pleasures of that role. Their continued engagement with this set of texts means a constant and often conscious reworking of their relationship with the comic and with other, especially male, fans as well as non-readers. Yet readers interviewed maintained a relationship with these texts and described them as offering a number of, sometimes contradictory, pleasures. In effect, as Barker suggests, the contract that they were offered by these texts was far more satisfying to them than that offered by those aimed at a primarily female audience (1989, p.256), even if the identity that resulted from accepting that contract was difficult to occupy. In this relationship with fandom as adults, as well as those relationships of readers who were involved with other kinds of comic in the past, there is evidence of a continual reworking of female identity in relation to media texts.

Conclusion

In this book, I have focused on a history of girls and girlhood in relation to comics in Britain. I see this history as an important one, but one which has been largely neglected as a research subject within the academy and in popular accounts of youth culture. I have drawn parallels between the treatment of girls' comics and the way in which girls' culture in general has often been dismissed as consumer-orientated, non-resistant and of little interest to the academic (as McRobbie and Garber noted (1976)). This neglect of girls' comics has been partly generated by the way in which, as I have outlined, they have been seen consistently as having a lower status than comics for boys. Further, I have, through working with interviews and written accounts, engaged with issues of memory and popular culture.

The lower status of girls' comics came about, ironically, because they have been seen as 'better' than most comics, in being more acceptable to teachers, parents and other adults, and 'worse' for precisely the same reason. Making comics for girls acceptable to gatekeepers and readers meant that producers had to negotiate a fine line between adventure and 'proper' girlhood. This returns us to notions of a domestic gatekeeper, as envisaged by Lewin (1943). Whilst Lewin's work was about food and gatekeeping, the idea of the gatekeeper of cultural artefacts is similar regarding choice and access. The emphasis on the girl who was appropriately 'girlish' and was offered, in terms of content, 'suitable' reading, involved massive compromise between the desires of actual readers and notions of girlhood held by adults and readers. Thus, these comics have often been characterized, along with other popular culture for girls, as part of a painfully conservative and narrow range of products. Hence the gender of the audience contributes to the perception of these comics as less valuable, which has often led to their dismissal by many of those interested in comics.

However, throughout I have also suggested that many of the assumptions about the creation of comics specifically for girls need reconsideration. The growth of the comic for girls in the post-war period was a major shift in periodical publishing and titles reached a large number of girls over several generations, potentially influencing post-war conceptualizations of British girlhood. Such conceptualizations should be understood as both actual girls' self-image and adults' (especially teachers and parents) perceptions of what girlhood consisted of. In analyzing these constructions of girlhood, I have charted the way that the girls' comic changed during the period. Whilst seemingly offering a consistent model of middle-class girlhood (or rather, having been characterized as doing so), these comics actually adapt to changes in education, particularly those titles targeting working-class girls. They also show evidence of the impact of the growth of consumerism and the growth of the concept of the teenager. Further, in response to both developments, the girls' comic, far from being only one type of comic, was increasingly subdivided according to the age and class of the intended reader throughout the late 1950s and early 1960s, in an attempt at niche marketing.

Thus, whilst girls' comics offered models of girlhood and femininity to each generation, these models constantly fragment and change over time and according to class. They are not even coherent within single titles. As Barker's (1989) analysis reveals, there are many different types of narrative within each of these comics. What the publishers offered was not generally consistent, with stories of female solidarity such as 'The Four Marys' undermining and being undermined by those that focused on suffering. Further, Barker identifies elements of girls' comics, such as the problem pages, as offering a very different model to that of the narratives. The contents do not give the sense of a unified feminine self that the titles of the comics might imply. In addition, given the connotations of the comic strip format, it is difficult to see these texts as offering straightforward models of girlhood and femininity.

I have explored the range of subject matter in girls' comics, which expanded during the period, although many of their themes were inherited from early magazines for girls and from book publishing. During this period, producers incorporated new subject matter, reflecting changes in what they saw as suitable reading for girls. Changes also occurred in relation to format, with photo-stories becoming the dominant form of storytelling in comics for girls in the mid-1980s. This change had a huge impact on the type of narratives offered, refocusing the comics on stories of everyday life. However, I have not embarked on a textual analysis of girls' comics, but instead focused predominantly on readers' memories of comics. These memories were often about extra-textual meanings and suggested that the comic acted as an important signifier of girlhood, relationships and identity.

Memories took several forms in the research. The comic as object, or even at the level of a title, acted as a trigger. The first was an initial flood of memories that was very powerful. It seemed to overwhelm those interviewed, as if a forgotten self had suddenly come to the forefront of their thoughts. The title of a comic would trigger memories of stories, characters, other titles and then, quite often, questions. However, there were often comments about how the paper felt, or the scent of the ink.

Where comics were actually present, they were touched, smelt and only after that actually opened, flicked through, often with exclamations about stories or images. Memory incorporated the materiality of the comic, the tactile aspects of the object, as well as narratives and images. Aspects of the comic that were non-narrative, especially the gifts and cut out dolls were mentioned at various points. The physical memories were particularly attached to the girls' comics, not other titles read by girls. Checking the date of publication was also an important action, with people commenting that titles were before their time. One might lose an interviewee altogether, as they drifted into reading stories. They would also often comment as to whether the edition they were reading had stories they recognised, sometimes becoming confused at seeing a familiar narrative in an edition from after they stopped reading the title. Nostalgia was rarely present, and memories, as we have seen, were not always happy ones, especially given the way that texts linked with networks of relationships, with parents, friends, siblings and professionals. I return to memory later in this conclusion.

In addition to charting a history of girls and girls' comics, I have indicated that female readers for a range of titles aimed at boys and mixed audiences have, and indeed do, exist. Consequently, I have considered both comics for girls and comics read by girls in this monograph, categories, I argue, which are by no means identical. Memories also included how one related to other through comics and practices around comics, such as shared reading and swapping, as we have seen. This took place across all genres.

In this monograph, then, in focusing on reader accounts I have dealt with readers' understandings of comics, juxtaposing memory with critical writing on comics and aspects of production. In doing so, I have uncovered connections between these various accounts, particularly the impact of writing about the mass media of the 1950s and earlier upon teachers and, in turn, readers. As a result, this book is in part a study of the underlying assumptions of much of the academic and educational work on comics and their readers that has appeared since the 1950s. Whilst I feel that much of this work is illuminating, revealing shifts in both models of girlhood and attitudes towards the comic, it was often caught up with models of 'media effects' and positions the child as a passive, unquestioning consumer.

During the course of this monograph, I have also addressed the question of why girls' comics developed and why they disappeared. I have suggested that the creation of comics for girls was a paradox, given that the medium has consistently been seen as a male province in Britain, even when comics have sold in large numbers to female readers. However, the major campaigns vilifying the form created a climate in which girls' comics were seen as a partial answer to the problems of other comics (those that had significant mixed audiences) and a way for producers to maintain sales through the development of new markets. Ideologically, girls' comics, whilst also proving to be profitable, made points about the 'niceness' of British comics, which suggested that they were preferable to titles from abroad. Producers, one could speculate, expected girlhood (understood as polite, nice, middle-class and decorous) to be seen by parents and commentators as exercising a moderating effect on comics in much the same way that girls might once have been accepted into a boys' school: that is, on the basis of their 'civilizing' influence.

If the creation of comics for girls is problematic, the question of why girls' comics disappeared has a clearer answer, as has the question of why female audiences for comics in general shrank between the 1960s and the early 2000s. I have argued that the disappearance of girls' comics and lack of female interest in the medium comes about for a number of reasons, but primarily because comics were replaced by the magazine as a vehicle for popular cultural meanings of girlhood, femininity and consumption. Tinkler (1995) argues that the girl was a category addressed (and created) by producers as a new market by the magazines of the late nineteenth and early twentieth centuries. Girls' comics, in their turn, were part of the intensified focus on the girl as consumer in the 1950s and on, but finally became the victims of consumerism, for, as consumerism expanded, girls' comics were left behind. Consumer industries throughout the 1950s and on increasingly created children's culture (and childhood) as a network of products where the objects offered for consumption were inter-related. Comics played little part in the overall meanings of that network, as they were, significantly, not usually tied in to a large range of other commodities (the exceptions include *Jackie*, which combined comic and magazine forms). This absence of links with other commodities is suggested by the way that readers' memories of comics were often tied to memories about friendships and other relationships. Girls' comics were tied into a web of 'comicness', perhaps, but not necessarily tied to other media. In effect, comics were increasingly not part of the consumption net, or web, as Jean Baudrillard describes it. According to Baudrillard 'few objects are offered alone, without a context of objects to speak for them…[The] object is no longer referred to in relation to a specific utility, but as a collection of objects in their total meaning' (in Poster, 1988, p.31). Magazines, in contrast, promoted a lifestyle focused largely on merchandise (and thus girlhood identity was confirmed by a range of inter-related and cross-promoted objects).

In this reading, comics went from central to peripheral in terms of girls' culture over several generations because of lack of reinforcement. Publishers contributed to this process in that the success of *Jackie* in the 1960s and on meant a refocusing of titles for girls onto non-comic strip materials which were cheaper to make, given that most comprised mainly adverts and were subsidized by the producers of the products. In effect, the publishers put themselves out of the business of creating comics for female readers in that the magazine offers a better 'fit' or, perhaps, a more acceptable 'contract' to girls.

Other reasons for the falling popularity of the girls' comic could include the consistent tensions between how the comic is understood and conceptions of girlhood. As I suggest above, the comic has invariably retained a maverick status, a charge of being disreputable and male-orientated, even given the development of the girls' comic. Comics have, as I have indicated, also been associated in various studies with working-class-ness, low literacy levels, and a lack of aspiration. In effect, the comic is considered 'vulgar', a term which judges them in terms of taste and class, reflecting Bourdieu's notion that 'good taste' and its consequences become, as Springhall (1998) outlines it 'operations of social domination and subordination' (p.139). Irrespective of the intent of the publisher, these perceptions of the medium can undermine the actual content of comics, even when they are intended as entirely 'wholesome': that is, acceptable to middle-class adult gatekeepers as well as children and young people.

What the examples about class and the comic in Chapter 4 suggest is that girls (as embodying 'proper' girlhood) may be compromised by contact with comics as a medium. Characterizing the comic as a compromise of 'proper' girlhood reveals attitudes to comics that are consistent with the formal campaigns against comics of the 1950s, and subsequent concerns about comics voiced in the 1960s until the early. In general, the comic campaigns and later concerns depicted an inherently problematic medium (as is the case in the writing of Pumphrey). Girl readers, where they appear in case studies, were usually considered as representative of a single, homogenized group to be protected from unsuitable topics, or depicted as one of a delinquent few. Girls, it is implied, must be protected from any temptation to behave in the 'inappropriate' ways that the subject matter of any given comic might encourage, and thus girls' comics were likely to be blander than boys' comics.

However, the associations of the comic mean that through its very form, no matter how anodyne the content, the comic is an undermining of 'proper' girlhood, a contaminant that will result in the girl being seen as not 'respectable'. Reading comics was, then, a point of tension in relation to respectability, and as Skeggs argues, 'Respectability would not be of concern... if the working classes... had not consistently been classified as dangerous, polluting, threatening, revolutionary, pathological and without respect (Skeggs, 1997, p.1). As Skeggs outlines, being respectable legitimates the individual working-class girl or woman, which means that much is at stake in maintaining respectability. In effect, one could argue that girls' comics did not so much succeed in moderating the comic as in compromising girlhood. In this reading the preconditions for girls' comics to fail in the long term were inherent within the genre, in that the message of the medium and the message of the contents undermine each other in various ways. The girls' comic may, then, have partly disappeared because of an overall incompatibility with definitions of femininity. The magazine, in comparison, was a format associated with female readers, as Winship (1987) confirms.

As the second chapter describes, there may have been other contributory factors to the end of the girls' comic, including institutional practices such as the repetition of stories. Whilst the humour comics often used slapstick, which was less likely to lose relevance or be seen as old-fashioned if repeated, in the girls' comics repetition was more problematic. One could say that recycling from a back catalogue of owned materials to create new spin-offs is an important aspect of the approach of cross-media firms today. However, in many cases this recycling involves updating (rarely done in girls' comics) or is done with the nostalgia market in mind. The latter is an approach rarely used with girls' comics, although the annuals (which were often continued well after a title had been cancelled) could be seen in this way. This was because the stories often tied in with activities for girls that were subject to fashion. Ballet (popular in the 1950s and 1960s), for instance, was replaced by gymnastics in the 1970s. Failing to focus on a newly fashionable activity, or to recognize when a set of stories were redundant, meant a comic could lose readers. A combination of publishers responding in limited ways to changes in girls' consumption patterns through the narratives, but not changing their practice of repeating older stories, may have contributed to the girls' comics fall in popularity.

It can also be speculated that the girls' comic died because there was no real progression for girl readers to an adult equivalent or into nostalgic collecting (there was little fandom or a collectors market for girls' comics until recently). The experience of girl readers is very different to that of boy readers, for whom, as the twentieth century ended, comics were increasingly a medium to grow up with and read as an adult, rather than just a phase in reading. If girl readers chose to read boys' comics, particularly superhero ones; television programmes, films and toys, initially spin-offs from the comics, provide both a context, and, as the collectability of these texts grows, a distinct form of fan-orientated consumption in relation to comics, reinforcing the reader's identity as fan.

Finally, I would argue that the varied discourses about a range of comics contributed to a scenario where, from the point-of-view of adults of both left and right wing persuasions, there were no 'appropriate' titles for female readers. For instance, in Chapter 3, I described how an influential strand of feminist writing about children's literature had an impact on the comic. As shown in Chapter 5, many of the readers who chose to reject British girls' comics remembered reading them from a feminist perspective as repressive, as a trap for the working-class or otherwise 'vulnerable' girl reader. Such readers found that the alternative titles they turned to were also considered problematic, predominantly because of the images of women they contained. Whilst real readers might choose to ignore these perspectives on girls' and other comics they were inevitably caught up in various discourses which had an impact on them as child readers, and as adults mediating the form for later generations. Such contradictions are at the heart of the disappearance of the girls' comic and part of the reason why girls' reading of comics in general declined.

As I have shown, British girls' comics faded out by 2001. It was not until after this point that the publication of manga for female readers re-engaged girls with comics and led to British women and girls creating comics of all kinds in much larger numbers. Having outlined various reasons for the creation and disappearance of comics specifically for girls, I move on to address what readers reported about using comics and about what comics meant to them. Responses were very diverse, crosscut by age, class, and other factors. As I suggest above, however, in general their meaning was bound up with attitudes towards comics and girlhood on the part of both readers and their adult carers. They responded in various ways to what they saw as the status and meanings of comics and the models of girlhood and femininity they felt girls' comics offered. Some readers characterized those comics as offering aspirational images, whilst others saw them as about conforming to norms of girlhood and rejected them. For all these readers, however, these publications were intimately tied to a sense of self, of girlhood, and perceptions of class position.

Whilst there were common themes in how readers understood girls' comics in general, what specific girls' comics meant to readers varied over time. Responses to comics for girls did change over several generations of readers, as we have seen. These changes meant that the comics of one generation often meant something very different to the next. Readers' memories of their responses to comics include notions of generation and peer group. *Girl*, for instance, begins as a text celebrated by readers for the active heroines it contains and the high quality colour printing. To many of the later generations of comic readers, in contrast, it is seen as 'twee' in comparison to titles like *Bunty*. In relation to paper quality too, *Girl* acts as a point of contrast, as the paper for *Bunty* is described as 'fuzzy' and is seen by readers as preferable to comics on 'shiny' paper. Class too, even if not articulated as anything more than a reference to 'posh' girls and 'snobs', is central to the shift between the two titles, with the readers of *Bunty* clearly locating *Girl* readers as middle-class and themselves as different from *Girl* readers. Even when also middle-class, readers saw titles they did not read as representing another kind of girl (usually 'posher' than themselves). Readers tended to see what they characterized as 'their' comic as offering aspirational images that were meaningful, whilst titles seen as belonging to others represented the unobtainable or the undesirable. Models of girlhood and notions of class were often indistinguishable in readers' accounts as well as being apparently synonymous in many of the comics, showing that these discourses overlapped both in memory and within the texts.

Reading specific comics or narratives within comics sometimes cut across the boundaries of generation and perceptions of class, however, usually because of the institutional practices that meant that stories were repeated. Specific narratives became unbound from and rebound to different readers, who, despite being from disparate generations and backgrounds may, therefore, share experiences of comics. For instance, 'Bessie Bunter', initially located in *School Friend* in the early 1960s, was produced for a predominantly middle-class audience, but ended up in *Tammy* in the early 1980s, which had a much wider readership. That 'Bessie Bunter' combined humour with boarding school story meant that it had more chance of translating successfully from one generation to another than other stories that did not contain those elements. In addition, readers had sometimes read comics as both children and adults, so experiencing considerable continuity in their reading, or had subsequently revisited comics with their own children. There were also continuities in the ways that readers rejecting girls' comics, whether in favour of the *Eagle* or of *Batman*, reported their response to girls' comics. As I have mentioned, the term 'wet', even for readers of the 1980s, was a common one. These continuities, as well as breaks, in comic reading, complicate attempts to map girls' (and women's) relationships with comics.

Although what specific comics meant changed over a period of years, the pleasures of girls' comics were fairly consistent. The main attraction was that they did, after all, address girls specifically and offered narratives about girls. Comics for girls offered a mixture untypical of other media in allowing adventure as well as feminine glamour (often combining them in figures like the ballerina). Characters could be static and visually pleasing, but also involved in modified hero narratives where the motivation for action was personal rather than abstract. Actual girl readers clearly did respond to these images, with variables being class, era and age. There was considerable devotion to some characters, for instance 'Valda' (who appeared from 1969-1982 in *Mandy*) which showed the importance to readers of these active yet feminine figures. The kinds of activity heroines engaged in were much commented upon, often reflecting the growing accessibility of various sports to working-class readers. For instance, swimming, dance (especially disco) and gymnastics were important to the narratives of the 1970s. As with ballet in the 1950s, these images of girls were aspirational in allowing readers to explore fictional older or otherwise alternative selves. As I have suggested, there was considerable playing out of group narratives (such as 'The Silent Three') amongst friends. This play also amounts to a performance of girlhood, emphasizing that it is a construction, and that readers inhabited it only with difficulty and with practice.

Other activities related to these comics had similarly aspirational functions, as shown, for example, in one reader's report of becoming a fashion designer having been inspired by cutting out *Bunty*'s paper dolls. Emotional exploration was also possible, through both stories of friendship like 'The Four Marys' in *Bunty* and also narratives of suffering, through the isolated heroine. Readers described sharing the emotional states of the characters, finding similar tensions and pleasures in their own lives. All respondents reported, as girls, having used the comic in a negotiation of self and other, and the comic and self-image were connected through the interplay of many identities.

The girls' comics featured communities of girls in only a few of the narratives, although these stories tended to feature out of proportion to their number in readers' accounts of their memories of girls' comics, suggesting their popularity. These stories and girls' comics in general seemed to have fulfilled the function for readers of consolidating a notion of girlhood as community. Whilst stories tended to emphasize the girl alone, shared reading and swapping meant that girl readers were not usually isolated. Further, readers' pages, whether focusing on problems or about looking for pen-pals, also emphasized collective girlhood. For most girl comic readers the production of meaning was social, shared amongst friends. As Jenkins says, 'for most fans meaning-production is not a solitary and private process but rather a social and public one' (Jenkins, 1992, p.75). In effect, whilst not characterizing themselves as fans of particular comics or of girls' comics in general, the groups that readers were part of, and their sense of belonging, were very typical of fan activity. As fissures around titles with regard to class and generation suggest, however, this was not a holistic girlhood of sameness, but one that did offer readers a peer group. The pleasures of belonging were also joined by pleasures in ownership, in addition to readers enjoying specific narratives or characters.

The comics also contained, according to readers, 'clues', or perhaps cues, as to how to understand or behave. Romance in particular, especially in the 1950s and 1960s, was identified as something that comics offered 'clues' about. Whilst readers were often very positive about what their comics offered them, such comments both emphasize the comics' potential role as training texts and reinforce Walkerdine's argument that femininity is not 'natural' (1984). This notion of comics as training texts encouraging the performance of girlhood could be seen as supported by the way that readers' accounts sometimes offered full reading histories, which described reading as a process of progression from one title to another. Readers discussed moving through a sequence of comics, in which each title had a symbolic importance to peer group or family as an indicator of age or maturity on a path to adulthood. Moving to the next title was an important 'transformative moment', to borrow Stacey's (1994) term, and a personal marker. The comic as marker could also be seen as indicative of an increasing mastery over oneself.

However, as Rose describes it, such markers may actually be about adult control of the child, '...securing the child's rationality, its control of sexuality or of language (or both)' (Rose, 1992, p.10). The child's mastery of the self and the world, Rose argues, is secured through fiction written by adults. I would argue that Rose's argument could be extended to include comics. In this reading, the role of the child is secondary to that of the adult as, inherently; all fiction for children is a projection of adults' concerns about children. Fiction reveals, Rose asserts, that adult concerns are about controlling children, but also about developing the child's self-discipline as part of that control, as well as revealing concerns on the part of the adult about their mastery over their inner child. Thus, fiction for girls, in contributing to the construction of an identity as 'girl' could be seen as being about containing and controlling actual girls. Children's fiction can be seen as part of this control, in that, as Rose argues, 'there is no child behind the category children's fiction, other than the one which the category itself sets in place, the one which it needs to believe is there for its own purposes' (Rose, 1992, p.10). She identifies fiction as part of a barrier between adult and child, defining the child and thus establishing parameters for adult behaviour and part of what adults' demand of the child.

Given such a reading it may seem paradoxical to suggest that readers could see girls' comics as positive. Yet in readers' memories of comics they characterized the contents of these comics as having offered them freedom, at least from adult and male control, through construction of an identity as a girl, i.e. not adult and not woman. In this, as I have suggested, they may create a private 'girl' time and space. Reading girls' comics could be characterized as being about resisting (as well as marking) becoming older and becoming women. There was, in addition, a sense in which reading even girls' comics was seen as a rebellion against 'proper' girlhood, stimulated, I would argue, by the connotations of maleness and working-class-ness associated with the comic form. Adult gatekeepers' lack of approval meant that comics were not commonly used as rewards or as cross-generational bonding. Being forbidden comics, or specific titles, gave the whole medium connotations of rebellion in relation to parents or school, making the comic more attractive to readers. Parental control of reading was a central part of many accounts of comic reading and therefore important to how readers used them. As David Buckingham outlines, young peoples' relationship with various media is heavily determined by its regulation by adults such as parents and teachers, and by the more distant control of the state. However successful young people may be in their struggle to avoid this kind of regulation, the meanings and pleasures they derive from the media are bound to be at least partly defined by it (Buckingham, 1993, p.15).

Further, Rose, in relation to children's fiction, describes 'how these different forms of writing, in their long and continuing association with childhood, have been thought about for children' (Rose, 1992, p.9). This statement points out the differences between adults' and girls' understandings of the girls' comics. What is also clear is that using the comic as marker and rebellion involved the reader in oscillating between two opposing views about the comic. The tension between rebellion and conformity was clear in some of the interviews, reflecting the '[opposed] conceptions of childhood that circulate within popular discourse' (Jenkins, 1992, p.35). Here the reading process engages the reader in an act of negotiation, whilst still offering pleasure, as Gledhill (1988) suggests. The pleasures of these comics were, then, often contradictory in that they attracted disapproval but could also be part of being a 'good' girl.

Readers who remembered rejecting girls' comics often claimed that they had done so on the basis that they saw girls' comics as tools used by adults and peers to coerce them into conforming to behaviour and attitudes considered 'appropriate', rather than offering them a pleasurable reading experience. As these readers reported, continuing to read *Bunty* when peers moved to *Jackie*, or reading comics for boys, could be seen by peers (as well as adults) as 'suspicious' and result in that reader being policed. As I note, the use of comics as markers of a passage, a 'progression', through girlhood was not necessarily a wholly positive one. Such a movement past a number of markers was seen by these readers as less about personal change, and instead more directive, moving them along the lines of proper girlhood and femininity. These readers regarded girls' comics as representing compulsory femininity and heterosexuality.

The connotations of the comic format, for readers who rejected them, could not outweigh the connotations of the labelling of these comics as 'for girls'. For example, in the Hulton group in the 1950s, all readers were expected to move from *Robin* and *Swift* to either *Eagle* or *Girl*. Most of the Hulton titles are bird names so the sudden branching off of a gender-divided title, the very existence of *Girl,* in fact, suggests that girls are set apart and have a separate identity and subject matter appropriate to that identity. In this reading such titles do construct a myth of girlhood in which girls are turned into manageable images and stories that are then offered back to the actual readers. Girlhood can perhaps be seen in these texts as detached from the lived experience of readers, as 'myth' in the sense intended by Roland Barthes, that which transforms 'history into Nature' (1972, p.129). If one assumes that the girls' comic was the limit of girls' reading, then the comic's role as reinforcement is an important one.

The conflation of comic and gender role may have led some female readers to reject girls' comics, understanding their rejection as one of both text and models of girlhood. In making this analysis, readers were very much in line with the feminist analysis of girls' comics. For readers rejecting the girls' comic, rebellion was the key term used to typify their reading choices. These readers saw themselves, in reading 'otherwise', as overtly oppositional, rebelling against the models of girlhood and femininity they perceived in school, peer and family groups. One could characterize their intention as to use reading as a site of resistance, to be subversive.

For those rejecting the girls' comic, identity was formed around being 'not-girl', an attempted escape from gender assumptions. Whilst those who swapped comics negotiated middle-class-ness and other issues through inhabiting different spaces temporarily, this other, smaller group refused it altogether. Those who reject the girls' comic break with the group who swap comics, something that is reflected in the way that sections in Chapter 5 address a very different set of texts and use rather different terms of reference, including the language of fandom. There was often a similar response to class as expressed in girls' comics. American comics, whilst having connotations of class in a British context through their format, were not, in their narratives, seen as bound up with class structures.

'Other' comics, particularly American superhero titles, were remembered as appealing to readers because they offered 'exotic' and adult worlds. These comics also offered images of men and women in largely professional rather than romantic relationships. The geographical distance of America (along with the age of the protagonists) meant that these comics came to represent a 'symbolic spatial location' (Stacey, 1994, p. 234) to these female readers as girls. In this space, they could move beyond what they perceived as the limits of British girlhood. Whilst the distinct national identity of British comics was seen by many commentators on the comic (until the 1970s at least) as a bastion against American culture, American comics facilitated these readers' rejection of what they saw as British middle-class values. Readers did, however, sometimes remember that they read against the grain of these comics and despite their affection for these titles acknowledged their limits.

Reading comics for boys was perceived by these readers as adults and as girls (and often, they reported, by their peers and families) as transgressive of the norms of girlhood. There was a blurring of gender boundaries involved in reading otherwise, but readers were also caught in a bind in that what were alternative comics (in the context of the British girls' comic) were also characterized as problematic. In particular, those comics containing images of superheroines gained critical attention, as we have seen, from both feminist and anti-feminist commentators. In addition, it is possible to see reading comics aimed at a male audience in another, more critical, light. Girls who chose such comics privileged male reading and thus participated in dismissing female reading and readers. Therefore, this group of readers was often marginalized with regard to both comics' culture and feminism. These readers remembered establishing what they felt was a different kind of girl identity, but also felt themselves to be isolated from other girls as a result.

One can conclude that these readers of other comics perform a non-feminine identity, one that is also difficult to inhabit. Whilst some readers preferred comics for girls and others rejected them, the majority of readers reported having read both mixed gender and boys' comics alongside girls' comics. This was, however, not as a result of purchasing these 'other' comics - which was usually a flash point with parents, as the readers who rejected the girls' comic and bought boys' comics confirmed - but through swapping. Exchange was an important aspect of both girls' and boys' comic usage. Swapping comics was largely clandestine and so did not draw attention to participants' cross-gender reading. There are a number of ways to interpret this practice. One could, for instance, speculate that swapping comics would make the readers aware that the subject matter, presentation and assumptions about girlhood and boyhood in these comics were very different. Indeed, it is possible that swapping made children more aware of gender roles and aware that other kinds of narrative were deemed unsuitable for them on the basis of gender. Thus swapping might reinforce rather than break down gender roles.

However, other ways of understanding swapping undermine any notion of comics as reinforcing gender roles. Being restricted to girls' comics was often seen in readers' accounts as adults limiting the girl. As the reports of girls rejecting the girls' comic suggest, the girl had to agree to accept the comic as marker. Sean Griffin argues that '[a] child's ability to use objects created by the dominant hegemonic system in defiance of adult standards acts as a point of 'negotiation' or even 'resistance'...' (in Kinder, 1999, p.104). In this reading, swapping on a huge scale represents a resistance to gendered reading material. Even those readers who characterized their reading as a progression from *Twinkle* to *Bunty* to *Jackie* said that they had participated in swapping, not only with female friends for other comics for girls but also with boys (although male reading of girls' comics is little spoken of).

Further, readers who swapped comics, and especially those that rejected girls' comics, could be seen as insisting on complicating the gender boundaries that impinged on them. Readers' use of titles aimed at male, female and mixed audiences suggests a range of models of girlhood, childhood and boyhood that change over time, and with the age of the child, with readers oscillating between models, resisting fixed identity. As Griffin asks, with regard to the 'Davy Crockett' craze in America in the 1950s, given his argument that the gender roles of that era were strictly demarcated, '...what were girls doing wearing coonskin caps and holding rifles?' (in Kinder, 1999, p.115). He goes on to say that despite marketing aimed at girls which promoted 'Polly Crockett' dolls and outfits, most women he interviewed remembered having the same hat as the boys, nor did they recall playing a female role (in Kinder, 1999, p.116). There may be adult-generated preferred uses of media texts, but there is also child resistance. I would argue that in each generation of girl comic readers, some, in effect, choose to wear coonskin caps, resisting the materials offered to them. The existence of a readership that persisted in rejecting the girls' comic and magazine could act in a symbolically meaningful way for both girl and woman readers, giving them a further stake in the comic format.

In yet another reading, the practice of swapping could be seen as part of girls' activity as 'textual poachers'. The 'scriptural economy', as Jenkins says, may be dominated by textual producers (and institutionally sanctioned interpreters) working to restrain the 'multiple voices of popular orality, to regulate the production and circulation of meanings' (Jenkins, 1992, p.24). However, the girl reader, in this reading of girls' use of comics of all kinds, produces popular meanings, like that of the fan of any age 'outside of official interpretive practice' (Jenkins, 1992, p.26), whether educational, adult or feminist. Reading practices and the use of reading as exploring and understanding identity can be seen as actively fragmenting and reassembling materials according to the readers' blueprint. Such activities can be seen as positive articulations of identity despite the fact that 'like the poachers of old, fans operate from a position of cultural marginality and social weakness' (Jenkins, 1992, p.24). Although this would apply still further to children, particularly given their economic dependence, Jenkins argues that this does not mean that one passively accepts ideological messages (Jenkins, 1992, p.27). Instead, children as fans may use, reuse and rewrite comics for their own purposes.

Whilst I am wary of characterizing girl readers as utterly free textual poachers, neither can I see them as dupes. Readers' accounts of their memories of comics offer a range of reading practices and responses to girls' comics in particular (but also comics in general) that can be understood in a number of ways and so resist simple categorization. Readers' accounts show that the British girls' comic was used by most as a representation of a kind of British girlhood, no matter how contradictory the texts were, but their responses to them emphasize diversity rather than conformity. The range of responses and changes in titles combine to confirm that, as Rose argues, 'there is no children's book market which does not, on closer scrutiny, crumble under just such a set of divisions-of class, culture and literacy-divisions which undermine any generalized concept of the child' (Rose, 1992, p.7). I have tried to show how appropriate this is in relation to notions of the girls' comic and girlhood and of reading in this medium in general.

Whilst girls' comics can be seen as enforcing a feminine career, to see them only in this light misses out on how the comics themselves changed and how some readers' rejected girls' comics or found alternative titles. Overall, it is possible to see the eventual failure of the girls' comic as more of a confirmation of the feminine career in focusing female readers on the more effectively consumerist model of the magazine.

So how did readers remember comics? From the start of this monograph, I have emphasized that my concern is with understanding women's experiences of reading comics, their memories of the form. In exploring comics and readers in this way, I see a parallel with research done in relation to other media and memory. For instance, writing specifically of popular film, Kuhn argues that,

> memory work presents new possibilities for enhancing our understanding not only of how films work as texts, but also of how we use films and other representations to make our selves, of how we construct our own history through memory, even of how we position ourselves within wider, more public histories. (Kuhn, 1992, p.243)

Comics, as a major medium in Britain during the twentieth century (albeit a problematic one) can also be understood as part of that construction of personal history and positioning within public ones. Such an approach could be seen as a necessary balance to statistical work on audiences, ensuring, as Jackie Stacey states (also in relation to popular film), that the history of audiences does 'not...remain at the purely quantitative level' (1994, p.63).

Theoretically, as I discuss in Chapter 1, memory and experience have been seen as problematic within the academy in the past. In working with memory I am aware of the questions that emerged around the legitimacy of oral history, about the reliability of memory and about how representative an account can be of a community or era, given how we select and construct memory. As Stacey states, 'memory is not a straightforward representation of past events to which we have direct access and which we can in turn retell to others' (1994, p.63). Like Stacey and Kuhn, however, I feel that readers' responses offer an entirely different way of understanding the texts which complements and at times, undermines other readings (Kuhn, 1992, p.236). In addition, as Stacey argues, highlighting the production of memories means recognizing that the 'real' past cannot exist 'separately from our retelling of it' (1994, p.70).

Further, this monograph brings together academic writing on comics with readers' understandings of the medium. In juxtaposing these differing versions of the history and readership of comics I draw together what Kuhn says could be seen as entirely different registers, balancing 'memory/feeling...against explanation/analysis' (Kuhn, 1992, p.237). Consequently, I have concluded that, as Tony Bennett wrote, 'the text that the critic has on the desk before her or him may not be the same as the text that is culturally active in the relations of popular reading' (Bennett, 1983, p.225). What Kuhn suggests is that using both broadens our understanding of both the subject chosen and the academy. In addition, in also drawing on accounts by other adult mediators of the form I contrast the official cultural image of comics with readers' views. I also suggest that academic accounts, too, are caught up in, are products of, and in turn influence, their cultural moment. The comparison of all these various discourses about the comic suggests that we must constantly ask questions about all the many approaches that have been used to understand these publications.

This monograph is, then, a readers' history of comics that I nonetheless see as only a partial picture of memories of comic reading amongst British girls throughout the 1950s to 1980s. Even given that it can offer only a partial picture, it nonetheless has to account for significant variations amongst readers as to the role and importance of comics in their lives. These variations have to be seen, in part, in the light of work on memory. As Stacey (1994) describes:

> What gets remembered and what gets forgotten may depend …[not only on the text] …but also upon the identity of the [reader]. … The ways in which their lives had changed, and the feelings they had about their past, present and future selves, will have been amongst the factors determining the memories produced for the purposes of this research. (p.70)

Whilst one might have assumed that the memories of comics would be uniformly straightforward, interviews and letters from readers offer a rather different picture. As in the case of Frazer, I too have found that 'readers take a critical stand vis-a-vis texts' (Frazer, 1987, p.407), both in their remembered girlhood relationship with comics and in the self-conscious analysis of memory.

Each reader places comics in different ways in their autobiography, reflecting both what they brought to that text when it was first encountered, as well as what the reader has since learnt. In some cases, memories of comics constituted what Stacey calls 'treasured memories'. It may be, as Stacey (1994) argues, that such memories of the role of the text in relation to a younger self might work as 'personal utopias', offering escape from everyday life (p.64), but I found little to suggest this. She (1994) argues that such memories are 'particularly significant in conserving a past self and thereby guarding against the experience of loss. 'Treasured memories' may thus signify past selves or imagined selves of importance retrospectively' (p.64). She sees this

investment in certain memories as based around 'transformative moments', which in this case would link transitions from comic to comic and beyond to the passage through girlhood and self-transformation.

Stacey's notion of memory as 'treasure' fails, however, to account for the appearance of memories that could be characterized as 'trauma'. Memories about the rejection of the girls' comic, or of unhappiness in relation to reading, or even of reading as a consolation in the light of other problems, may also be similar moments of transition, of personal transformation. Such moments, whilst certainly invested in, were not described as treasured in any way. Thus, the unhappy, but nonetheless important, memory may fulfill the same function as those that are treasured.

As discussed in this monograph, women's memories of comics revealed that readers had intense and complex relationships with both childhood reading and child selves. Memory is not, as Stacey confirms, straightforward, involving, as it does, '[a] set of complex cultural processes: these operate at a psychic and social level, producing identities through the negotiation of 'public' discourses and 'private' narratives' (1994, p.63). Reading was a focus for issues around femininity, the self, and, in many cases, feminism. In discussing them, the readers, as Kuhn (1995) describes, created their own 'memory- stories' which are now circulated here as 'memory texts', 'secondary revisions of the source materials of memory' (Kuhn, 1995, p.4).

However, there were several notions that had a noticeable impact upon the vast majority of female readers' memories of comics. These were centered on the gender and age group that comics were appropriate for and the comic as 'problem'. In relation to the former, I began this monograph by asserting that comics have often been seen, in Britain and America at least, as an immature medium for immature people. Such a perspective could be seen to reflect what John Springhall (1998), in his account of moral panics, argues in relation to Bourdieu's ideas about taste. Springhall asserts that notions of taste '...might also be applied to age relations, exploring how certain denigrated forms of amusement come to be associated with a prepubescent age group...while other tastes, values and hierarchies are established as culturally adult' (1998, p.139). This assertion about adult and child tastes can be seen as cross cut by gender in relation to comics.

In Britain, the way that comics have been consistently viewed as problematic has meant that they have attracted official and parental disapproval. In particular, comics were often seen as a medium that may undermine the young, in terms of either literacy or morality, resulting in a policing of readers and an insistence that the comic strip should address only 'suitable' topics for children in gendered ways. Lynn Spiegel has described television in a similar way, arguing that it too has 'been seen as a threatening force that circulates forbidden secrets to children...[and that as a result] adult culture has continually tried to filter the knowledge that mass media transmit to the young' (Spiegel, 1993, p.265). As Amy Kiste Nyberg says of the American experience, 'adults' concern stemmed in large part from fears that children's culture, especially the control of leisure reading, had escaped traditional authority' (1998, p.viii). Fears about 'media effects' run through historical accounts of the comic. Comics makers have variously been seen as creating addictive 'rot' or 'glamorous' (and therefore dangerous) worlds, and sometimes both, as Hoggart's thoughts on comics indicate.

As I have shown, this image of the comic as 'problem' has persisted despite the flexibility of the medium, which can address almost any topic and all age groups. The image of the comic as 'problem', readers' accounts suggest, had a significant impact upon the relationship of female readers with comics and so is a useful framework.

In addition to these three notions, a common thread in discussing comics seemed to be a belated recognition, by the adults interviewed, of their childhood sophistication in understanding texts of all sorts. Reflecting on memories of comics sometimes led to a reassessment of perspectives on childhood. In this, the readers' memories mirror what Kuhn describes in relation to her memories of the film *Mandy*. She argues that 'the analytical material of this case history is less a child's response to a film than a child's response admitted to adult memory: for the child's reading returns only in the adult's interpretation' (Kuhn, 1992, p.243). What Kuhn emphasizes is how history is an interpretation, a temporary answer to any given question, and not a final one, given that interpretations of memory by both the individual reader and by the critical writer are never neutral or descriptive, but always selective and constructed. Interviews show signs of re-writing, inevitably, although my comparisons of accounts produced during the 1950s to the 1980s and readers' recollections as adults do occupy very similar ground.

I do not want to stop discussion and argument by insisting on personal truth, but to illustrate that memory work adds a set of productive complications to our understandings of comics. One complication was about how readers remembered time and date. In terms of memories, readers in the post-war period used their personal journey through school, or the type of school they attended, as markers along with the titles of comics. Identifying oneself as being at a specific stage of girlhood was also important. For example, being recognized by adults and peers as a teenager (at whatever age that that transition was seen as occurring) was often more noteworthy for readers than any sense of specific date. Finally, the comics themselves, in frequently being published for ten years or less, acted as readers' shorthand for a specific period, hence my inclusion of a comic checklist, and the inclusion of publication dates in the main text when a comic is first mentioned.

The most important complication is that within readers' accounts I found evidence of two major ways of thinking about comics in general, and about girls' comics in particular, one official and applied in their professional lives, another personal and about their childhood. The former was influenced by the notions I outline above about the gender and age of readers and the perception of the comic as 'problem'. As adults, readers tended to articulate the former, dominant position on comics. Personal memories were buried beneath official understandings of the form as problematic. Thus the former was uniformly disapproving, whilst the latter encompassed a range of responses to girls' and other comics and varied from enthusiasm to hatred.

This multiple understanding of the comic could be interpreted as negotiation, once more returning to Gledhill's (1988) understanding of how readers deal with contradictory imperatives. Yet, Gledhill, in using the term negotiation, implies an active and conscious process. Kuhn (1995), in contrast, is more open to notions of internal negotiation. Whilst discussing memories of comics seemed to trigger such negotiation, it often seemed as if the two views of the medium had not been previously juxtaposed by readers. It may be that these two views were seen by readers as belonging to separate stages in life, adulthood and childhood, and thus were not seen as contradictory or overlapping. Alternatively, one can conclude that these processes of negotiation are not a matter of conscious balancing, but rather of internal and unconscious rebalancing of fragments of our identity. In exploring memories of comics, it becomes clear that readers were, as it were, in several minds about the medium, seeing it as a form to be both embraced and rejected.

They were also in several minds about the models of girlhood that they saw girls' comics as offering or representing. Even though, as I describe, the actual content undermined coherent notions of girlhood in many of the comics for girls, to many readers the comics carried connotations of a proper girlhood that they had to negotiate. Readers seemed to see the texts as indicating what they should become, but they were not just sponges. Rather, they performed a great deal of work in interacting with, giving into, opposing and resisting the possibilities that these texts offered for creating meaning. However, readers might also ignore their own experience in the face of the view of girlhood put forward in the texts, which, as I have argued, shifted across generations. In addition, the differing connotations of form and content further complicated girls' relationship with comics. These various splits offer us a way of understanding how for instance, conformity and rebellion could be centered on the same comics and, in turn, how those comics had an impact upon girls' identity. Thus, some reading was intended to be resistant, but this was not always the case, showing that the notion of 'resistance' is often an oversimplified one.

In adult memory, girls' comics were recalled as vitally important to the child self, but this was overlain by what could often be characterized as the adult self's mild embarrassment at having felt such powerful emotions about 'trivia'. Yet many readers acknowledged the importance of comics through the way that they had kept one or two 'special' comics (often those in which they had featured as prize-winners) well into adulthood. In effect, past and present selves intertwined. Comics also functioned as reminders of past selves, and were tied in with a much wider network of personal associations (acting as triggers), although there was enough overlapping between accounts to suggest some common strands. These overlaps were primarily about tensions around girlhood, class, gender and comics.

Requests for memories of comics possibly allowed the recreation of a past self 'and its relationship to past ideals of femininity' (Stacey, 1994, p.227), as Stacey says is the case with memories of film texts. Stacey argues that '[m]emory constructs the past as a selection of 'treasured' moments which may have become 'fixed' or 'frozen' with the passage of time. Such a fixing may be the result of their repeated recirculation or indeed of the attempt to preserve them' (1994, p.227). Comics acted as physical reminders of key moments in girlhood and helped to locate them in time and in socio-historical context.

Yet whilst Stacey focuses on nostalgic desire for the past self, what interviews about comics revealed ranged much more widely than that, with many reporting memories bound up with tensions, trauma and often anger. Although readers felt comparatively 'safe' talking about comic reading, interviews were often revealing, particularly of tensions around education and class. One aspect of this very different kind of memory was concerned with peer pressure. Myra Macdonald, in exploring the various approaches used by different disciplines in defining and redefining femininity, at one point describes the work of the psychologist Lawrence Kohlberg in the 1970s and his identification of girls' recognition of social pressures from both adults and peers. In addition, girls were also aware of how those pressures operate (Macdonald, 1995, p.18). Comics, as readers' accounts confirm, could form part of that pressure, as well as enabling the reader to find ways of coping with it. So, whilst nostalgia played a part in accounts, readers, in the responses to comics they describe, also recognized the roles that various texts played in their relationships with friends and authority.

Comics were part of memory, for most of these readers, rather than part of an active, current collecting of girls' comics. Lack of female collecting could be seen to suggest that these comics were unimportant, but they were important in memory. However, girls' comics were frequently remembered as a 'phase one goes through', a culture that one was part of as a child, but moves on from as an adult. The difference between that and the collecting culture around boyhood texts that currently exists for men reflects gender differences in adult consumption patterns. In an interview, a female collectibles dealer said that women were reluctant to buy things they liked if those things were just for themselves, but male purchasers had no such qualms. Women, she argued, seemed to characterize such spending as selfish, and so could not revert to, or indulge, a childhood self so easily. Thus, the lack of collecting by women is suggestive of differences in relationships with economic power and notions of gender and responsibility.

However, the gender differences in adult consumption patterns between male and female readers seem to break down when confronted by those few female comic fans, who do purchase for their own pleasure. The girls who read 'other' comics often became adult comic collectors, participating in a more 'male' form of ownership and exhibiting similar continuity in reading. Comparing both lists of titles and when certain titles were read was a way of building a shared picture of comic reading with the interviewer. Yet, these readers too, in consistently and consciously attempting to reject models of femininity, remain in negotiation with notions of economic power, gender and responsibility. In enjoying these 'other' comics one could, readers felt, escape from the limits of the 'Britishness' of British comics, associated by readers with what were seen as restrictive discourses of class, gender and age. For some, these comics were a clear statement about being part of a subculture, rather than a national culture: either comic fandom, or, for instance, 'goth' culture, where some comics have had an impact. However, as I suggest, whilst these readers were attempting in some ways to 'escape' femininity, it nonetheless had a huge impact on them in that they were predominantly seen by male fans as swooning over characters rather than being 'serious' about comics. Reading 'otherwise' demanded that female readers prove themselves as 'real' (i.e. male heterosexual) fans. Thus, where gender differences did not negate female collecting of comics entirely there was still an insistence that women consume comics differently.

Gender differences in adult consumption patterns may also reflect differing gender relationships with past selves. As I have indicated, many women who had read comics- and particularly those who had read girls' comics- reported that their interviews or letters were the first time for many years that they had thought consciously about their comic reading. Yet once they began to think about comics they recalled both the importance of these texts and the passion they had generated. In rarely focusing on this childhood relationship with a medium seen as problematic, and often related to resistance or conformity to feminine norms, the readers could be seen as writing out problematic aspects of their girlhood, in effect 'burying' certain aspects of their child selves, particularly those relating to rebellion or aspiration.

For some readers this 'burial' of a problematic child self in memory was preceded by a literal discarding of their comics at the 'end' of childhood. As I showed this moment of destruction was often not chosen, but performed by a parent as a statement that the child had grown up. This too conforms to the idea of the girls' comic as a training text, in which the last aspect of the training was letting go of both girlhood and the texts and practices relating to it. Whilst this destruction was, as I also note, something that happened to male readers as well, there is a significant difference in that male readers often return to comics, whilst female readers typically do not. Women readers rarely replace lost childhood collections in adulthood. Doing so would, in a sense, mean returning to a childhood self that was lost along with the collection. For male readers, then, there was a sense of continuity with their childhood selves, but the majority of women were not similarly at ease, implying a break, or fracture, in a sense of self.

The fractured sense of self in feminine subjects revealed by both gendered collecting patterns and memories of girlhood and comics, suggests that femininity is a difficult position to inhabit. Readers' memories do not suggest a simple opposition between pleasure and regulation within girlhood, but instead a fragmentary self and, therefore, complex negotiations around girlhood and femininity. There can be no grounding in a firm sense of femininity because it dissolves across any number of boundaries and is refracted (or manifests itself) through other divisions such as age and class.

In conclusion, adult memories of comics allowed readers to show their awareness of the position of inequality they had held as girls and were also a focus for readers in connection with their relationships with peers, parents and other adults in authority. However, whilst this is a charged medium for girl readers for many reasons, as we have seen, how one matched up to the image of girlhood which comics were seen as offering was a particular concern. Rejecting or accepting the girls' comic in particular was, during the 1950s to the 1980s, an important aspect of locating oneself in relation to the models of girlhood and femininity of a specific era. The vast majority of women with whom I discussed comic reading, no matter what they read, positioned themselves primarily in relation to the girls' comic. Thus, the most important aspect of readers' accounts of comics (of all kinds) was the way that these texts were a focus of tension and exploration around identity. Seeing these texts in such a light emphasizes Stacey's comment about identity, that '...be it gender, sexuality...[identity] should be seen as partial, provisional and constantly "in process"', but also reinforces her assertion that 'identities are fixed by particular discourses, however unsuccessfully, temporarily or contradictorily' (1994, p. 226, my emphasis). In recognizing these tensions around the comic, readers problematized their girlhood identities, something seen by Stacey as an 'important political and theoretical move' (1994, p.226). Whether seen as reinforcing, or potentially being used to undermine, femininity, comics were recognized by readers as part of the construction of their identity as girls and so, like magazines, comics (even when not aimed at girls) are sites of intense reworking of female identity.

Appendix 1

A Note on Interviews with Children in Accounts of Reading in the 1960s

The differences between retrospective accounts by readers and those accounts collected contemporaneously give a sense of the way that memory might be re-written. Although these are necessarily different interviewees, there were some common observations made in the contemporary accounts which had no equivalent in the research I conducted. For instance, Pumphrey despairs of understanding the appeal comics have for readers because in the questionnaires 'When they 'liked' a comic it was because they 'liked' it or because it was 'funny'' (1964, p.7). The adult accounts I received, although more distant from the reading experience, were usually clearer about a comic's appeal, reflecting the critical vocabulary of an adult.

In reporting that children cannot explain the charm of their comics, Pumphrey fails to recognize the critical perceptions displayed in outlining the limits of comics. One nine year old, for instance, demanding more exciting stories in girls' comics, commented 'I think that *Princess* is not very interesting. The story about Sue is not very good she never gets kidnapped or never anything good happens' (Pumphrey, 1964, p.20). Pumphrey sees this as revealing her fears rather than indicating her critical judgement, implying that the texts she reads have frightened her. He adds that girls resented what they saw as 'boys' stories' in titles like *The Beezer*, and wanted more action in all of the comics they read. This leads me to conclude that the female reader was aware of bias in some of the titles aimed at a mixed audience, but in demanding that titles for girls be more like those for boys, they also reveal their familiarity with both sets of texts. This tiny snapshot shows a female readership driven by a desire to see more adventure stories. It also suggests that children were capable of being critical about comics. This in turn implies that comments in my interviews about the limits of these comics are not something that readers simply adopted as adults, but reflect the critical thinking of their child selves.

A significant limitation of Pumphrey's research lies in the main question he asked readers: whether comics could be improved, and, if so, how. This research obviously functions as a call to the producers to change their products rather than as an account of readership. Nonetheless, the comments by readers made in the section concerned with twelve to fifteen year-old girls also suggest a readership that did not accept without question either the stories or the activities offered to them. They complain about the number of adverts and exhibit considerable scepticism about whether the products in those adverts do what the advertisers claim. There is a demand for more stories in strip and text format, including pop star and other biographies, and for less repetition. One thirteen year old said 'Hosts of the stories in girls' comics are about ballet dancers, pony riders or swimmers. I gave up my comic about a month ago because of this boring repetition' (Pumphrey, 1964, p.23). Similar sentiments applied to romance comics.

The emphasis on repetitiveness seen in children's accounts was not usually an issue in memory-based accounts. My reading of the comics showed that they were repetitive, which raises questions about whether one aspect of re-writing autobiography involves 'editing out' such repetition. Where comments about repetition did appear was in relation to the notion of regular reading. A number of respondents reported a sense of pleasurable ritual in reading comics. This ritual is also evident in McRobbie's account of reading practices in the 1980s. Here '[Jackie] punctuates the end of the week and thus creates a feeling of security' (McRobbie, 1991, p.142).

One aspect touched on by Pumphrey's research which did emerge in memory-based accounts, was a moment of realization on the part of readers that they were outgrowing many of their comics and had begun to see them as for a younger audience. This correlates with memories of shifting from one title to another because other titles seemed more grown up.

Alderson (1968) too gives a limited space to the voices of readers, this time in regard to romance titles. Like Pumphrey, she shows considerable puzzlement about their choices and reasoning. However, she does identify at least four aspects that were also clear from my interviews, those being borrowing and swapping, readers' enthusiasm, a sense of community against authority and readers' critical ability. For instance, Alderson notes the enthusiasm of the readers in terms of quantity, as readers might look at up to seven titles a week (1968, p.98) and in terms of their content of stories, fashion and pop. She also recognized their links with other readers, which often involved borrowing what their parents read. She identified the reader's ability to analyze the texts and their acceptance that the romance stories are 'dream-worlds' (Alderson, 1968, p.98). Readers also identified reading comics and magazines as resistant: 'The books they make us read are like fairy stories...They confiscate our magazines if we read them in the classroom. They want us to read old-fashioned books' (Alderson, 1968, p.100, her emphasis).

However, Alderson largely addresses texts (seen as limiting), not readers. As with Pumphrey, much of what she says about comics contrasts sharply with what is revealed by her interviews with actual readers. Alderson flags up a number of practices that emerged in my interviews: reading as resistance, swapping, and being critical of the texts. Nonetheless, the readers seem to be more critical in their analysis and more constructive in their use of the text than the writer acknowledges.

Without this critical material from the 1960s, the reader's analysis of, and distance from, the comics might be identified as something that occurred only in adulthood. These commentaries suggest that what readers remember might actually correlate more closely to what happened at the time than might be anticipated. As such, what Pumphrey and Alderson say proved useful tools in testing and supporting conclusions drawn from memories of comics.

Appendix 2

Comics and Magazines Checklist

Throughout this book a range of British comics and magazines are mentioned. This appendix is intended to be a quick guide to what was published when and by whom. The appendix is divided into three sections.

The first is a list of comic titles, publishers and dates of publication, where available. In addition, I include magazines and story papers discussed in the dissertation, which are labelled as such, and the comics for boys and mixed audiences that are mentioned. The magazines and story papers did not, generally, incorporate comic strips.

The second list is of named, authored works mentioned in the dissertation, and the third covers stories.

Comic and Magazine titles

19 (IPC SouthBank) 1968-2004. Magazine.

2000AD (IPC/Fleetway Publications/Egmont Fleetway/Rebellion) 1977-date

Action (IPC) 1976-1977.

Ally Sloper's Half Holiday (WJ Sinkins/The Sloperies) 1884-1914.

Beano, The (DC Thomson) 1938-date.

Beezer, The (DC Thomson) 1956-1990.

Beezer and Topper 1990-1993.

Bimbo (DC Thomson) 1961-1972. Nursery comic. Became *Little Star* 1972-1976.

Blue Jeans (DC Thomson) 1977-1991. Photo-stories and later magazine.

Bobo Bunny (IPC) 1969-1973. Nursery comic.

Bonnie (IPC) 1974-1975. Merged with *Playhour*.

Boyfriend (City Magazines Ltd) 1959-1967. Title change to *Trend & Boyfriend* 1966 and then *Boyfriend & Trend* 1966. Merged with *Petticoat*, a magazine.

Boys' Own Paper (Religious Tract Society) 1879-1967. Story Paper.

Bunty (DC Thomson) 1958-2001.

Bunty Story Picture Library For Girls (DC Thomson) 1963-1997. Monthly.

Buster (Fleetway /IPC) 1960-2000.

Cherie (DC Thomson) 1960-1963. Merged with *Romeo*.

Chips See *Illustrated Chips*.

Classics Illustrated (Elliot Publishing Co. (1941–1942), Gilberton Company, Inc. (1942–1967), Frawley Corporation (Twin Circle), (1967–1971).

Comic Cuts (Amalgamated Press) 1890-1953.

Commando (DC Thomson) 1961-date.

Cosmopolitan (Hearst Corporation) 1965-date. Magazine.

Crisis (Fleetway Publications) 1988-1991.

Dandy, The (DC Thomson) 1937-2013.

Deadline (Deadline Publications Ltd) 1988-1995.

Debbie (DC Thomson) 1973-1983.

Debbie Picture Story Library for Girls (DC Thomson) 1978-1993. Monthly.

Diana (DC Thomson) 1963-1976. Merged with *Judy*.

Dreamer (IPC Magazines Ltd) 1981-1982. Photo-stories.

Eagle (Hulton Press Ltd/ Odhams Press Ltd/Longacre Press) 1950- 1969.

Eagle (IPC) 1982-1994.

Emma (DC Thomson) 1978-79.

Esmeralda (Gresham) 1971-1972. Merged with *Bobo Bunny*

Fab 208 (Fleetway Publications) 1966-1982. Magazine, originally launched in 1964 as *Fabulous*.

Fast Forward (BBC Magazines) 1989-1995. Magazine.

Film Fun (Amalgamated Press/Fleetway Publications) 1920-1962. Merged with *Buster*.

Gem, The (Amalgamated Press) 1907-1939. Story paper.

Girl (Hulton Press Ltd/ Odhams Press Ltd/Longacre Press) 1951-1964. Merged with *Princess*.

Girl (IPC Magazines Ltd) 1981-1990.

Girls' Crystal (Amalgamated Press) 1935-1963. As a comic from number 909 in 1953. Merged with *School Friend*.

Girl's Diary (Famepress) 1964-1966. End date uncertain.

Girls' Friend (Amalgamated Press) 1899-1931. Story paper.

Girls' Home (Amalgamated Press) 1910-1915. Story paper.

Girl's Own Paper (Religious Tract Society) 1880-1956. Story paper merged with *Heiress* 1950-1956.

Girls' Reader (Amalgamated Press) 1908-1915. Story paper.

Girl's Realm (Hutchinson/Bousefield/Cassell) 1898-1915. Story paper.

Honey (Fleetway/IPC) 1960-1986. Magazine.

Horse and Pony (Redan Co/EMAP Active) 1995-2010. Magazine.

Hotspur (DC Thomson) 1933-1981. A story paper until 1959.

Illustrated Chips (Amalgamated Press) 1890-1953.

Jack & Jill 1954-1985. Nursery comic.

Jackie (DC Thomson) 1964-1993.

Jinty (Fleetway) 1974-1981. Merged with *Tammy*.

Judy (DC Thomson) 1960-1991, *M & J* from 1991-1997. Merged with *Mandy*.

Judy Picture Story for Girls (DC Thomson) 1963-1998. Monthly.

June (IPC Magazines Ltd/Fleetway Publications Ltd) 1961-1974. *Poppet* merged into it in 1964, with *School Friend* following the next year and *Pixie* in 1973. Merged with *Tammy*.

June & School Friend Picture Library (Fleetway Publications) 1965-1966. Monthly.

June & SF and Princess Picture Library (Fleetway Publications) 1966-end date unknown. Monthly.

Just 17 (EMAP) 1983-2004. Magazine.

Lady Penelope (City Magazines Ltd) 1966-1969. Title change to *Penelope*. Merged with *Princess Tina*.

Larks (AP) 1927-1940. Merged into *Comic Cuts*.

Lindy (IPC Magazines Ltd) 1975. Merged with *Jinty*.

Look & Learn (Fleetway Publications) 1962-1982.

Lucky Star (Newnes & Pearson) 1935-1957. Magazine.

Magnet, The (Amalgamated Press) 1908-1940. Story paper.

Mandy (DC Thomson) 1967-1991. *M & J* from 1991-1997 when merged with Judy.

Mandy Picture Story Library for Girls (DC Thomson) 1978-1997. Monthly.

Marilyn (Amalgamated Press) 1955-1965. Merged with *Valentine*.

Marty (C. Arthur Pearson) 1960-1963. Merged with *Mirabelle*.

Mates (IPC Magazines Ltd) 1975-1981. Photo strips and later magazine. Merged with *Oh Boy*.

Melanie (IPC Magazines Ltd) 1973-end date unknown.

Mirabelle (C. Arthur Pearson/IPC Magazines Ltd) 1956-1977. *New Glamour* merged into it in 1958, followed by *Marty* in 1963 and *Valentine* in 1974. Became a magazine.

Misty (Fleetway) 1978-1980. Merged with *Tammy*.

Mizz (IPC Magazines Ltd) 1985-date. Magazine.

More (Emap) 1988-2013. Magazine.

My Guy (IPC Magazines Ltd) 1978-1994. Photo-stories and later magazine.

New Glamour (IPC Magazines Ltd) 1956-1959 Merged with *Mirabelle*. Had been a story paper, *Glamour*, which was re-vamped as a comic.

Nikki (DC Thomson) 1985-1988.

Oh Boy (IPC Magazines Ltd) 1976-1985. Photo-stories and later magazine. Merged with *My Guy*.

Over 21 (MS Publishing) 1972- 1988. Magazine.

Patches (DC Thomson) 1979-1989. Photo-stories and later magazine.

Penny (IPC Magazines Ltd) 1979-1980. Merged with *Jinty*.

Peg's Paper (C. Arthur Pearson) 1919-1940.

Photo Love (IPC Magazines Ltd) 1979-1981. Merged with *Oh Boy*.

Photo Romance (IPC Magazines Ltd) 1973.

Photo Secret Love (IPC Magazines Ltd) 1980-1981.

Pink (IPC Magazines Ltd) 1973-1980. Merged with *Mates*.

Pixie (IPC Magazines Ltd) 1972-1973. Merged with *June*.

Playbox (Amalgamated Press) 1925-1955. Merged into *Jack & Jill*.

Poppet (Fleetway) 1963-1964. Merged with *June*.

Princess (Fleetway Publications/IPC Magazines Ltd) 1960-1967. It absorbed *Girl* on 3 October 1964. On 16 September 1967 it merged with *Tina* to become *Princess Tina*.

Princess Picture Library (Fleetway Publications) 1961-1966. Monthly.

Princess Tina (Fleetway Publications/IPC Magazines Ltd) 1967-1973. Merged with *Pink*.

Rainbow (Amalgamated Press) 1914-1956. Nursery comic.

Robin (Hulton Press Ltd/Longacre Press/Odhams Press Ltd/IPC Magazines) 1953-1969. Nursery comic. Merged with *Playhour*.

Romeo (DC Thomson) 1957-1974. Merged with *Diana*.

Roxy (Amalgamated Press/Fleetway) 1958-1963. Merged with *Valentine*.

Sally (IPC Magazines Ltd) 1969-1971. Merged with *Tammy*.

Sandie (Fleetway) 1972-1973. Merged with *Tammy*.

School Friend (Amalgamated Press/Fleetway/IPC) ran from 1919-1929 as a story paper and 1950-1965 as a comic. Merged with *June* to become *June and School Friend*.

School Friend Picture Library (Amalgamated Press) 1962-1965. Monthly.

Schoolgirls' Own (Amalgamated Press) 1921-1936. Story paper. Merged with *The Schoolgirl*.

Schoolgirl's Picture Library (Amalgamated Press) 1957-1965. Merged with *June & School Friend Picture Library*. Monthly.

Schoolgirls' Weekly (Amalgamated Press) 1922-1939. Story paper.

Seven (Gresham/Wells Gardner Darton) 1971. Changed to *Esmeralda*.

Shocking Pink (Shocking Pink Collective) 1982, 1987. Quarterly.

Shout (DC Thomson) 1997-date. Magazine.

Smash Hits (EMAP) 1978-2006. Magazine.

Sonic the Comic (Fleetway Editions/Egmont Magazines) 1993-2002.

Spellbound (DC Thomson) 1976-1977. Merged with *Debbie*.

Sugar (Attic Futura/HFUK/NatMags/Hearst.) 1994-date. Magazine.

Swift (Hulton Press Ltd/Longacre Press/Odhams Press Ltd) 1954-1961. Merged with *Eagle*.

Tammy (Fleetway) 1971-1984. Merged with *Girl*.

Tiger (Amalgamated Press /Fleetway Publications/IPC Magazines Ltd) 1954-1985.

Tina (Fleetway Publications) 1967. Merged with *Princess*. Title change to *Princess Tina*.

Topper, The (DC Thomson) 1953-1990. Merged with *Beezer, The*, 1990-1993.

Tots TV (Redan Co) 1996-end date unknown.

TV21 (City Magazines Ltd) 1965-1971. Began as *TV Century 21*. Merged with *Tornado*, *Joe 90* and *Valiant*.

Tracy (DC Thomson) 1979-1985.

Trend (City Magazines Ltd) Dates unknown.

Twinkle (DC Thomson) 1968-1999.

Valentine (Amalgamated Press) 1957-1974. Merged into it during its run were *TV Fan* in 1960, *Serenade* and *Roxy* in 1963, and *Marilyn* in 1965. Eventually merged into *Mirabelle*

Victor (DC Thomson) 1961-1992.

Viz (Dennis Publishing) 1979-date.

Wizard (DC Thomson) 1922-1978. Story paper until 1970.

Woman (IPC Magazines Ltd) 1937-date. Magazine.

Comics and Graphic novels

Bennett, C. (ed.) (1997) *Women out of Line*. London: Fanny.

Smith, E. (ed.) (1998) *GirlFrenzy Millennial*. Hove: Slab-o-Concrete.

Sweet, L. (1997) *Unskinny*. London: Quartet.

Talbot, B. (1996) *The Tale of One Bad Rat*. London: Titan Books.

Varty, S. (ed.) (1978) *Heroine*. Birmingham: Ar:Zak, Birmingham Arts Lab.

Specific Stories, Series & Characters in Girl's Comics

Gives title, series or character name, followed by comic in which they first appeared and any other details (where known).

'Alona, the Wild One'. *Princess*, (AP), 1964-1967 and *Princess Tina*, (Fleetway/IPC), 1968-1972. By Jean Sidobre.

'Angela, Air Hostess'. *Girl*, (Hulton), 1958-1961. Written by Betty Roland and drawn by Dudley Pout.

'Belle of the Ballet/Belle and Marie'. *Girl*, (Hulton), 1952-64 and *Princess*, (AP), 1964- 67. By George Beardmore, Stanley Houghton, Terry Stanford & John Worsley. Drawn by Harry Lindfield from 1962 onwards.

'Bella at the Bar'. *Tammy*, (IPC), 1974-1984. Art by John Armstrong. Writers included Jenny McDade, John Wagner, Primrose Cumming and Malcolm Shaw. A gymnastics story that ran for nearly the entire life of the comic.

'Beryl the Peril'. *Topper*, (DC Thomson), 1953-1990. Initially by Davey Law (Gifford, 1987, p.21).

'Bessie Bunter'. *School Friend*, (AP). 1919-1929 as a story by Charles Hamilton. In 1963 began as a comic strip by Cecil Orr. Then in *June*, (Fleetway), 1964-1974 and *Tammy*, (IPC), 1974-1981.

'Beth Lawson - Nurse of the Outback'. *Princess*, (AP), 1963.

'Bimbo'. *Bimbo*, (DC Thomson), 1961-1972. By Bob Dewar.

'The Black and White Life of Shirley Grey'. *Tammy*, (IPC). 1981 Art by Diane Gabbot.

'Blind Bettina'. By Benita Brown. Unable to trace.

'The Button Box'. *Tammy*, (IPC), 15 Jan 1983. By Alison Christie & Mario Capaldi.

'Cathy's Friend from Yesterday'. *Mandy*, (DC Thomson), 1972. By Benita Brown.

'Children of Misery'. *Bunty*, (DC Thomson), 832, Dec 22 1973.

'The Comp'. *Nikki*, (DC Thomson), 1985-2000. Next appeared in *Bunty*. By Ron Lumsden.

'Damien Dark'. *Spellbound*, (DC Thomson), 1976-1977. Damian Darke was a regular narrator of weekly spooky stories.

'Doll's Hospital'. In 'Nancy the Little Nurse', *Twinkle*, (DC Thomson), 1968-1999. Drawn by Sabine Price.

'ET Estate'. *Tammy*, (IPC), Jan. 15 1983. Written by Malcolm Shaw.

'The Farleys must be First'. *Bunty*, (DC Thomson), 832, Dec 22 1973.

'The Fat Slags'. *Viz*, (Viz/John Brown) 1989-date. Created by Graham Dury.

'The Four Marys'. *Bunty*, (DC Thomson). 1958-2001. Artists Bill Holroyd, James 'Peem' Walker, Selby Donnison, Jim Eldridge, Barrie Mitchell.

'Gelda from the Glacier' *Bunty*, (DC Thomson).

'Girl Annuals'. *GirlFrenzy Millenial*, Slab-o-Concrete, 1998, p. 20. By Corinne Pearlman.

'Glory Gold' See 'Westward the Wagons'.

'The Growing Up of Emma Peel'. *June and Schoolfriend* (Fleetway) From issue 52, January 29, 1966 and ran for a further eleven instalments, concluding in issue 63, April 16, 1966.

'The Happy Days'. *Princess*, (AP), 1960-1967, *Princess Tina*, (Fleetway/IPC), 1967- 1972, *Pixie*, (IPC), 1972-1973. By Andrew Wilson & Jenny Butterworth.

'Hateful Heather'. *Mandy*, (DC Thomson), 23 June 1984. By Benita Brown, fourteen issues.

'Heartbreak Hospital'. *Shocking Pink*, (SP Collective), Spring 1987, p.4-5.

'Home & Away'. *Bunty Summer Special*, (DC Thomson), 1998.

'Jane Bond: Secret Agent'. *Tina*, (Fleetway), 1967, *Princess Tina*, (Fleetway/IPC), 1967-1970. Drawn by Michael Hubbard.

'Keyhole Kate'. *Dandy*, (DC Thomson), 1937-1955 and *Sparky*, (DC Thomson), 1965- 1974. Drawn by Allan Morley (Gifford, 1987, p.120). Reappeared in *The Dandy* in the late 1980s and early 1990s drawn by Sid Burgon before being dropped and later revived again. The revived strip was drawn by Tom Paterson and Trevor Metcalfe in *The Dandy*, until it was finally dropped in 2007.

'Kitty Hawke and her All-Girl Aircrew'. *Girl*, (Hulton), 1951-1952. By Ray Bailey.

'Lettice Leaf: The Greenest Girl in the School'. *Girl*, (Hulton), 1951-1964, *Princess*, (AP), 1964-1967. By John Ryan.

'Lucky's Living Doll'. *School Friend*, (AP), 1963-1964, and *June*, (Fleetway), 1964- 1974. By Robert McGillivray.

'Man in Black'. *Diana*, (DC Thomson), 1974-end date unknown. A regular narrator of weekly spooky stories. Artist David Cuzik Matysiak

'Marie Curie'. *Girl*, (Hulton), 1959. By Chad Varah & Gerald Haylock.

'Mary Jo'. *Princess*, (AP), 1964-1967. Drawn by Tom Kerr.

'Millie Tant'. *Viz*, (Viz/John Brown), 1989-date. Sabin (1993, p.123) argues that both 'Millie Tant' and 'The Fat Slags' (introduced 1989/1990), were a response to complaints about 'Sid the Sexist' from left-wing and feminist press. By Simon Donald.

'Minnie the Minx'. *Beano, The*, (DC Thomson), 1953-date. Initially by Leo Baxendale, taken over by Jim Petrie in 1961 until 2001. Tom Paterson strips (2001 - 2008). Ken Harrison strips (2008 - 2012). Nigel Parkinson strips (2012 - present).

'Moira Kent'. In 'Dancing Life of Moira Kent' and 'No more dancing for Moira Kent', *Bunty*, (DC Thomson), 1958-1964. Drawn by Ron Smith.

'Moira, Slave Girl of Rome'. *Tina*, (Fleetway), 1967, *Princess Tina*, (Fleetway/IPC), 1967-1970. *Sandie Annual* 1976. Artist Alberto Salinas.

'My Brother's a Pop Star'. *Bunty*, (DC Thomson), 832, Dec. 22 1973. (Started in October 1973)

'The Mystery of Eilean Mor'. In 'Real Life Mysteries' *Girl*, (Hulton), 1959, p.8.

'Nancy the Little Nurse'. See 'Dolls' Hospital'.

'Nothing Ever Goes Right'. *Judy*, (DC Thomson), 21 Feb 1981 – 13 June 1981. Reprinted 14 October 1989 - 03 February 1990. Art by Paddy Brennan.

'No Time For Pat'. *Jinty*, (IPC), mid-1970s.

'On Stage'. *Princess*, (AP), 1966-end date unknown. Reprint from *The Chicago Tribune* 1957. USA.

'On to Oregon' Unable to trace.

'Outcast of the Pony School'. *Bunty*, (DC Thomson), 832, Dec. 22 1973.

'Pansy Potter the Strongman's Daughter'. *Beano, The* (DC Thomson), 1938-1954, *Sparky*, (DC Thomson), 1965-1975. By Hugh McNeill, but Pansy Potter in Wonderland was by James Clark from 1949-1953. Subsequently, Bill Hill, John Geering and Evi De Bono drew the *Sparky* revival. Also in The Beano 1989-1993, drawn by Barry Glennard.

'The Passionate Prince'. *Roxy*, 1, (AP), March 15 1958.

'Penny's Place'. *Bunty Summer Special*, (DC Thomson), 1998.

'Powder Potts'. *Bunty*, (DC Thomson), 20 October 1973 – 02 February 1974.

'Princess Anita'. In 'Princess Anita' 1954 and 'Anita, Princess in Disguise' 1958, *School Friend*, (AP), 1954-1958.

'Robbie of Red Hall'. *Girl*, (Hulton), 1952-1956. By George Beardmore & Roy Newby.

'Romy's Return'. *Tammy*, (IPC), Jan. 15 1983, p.3-5. By Charles Herring & Juliana Buch.

'Scream Inn'. *Shiver & Shake*, (IPC), 1973-1974, *Whoopee*, (IPC), 1974-1977. By Bryan Walker (Gifford, 1987. p.188). Children would write in with suggestions for characters who would then try and spend the night in the haunted house. The work thus tied into their actual, at the time relationship with the comic.

'Sid the Sexist'. *Viz*, (Viz/John Brown), 1982-date. By Simon Donald. See also 'Millie Tant' and 'The Fat Slags'.

'The Silent Three'. *School Friend*, (AP), 1950-1963. Written by Horace Boyten and Stewart Pride, and originally illustrated by Evelyn Flinders. Valerie Gaskell illustrated 'The Silent Three's Mermaid Mystery' (1956), 'Foiled by the Silent Three' (1957), 'The Silent Three and the Kidnapped Dog' (1958), and 'Only the Silent Three could help her' (1960).

'The Slave of Form 3B'. *Jinty*, (IPC), 13 March 1976-17 July 1976. Artist: Trini Tinturé.

'Sue Day' See 'The Happy Days'.

'Susan of St. Bride's'. *Girl*, (Hulton), 1954-1961. Written by Ruth Adam by drawn by Peter Kay.

'Tessa of Television'. *Girl*, (Hulton), 1958-1959. By Diana Potter and Leo Davy.

'Tiger Tim'. *Monthly Playbox*, (AP), 1904-13, *Rainbow*, (AP), 1914-1956, *Tiger Tim's Tales*, (AP), 1919-1920, *Tiger Tim's* Weekly, (AP), 1920-1940, *Tiny Tots*, (AP/Fleetway), 1956-1959, *Jack & Jill*, (Fleetway/IPC), 1966-1985. (Gifford, 1987, p.223).

'Tommy's Lucky Little Guitar'. *Roxy*, 1, (AP), March 15 1958, p.1.

'Trigan Empire'. *Ranger*, (IPC), 1965-66, *Look & Learn*, (IPC), 1966-82, *Vulcan*, (IPC), 1975-76. By Mike Butterworth & Don Lawrence (Gifford, 1987, p.231).

'Up-to-Date Kate'. *Diana*, (DC Thomson), 1963.

'Valda'. In 'The Return of Valda' (started 13 September 1976), 'The Amazing Valda' (10 February 1969 – 31 May 1969) and 'The Truth about Valda' (10 February 1968 – 22 June 1968) *Mandy*, (DC Thomson), 1968-1984. Artist: Dudley Wynn (Gifford, 1987, p.234).

'Vanity Fair'. *Girl*, (Hulton), 1959. By Sarah Peters & Leo Davy.

'Wendy and Jinx'. *Girl*, (Hulton), 1952-1964. Written by Michael and Valerie Hastings and drawn by Ray Bailey.

'Westward the Wagons'. *Tina*, (Fleetway), 1967. Artist: Jorge Moliterni.

'Wildcat of the Court'. *Bunty*, (DC Thomson), 20 October 1973 – 02 March 1974.

'Winning Ways'. By Benita Brown. Unable to trace.

Bibliography

Abrams, M. (1961) *Teenage Consumer: Part II*. London: London Press Exchange.

Ahmed, K. (1998) 'Bunty tries to spice up image'. *Guardian*, 12 Jan, p. 7.

Alderson, C. (1968) *Magazines teenagers read*. Oxford: Pergamon.

Andrews, M. & Talbot, M. (eds.) (2000) *All the World and Her Husband: Women in Twentieth Century Consumer Culture*. London: Cassell.

Ang, I. (1991) *Desperately Seeking the Audience*. London: Routledge.

Ang, I. (1996) *Living Room Wars: Rethinking Media Audiences for a Post-modern World*. London: Routledge.

Anonymous. (1993) *Mum's Own Annual*. London: Fleetway/IPC.

Arnold, M. (1960) *Culture and Anarchy*. London: Cambridge University Press.

Auchmuty, R. (1992) *A World of Girls: The Appeal of the Girls' School Story*. London: The Women's Press.

Auchmuty, R. (1999) *A World of Women: Growing up in the Girls' School Story*. London: The Women's Press.

Baker, S (2004) 'Pop in(to) the Bedroom: Popular Music in Pre-teen Girls Bedroom Culture' *European Journal of Cultural Studies* Vol. 7. No.1, pp.75-93.

Barker, K. (ed.) (1993) *Graphic Account*. London: Youth Libraries Group.

Barker, M. (1984) *A Haunt of Fears: The Strange History of the British Horror Comics Campaign*. London: Pluto Press.

Barker, M. (1989) *Comics: Ideology, Power and the Critics*. Manchester: Manchester University Press.

Barker, M. (1993) 'Seeing how you can see: On being a fan of 2000AD'. In: Buckingham, D. (ed.) *Reading Audiences: Young People and the Media*, Manchester: Manchester University Press, pp. 160-180.

Barker, M. (1997) 'Taking an extreme case: Understanding a Fascist fan of Judge Dredd'. In: Cartmell, D., Hunter I.Q., Kaye, H. & Whelehan, I. (eds.) *Trash Aesthetics: Popular Culture and its Audience*, London: Pluto Press, pp. 14-30.

Barker, M. & Petley, J. (1997) *Ill Effects: The Media/Violence Debate*. London: Routledge.

Barthes, R. (1972) *Mythologies*. London: Jonathan Cape. (First published 1957).

Baudrillard, J. (1988) 'For a Critique of the Political Economy of the Sign'. In: Poster, M. (ed.) *Jean Baudrillard: Selected Writings*, Stanford: Stanford University Press, pp.60-100.

Benjamin, W. (1970) *No. VI of the Theses on the Philosophy of History in Illuminations*. London: Fontana.

Bennett, T. (1983) 'Text, Readers, Reading Formations'. *The Bulletin of the Midwest Modern Language Association*. Vol. 16, No. 1, pp. 3-17.

Bergson, H. (2004) *Matter and Memory* London: Dover Philosophical Classics.

Bourdieu, P. (1984) *Distinction: A Social Critique of the Judgement of Taste*. Cambridge, MA: Harvard UP.

Braidotti, R. (1994) *Nomadic Subjects.* New York: Columbia University Press.

Brienza, C. (2011) 'Manga Is for Girls: American Publishing Houses and the Localization of Japanese Comic Books.' *Logos: Journal of the World Publishing Community*. Vol. 22, No. 4, pp. 41-53.

Brown, J. (1999a) *Quack! Oops! 20 Years of Viz.* Margate: Thanet Press.

Brown, J. A. (1997) 'Comic Book Fandom and Cultural Capital'. *Journal of Popular Culture*, Vol. 30, No. 4, pp.13-29.

Buckingham, D. (ed.) (1993) *Reading Audiences: Young People and the Media.* Manchester: Manchester University Press.

Cadogan, M. (1999) 'Girl Role Models in Comics and Story-Papers'. In: Pinsent, P. (ed.) *Pop Fiction: Proceedings from the 5th Annual British IBBY/MA Children's Literature Conference at Roehampton Institute.* NCRCL Papers 5, London: Roehampton Institute, pp. 53-59.

Cadogan, M. & Craig, P. (1986) *You're a brick, Angela! The Girls' Story 1839-1985.* London: Gollancz.

Camden Libraries and Arts. (1988) *Survey of comics & magazines for young people.* London: Camden Libraries and Arts.

Cartmell, D., Hunter, I. Q., Kaye, H. & Whelehan, I. (eds.) (1997) *Trash Aesthetics: Popular Culture and its Audience.* London: Pluto Press.

Chapman, J (2011) *British Comics. A Cultural History.* London: Reaktion.

Children's Literature Research Centre, Roehampton Institute. (1996) *Young People's Reading at the End of the Century.* London: Book Trust.

Chute, H (2010) *Graphic Women: Life Narrative and Contemporary Comics.* New York: Columbia University Press.

Danziger-Russell, J. (2012) *Girls and Their Comics: Finding a Female Voice in Comic Book Narrative.* Lanham: The Scarecrow Press.

Dellino, C. (1981) 'Comics that set a bad example'. *Sunday Times*, 15 Feb, p. 19.

Douglas, S. (1995) *Where the Girls Are: Growing up Female with the Mass Media.* New York: Times Books.

Drottner, K. (1988) *English Children and Their Magazines 1751-1945.* New Haven, Con.: Yale University Press.

Eco, U. (1986) *Travels in Hyper-Reality.* London: Picador.

Eshun, E. (2000) 'Wham! Bam! The X-Men are here'. *Independent on Sunday*, 6 Aug, Culture, p. 1.

Frazer, E. (1987) 'Teenage girls reading Jackie'. *Media, Culture and Society*, Vol. 9, No. 4, pp. 407-25.

Gaiman, N. (1998) 'Shameful Secrets of Comics Retailing: The Lingerie Connection'. In: Loubert, D. (ed.) *How to Get Girls (Into Your Store). A Friends of Lulu Retailer Handbook.* Pasadena: Friends of Lulu, pp.3-4.

Gale, G. (1971) 'Violent and Deformed - the prosecution case'. *Times Educational Supplement*, 5 Feb, p.6.

Gibson, M. (2013) 'Something for the Girls? Constructions of Class and Girlhood in Girl, Princess and Bunty' In: Carrington, B. (ed.) *The Final Chapters: Concluding Papers of Journal of Children's Literature Studies Wizard's Tower Press* (e-book) http://www.wizardstowerbooks.com/collections/non-fiction/products/the-final-chapters-bridget-carrington-pat-pinsent.

Gibson, M. (2011) 'Bella at the Bar' In: Gravett, P (ed.) *1001 Comics You Must Read Before You Die: The Ultimate Guide to Comic Books, Graphic Novels and Manga* NY: Universe Publishing.

Gibson, M. (2010) 'Graphic Novels, Comics and Picturebooks' In: Rudd, D. (ed.) *Routledge Companion to Children's Literature*. London: Routledge, pp.100-111.

Gibson, M. (2010a) 'What Bunty Really Did! Revisiting the Protagonist in Comics for Girls' In: McCleery, A & Brabon, B (eds.) *Scottish Comics*. Edinburgh: Merchiston Publishing. pp. 29-39.

Gibson, M. (2010b) 'What Bunty did next? Responses to Protagonists in the British Girls' Comic in Late 20th Century Comics and Graphic Novels' *Journal of Graphic Novels and Comics* Vol. 1, No. 2, pp. 121-135.

Gibson, M. (2009) 'Nobody, Somebody, Everybody: Ballet, Girlhood, Class, Femininity and Comics in 1950s Britain' in *Girlhood Studies*, Vol. 1, No. 2, pp. 108-128.

Gibson, M. (2008a) 'What you read and where you read it, how you get it, how you keep it: Children, comics and historical cultural practice'. *Popular Narrative Media*, Vol. 1, No. 2, pp, 151-167.

Gibson, M. (2008b) 'From 'Susan of St. Brides' to 'Heartbreak Hospital'. Nurses and nursing in the girls' comic from the 1950s to the 1980s'. *Journal of Children's Literature Studies*, Vol.5, No. 2, pp. 104-126.

Gibson, M. (2007) 'The Tale Of One Bad Rat: the child alone and the alternative and substitute family'. In: Bradford, C & Coghlan, V (eds.) *Expectations and Experiences: Children, Childhood & Children's Literature* Lichfield: Pied Piper Press.

Gifford, D. (1975) *The British Comic catalogue 1874-1974*. London: Mansell.

Gifford, D. (1985) *The Complete Catalogue of British Comics*. Exeter: Webb and Bower.

Gifford, D. (1987) *Encyclopedia of Comic Characters*. Harlow: Longman.

Girls Comics of Yesterday http://girlscomicsofyesterday.com/ (Accessed 3 July 2014).

Gledhill, C. (1988) 'Pleasurable Negotiations'. In: Pribram, E. D. (ed.) *Female Spectators: Looking at Film & Television*. London: Verso, pp. 64-89.

Gosling, J. (1998) *Virtual Worlds of Girls* http://www.ju90.co.uk/start.htm (Accessed 19 March 2015).

Gravett, P. (2011) *1001 Comics you must read before you die*. London: Universe/Cassell.

Gravett, P. & Harris Dunning, J. (2014) *Comics Unmasked: Art and Anarchy in the UK*. London: British Library.

Gravett, P. & Stanbury, P. (2006) *Great British Comics. Celebrating a Century of Ripping Yarns and Wizard Wheezes*. London: Aurum Press Limited.

Greenwood, James (1869) *The Seven Curses of London*. London: Stanley Rivers and Co. http://www.gutenberg.org/ebooks/45585 (Accessed 4 March 2015).

Griffin, S. (1999) 'Davy Crockett and Childrens' Space'. In: Kinder, M. (ed.) *Kids' Media Culture*, Durham: Duke, pp. 102-121.

Grimshaw, J. (1986) *Feminist Philosophers*. Brighton: Wheatsheaf.

Hagan, P. (1999) 'What happened to the comic heroines?' *The Journal*, 15 Feb, pp.42- 43.

Hague, I (2014) *Comics and the Senses: A Multisensory Approach to Comics and Graphic Novels*. London: Routledge.

Hall, S. (1987) 'Minimal Selves'. In: Appignanesi, L. (ed.) *Identity, ICA Documents 6*, London: ICA, pp. 44-46.

Hall, S. & Jefferson, T. (eds.) (1978) *Resistance through Rituals*. London: Hutchinson.

Heron, L. (ed.) (1985) *Truth, Dare or Promise: Girls growing up in the 1950s*. London: Virago.

Hoggart, R. (1957) *The Uses of Literacy*. Harmondsworth: Penguin.

Hunt, P. (ed.) (1992) *Literature for children: Contemporary Criticism*. London: Routledge.

Innes, S. (1998) *Tough Girls: Women Warriors and Wonder Women in Popular Culture*. Philadelphia: University of Pennsylvania Press.

James, A. & Prout, A. (eds.) (1997) *Constructing & Reconstructing Childhood*. London: Falmer Press.

Jenkins, H. (1992) *Textual Poachers: Television Fans and Participatory Culture*. London: Routledge.

Jenkinson, A. J. (1940) *What Do Boys and Girls Read?* London: Methuen.

Jenks, C. (1996) *Childhood*. London: Psychology Press.

Kaplan, A. E. (1983) *Women and Film: Both Sides of the Camera*. London: Methuen.

Kibble-White, G (2005) *The Ultimate Book of British Comics: 70 Years of Mischief, Mayhem and Cow Pies*. London: Allison and Busby Ltd.

Kinder, M. (ed.) (1999) *Kids' Media Culture*. Durham: Duke.

Kuhn, A. (1992) 'Mandy and possibility'. *Screen*, Vol. 33, No. 3, pp. 233-243.

Kuhn, A. (1995) *Family Secrets: Acts of memory and imagination*. London: Verso.

Lanyi, R. L. (1979) 'Trina, Queen of the Underground cartoonists. An interview'. *Journal of Popular Culture*, Vol. 12, No. 4, pp. 737-755.

Leavis, F. R. & Thompson, D. (1977) *Culture and Environment: The Training of Critical Awareness*. Westport, CT: Greenwood Press. (First published 1933).

Freeman, J (no date given) 'Lets Here It For The Girls' http://www.mistycomic.co.uk/ Lets—Here—It—For—The—Girls.html (Accessed 13/3/2015).

Lewin, K. (1943) 'Forces behind food habits and methods of change'. In: Committee on Food Habits *The Problem of Changing Food Habits, Report of the Committee on Food Habits 1941–1943*. Bulletin No. 108, Washington DC: National Research Council, National Academy of Sciences, pp. 35-65.

Lewis, D. (1998) 'Oops! Colin McNaughton and 'Knowingness''. *Children's Literature in Education*, Vol. 29, No. 2, pp. 59-68.

Lincoln, S. (2012) *Youth Culture and Private Space.* Basingstoke: Palgrave MacMillan.

McCloud, S. (1993) *Understanding Comics: The Invisible Art.* New York: Harper Perennial.

Macdonald, M. (1995) *Representing Women: Myths of Femininity in the Popular Media.* London: Arnold.

McRobbie, A. (1978a) 'Jackie: An ideology of adolescent femininity'. *Occasional Paper CCCS.* Birmingham: CCCS. Also in: Waites, B. & Martin, G. (eds.) (1982) *Popular Culture: Past and Present.* Milton Keynes: OUP. Also in: McRobbie, A (1991) *Feminism and Youth Culture: From Jackie to Just 17*, London: Macmillan, pp. 81-134.

McRobbie, A. (1978b) 'Working class girls and the Culture of Femininity'. In: Women's Studies Group, CCCS, *Women Take Issue: Aspects of Women's Subordination*, London: Hutchinson, pp. 96-108. Also in: McRobbie, A. (1991) *Feminism and Youth Culture: From Jackie to Just 17*, London: Macmillan, pp. 35-60.

McRobbie, A. (1980) 'Settling Accounts with Subculture: A Feminist Critique'. *Screen Education*, No.34, pp. 111-123. Also in: McRobbie, A. *Feminism and Youth Culture: From Jackie to Just Seventeen*, London: Macmillan, pp. 16-34.

McRobbie, A. (1991) *Feminism and Youth Culture: From Jackie to Just 17.* London: Macmillan.

McRobbie, A. (1997) 'More! New sexualities in girls' and women's magazines' In: McRobbie, A. (ed.) *Back to Reality? Social Experience and Cultural Studies*, Manchester: Manchester University Press, pp. 190-209.

McRobbie, A (2008) *The Aftermath of Feminism: Gender, Culture and Social Change.* London: Sage.

McRobbie, A. & Garber, J. (1976) 'Girls and Subcultures: An Exploration'. In: Hall, S & Jefferson, T (eds.), *Resistance through Rituals: Youth Subcultures in Post-War Britain*, London: Hutchinson, pp. 209-222. Also in: Gelder, K & Thornton, S. (eds.) (1997) *Subcultures Reader.* London: Routledge. Also in: McRobbie, A (1991) *Feminism and Youth Culture: From Jackie to Just Seventeen*, London: Macmillan, pp. 1-15.

McRobbie, A. & McCabe, T. (eds.) (1981) *Feminism for girls: An adventure story.* London: Routledge.

McRobbie, A. & Nava, M. (eds.) (1984) *Gender & Generation.* Basingstoke and London: MacMillan.

Millard, E. (1997) *Differently Literate: Boys, Girls and the Schooling of Literacy.* London: Falmer Press.

Moores, S. (1993) *Interpreting Audiences: The Ethnography of Media Consumption.* London: Sage.

Morris, S. & Hallwood, J. (1998) *Living with Eagles. From Priest to Publisher: The Life and Times of Marcus Morris.* Cambridge: Lutterworth.

Nelson, C. (1997) 'Mixed messages: Authoring and authority in British boys' magazines'. *The Lion and the Unicorn*, Vol. 21, No. 1, pp. 1-19.

Nyberg, A. K. (1995) 'Comic books and women readers: Trespassers in masculine territory?' In: Rollins, P. C. & S. W. (eds.) *Gender in Popular Culture: Images of Men and Women in literature, visual media and material culture*, Cleveland, OK: Ridgemont Press, pp. 205-225.

Nyberg, A. K. (1998) *Seal of Approval: The History of the Comics Code.* Jackson: University Press of Mississippi.

On These Days. (1998) BBC Radio 4. Broadcast on 17 Feb.

O'Connell, J. (1990) *More next week: a study in the socialization of young girls through British girls' comics.* BA thesis. Ulster: University of Ulster.

O'Neill, K. (1988) 'Knit yourself a Dutch cap!' *Comics Journal*, No. 122, p. 86.

Pearlman, C. (1998) 'Girl Annuals' In: Smith, E. (ed.) *GirlFrenzy Millennial*, Hove: Slab-o-Concrete, p. 20.

Pickard, P. M. (1955) *British Comics: An Appraisal.* London: Comics Campaign Council.

Pinsent, P. (ed.) (1999) *Pop Fiction: Proceedings from the 5th Annual British IBBY/MA Children's Literature Conference at Roehampton Institute.* NCRCL Papers 5. London: Roehampton Institute.

Pinsent, P. & Knight, B. (1997) *Teenage Girls and their Magazines.* NCRCL Papers 1. London: Roehampton Institute.

Pribram, E. D. (ed.) (1988) *Female Spectators: Looking at Film and Television.* London: Verso.

Probyn, E. (1994) *Sexing the Self: Gendered Positions in Cultural Studies.* London: Routledge.

Pumphrey, G. H. (1954) *Comics and your children.* London: Comics Campaign Council.

Pumphrey, G. H. (1955) *Children's Comics: A Guide for Parents and Teachers.* London: The Epworth Press.

Pumphrey, G. H. (1964). *What children think of their comics.* London: Epworth Press.

Reynolds, R. (1992) *Superheroes: A Modern Mythology.* London: Batsford.

Robbins, T. (2013) *Pretty in Ink. North American Women Cartoonists 1896-2013.* Seattle: Fantagraphics Books.

Robbins, T (2009) *The Brinkley Girls: The Best of Nell Brinkley's Cartoons from 1913– 1940.* Seattle: Fantagraphics Books.

Robbins, T. (1992) *A Century of Women Cartoonists.* Princeton: Kitchen Sink.

Robbins, T. (1996) *The Great Women Superheroes.* Princeton: Kitchen Sink.

Robbins, T. (1999) *From Girls to Grrrlz: A History of Women's Comics from Teens to Zines.* San Francisco: Chronicle Books.

Robbins, T. & Yronwood, K. (1985) *Women and the Comics.* London: Eclipse.

Rollins, P. C. & S. W. (eds.) (1995) *Gender in Popular Culture: Images of Men and Women in literature, visual media and material culture.* Cleveland, OK: Ridgemont Press.

Rose, J. (1992) *The Case of Peter Pan: Or the Impossibility of Children's Fiction.* London: Macmillan Press.

Rose, N. (1989) *Governing the Soul: The Shaping of the Private Self.* London: Routledge.

Rowbotham, S. (1973) *Woman's Conciousness, Man's World.* Harmondsworth: Penguin.

Royal Commission on the Press. (1977) *The Women's Periodical Press in Britain, 1946- 1976.* CLW Working Paper No. 4. London: HMSO.

Sabin, R. (1993) *Adult Comics: An Introduction.* London: Routledge.

Sabin, R. (1996) Comics, Comix and Graphic Novels. London: Phaidon.

Scott, J. (1998) 'Jinty Come Back!' In: Smith, E. (ed.) *GirlFrenzy Millennial*, Hove: Slab-o-Concrete, pp. 95-98.

Scott, J. *A Resource on Jinty: Artists, Writers, Stories.* http://jintycomic.wordpress.com/ (Accessed 3/7/14).

Skeggs, B. (ed.) (1995) *Feminist Cultural Theory: Process and Production*. Manchester: Manchester University Press.

Skeggs, B. (1997) *Formations of Class and Gender: Becoming Respectable*. London: Sage.

Smith, E. (ed.) (1998) *GirlFrenzy Millennial*. Hove: Slab-o-Concrete.

Spence, J. & Holland, P. (eds.) (1990) *Family Snaps: The meanings of domestic photography*. London: Virago.

Spiegel, L. (1993) 'Seducing the Innocent'. In: Solomon, W.S. & McChesney, R.W. (eds.) *Ruthless Criticism: New Perspectives in U.S. Communications History*, Minneapolis: University of Minnesota Press, pp. 264-265.

Springhall, J. (1998) *Youth, Popular Culture and Moral Panics*. London: Macmillan.

Stacey, J. (1994) *Star Gazing: Hollywood cinema and female spectatorship*. London: Routledge.

Stones, R. (1983) *Pour out the cocoa, Janet. Sexism in Children's Books* York: Longman Resource Unit.

Styles, M. & Watson, V. (1996) *Talking Pictures: Pictorial texts and young readers*. London: Hodder and Stroughton.

Syal, M. (1997) *Anita and me*. London: Flamingo.

Thornton, S (1995) *Club Cultures: Music, Media and Subcultural Capital* Cambridge: Polity Press.

Tinkler, P. (1995) *Constructing Girlhood: Popular magazines for girls growing up in England 1920-1950*. London: Taylor and Francis.

Tinkler, P. (2000) "A Material Girl'? Adolescent Girls and their magazines, 1920-1958'. In: Andrews, M. & Talbot, M. (eds.) *All the World and Her Husband: Women in Twentieth Century Consumer Culture*, London: Cassell, pp. 97-112.

Viz readership survey (1988) House of Viz/ John Brown Publishing.

Walkerdine, V. (1984) 'Some day my prince will come: young girls and the preparation for adolescent sexuality'. In: McRobbie, A. & Nava, M. (eds.) (1984) *Gender and Generation*, London: MacMillan, pp162-84. Also in Walkerdine, V. (1990) *Schoolgirl Fictions,* London: Verso, pp. 87-106.

Walkerdine, V. (1997) *Daddy's Girl: Young Girls and Popular Culture*. London: Macmillan.

Waller, R. (1999) 'Editorial', *The Journal*, 15 Feb, p. 8

Weiner, R & Gibson, M (eds.) (2011) 'Special Edition. Audiences and Readership'. *Journal of Graphic Novels and Comics* Vol.2 No. 2.

Wertham, F. (1954) *The Seduction of the Innocent*. New York: Rinehart.

Whelehan, I. (2000) *Overloaded: Popular Culture and the Future of Feminism*. London: Womens Press.

White, C. L. (1970) *Womens' Magazines 1693-1968*. London: Michael Joseph.

Whitehead, F., Capey, A., Maddren, W. & Wellings, A. (1977). *Children and Their books: The final report of the Schools Council Project on Children's Reading Habits, 10-16*, Basingstoke: Evans/Methuen Educational.

Williams, R. (1961) *The Long Revolution*. New York: Columbia University Press

Winship, J. (1987) *Inside Women's Magazines*. London: Pandora.

York, P. (1998) 'Wham bam, thank you Glam!' *Independent on Sunday*, 16 Aug, Culture, p. 4.

Index